easy
HIKING
in NORTHERN CALIFORNIA

More Than 100 Places
Anyone Can Hike This Weekend

ANN MARIE BROWN

Foghorn
Press

1-57354-062-5

51295

9 781573 540629

Library of Congress ISSN Data:

June 1999

Easy Hiking in Northern California:
More Than 100 Places Anyone Can Hike This Weekend

2ND Edition

ISSN: 1085-4665

Editor in Chief	Kyle Morgan
Maps	Kirk McInroy
Photo Credits	Ann Marie Brown
Cover Photo	Mark Gibson, Lassen Volcanic National Park

INTRODUCTION

I admit it; the idea for this book came from my own selfish perspective. Like so many of my friends and acquaintances, for years I had worked long hours in an office five or more days a week, putting in plenty of overtime and spending way too much time indoors. When I had time off, I tried to get out in nature as much as possible, but with all of life's demands, I rarely had more than a free morning or afternoon to spend outdoors.

In response to the complexity and demands of my life, I decided to take up a weekly ritual: Every Sunday morning, no matter what else was happening, I would take an hour or two to go for a walk in a beautiful outdoor place. I did this almost without fail for three years, only rarely missing a Sunday. It was during one of those walks that the idea for this book was born—a guide to more than 100 of the best short and easy hikes in Northern California, for those of us who want to feel the peace of wild places but are short on time and also frequently short on energy.

The greatest thing about the hikes in this book is that they are good for everybody, whether you have children in tow, or your grandma, or your spouse who thinks the outdoors is all mosquitoes and poison oak. The best test for these trails is to try hiking on one of them with someone who says they hate hiking, and just see if they don't have fun.

To choose the trails in this book, I walked every one of them, some of them many times over. I hiked many other trails that never made it in the book, often because they were too difficult or too dull to ensure that everybody would have fun. Sometimes I brought my less-than-enthusiastic-about-the-outdoors friends with me. Other times I borrowed my friends' kids and took them with me to see if they liked the hikes. Sometimes I made new friends on the trail—solitary female hikers like me, older hikers, hikers with babies in backpacks, and hikers with older kids wearing their own backpacks—and I asked them to suggest fun and easy trails.

What I found in researching this book is that there are plenty of trails designed for ordinary people, not just Mr. and Mrs. Hardcore Outdoors Enthusiast, and when people hike them, they feel pretty happy. It seems that fundamentally we aren't all that different from our canine companions whom we call man's (and woman's) best friend. We are happiest when we get to go for a good walk every day.

Hope to see you (and your children and grandmas) out there—

Ann Marie Brown

CONTENTS

Answers to Questions—p. 10
How to Use This Book—p. 16
Best Hiking Lists—p. 17

North Coast & The Redwoods—p. 19

Redding, Shasta, & Lassen—p. 43

Mendocino, Sonoma, & Napa—p. 67

Gold Country, Tahoe, & Plumas—p. 97

North San Francisco Bay Area—p. 131

East San Francisco Bay Area—p. 173

South San Francisco Bay Area—p. 185

Yosemite & Mammoth Lakes—p. 217

Index—p. 252

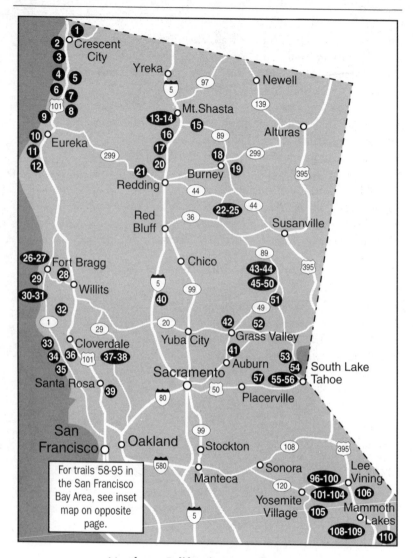

Northern California Easy Hikes

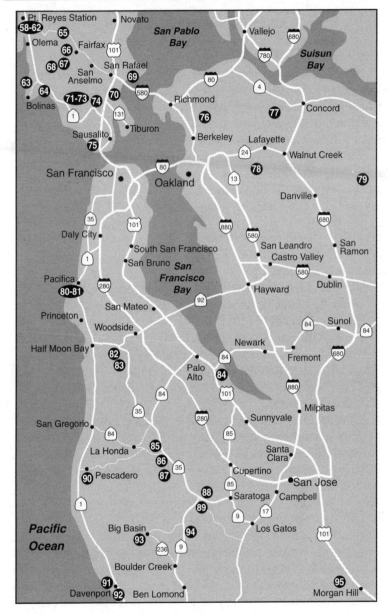

San Francisco Bay Area Easy Hikes (inset)

Hikes 58–75: North San Francisco Bay Area, pages 131-172

Hikes 76-79: East San Francisco Bay Area, pages 173-184

Hikes 80-95: South San Francisco Bay Area, pages 185-216

ANSWERS TO QUESTIONS

What's an Easy Hike?

An easy hike is one in which you don't have to carry a heavy backpack or plan for a week before you go. An easy hike is fun for families, or for older people, or for young and fit people who are tired of pushing all the time. An easy hike offers a good payoff—a reason for going besides just for exercise—whether it's a stunning view, a pretty waterfall, or a chance to experience the peace of an ancient redwood forest. An easy hike takes you away from pavement, exhaust fumes, and tour buses packed with the video camera-toting crowd. An easy hike leads you into wild places, but keeps you safely on trails and out of trouble.

How Were These Trails Selected?

First, I laid down a few rules, and then with only a couple of exceptions, I followed them.

- The trails had to be less than five miles long and walkable in under two and a half hours (round-trip).
- Every trail had to have something exceptional about it—a great destination or a reason for doing it besides the exercise.
- The trails had to be walkable by almost anybody, which meant no hikes with insanely steep elevation gains.
- The trails had to have the feel of true wilderness, so asphalt had to be avoided.
- All the trails had to start and end at the same place, so that no complicated transportation or car shuttles would be necessary.

Finally, I tried not to include any trails that are ridiculously well-known and hence overcrowded—hikes that get too much traffic to provide a peaceful nature experience.

Are Hiking Boots Necessary?

Boots are not always necessary for the trails listed in this book, but they can make things a lot more pleasant when the trail is unexpectedly wet and muddy, and they usually provide better traction and grip on a rocky or gravel-laden trail. Not only that, but they offer better foot and ankle protection than running shoes, tennis shoes, or whatever else you might wear. You don't need to spend a fortune on mountaineering boots, because these days you'll find tons of lightweight hiking boots on the market that feel as comfortable as your old tennis shoes but offer more protection for your feet. You can buy a decent pair for $60 or so, and if you plan to hike even once a month, they're worth it.

If you're hiking with children, they can usually get away with wearing sneakers or high-tops. But we adults with our weak knees and tired ankles usually need the support that hiking boots provide, especially for hikes that are in more extreme environments, like Yosemite or Mount Shasta, where trails tend to be more rough.

If you have hiking boots, don't forget to treat them with a waterproofing spray, repeated again every six months or so.

What Should We Bring on the Trail?

• *Food and water, first and foremost.* My hiking mantra is "Never be caught without a picnic." There's nothing like being hungry or thirsty to spoil a good time, or to make you anxious about getting back to the car. Even if you aren't the least bit hungry or thirsty when you park at the trailhead, you may feel completely different after 45 minutes or more of walking. A small daypack or fanny sack can keep you happily supplied with a quart or so of water and a few snacks. Carry them with you, always.

• *A map of the park or area you're visiting.* I've learned my lesson the hard way on this one. Most of the trails in this book are well signed, but that isn't always enough to keep you on track. For one thing, signs get knocked down or disappear with alarming frequency, due to rain, wind, or park visitors looking for souvenirs. For another, signs sometimes state the name of the trail you're walking on and sometimes state the name of a destination you're heading toward, but it isn't necessarily the information you need at that moment.

Get a map from the managing agency of the place you're visiting. All their names and phone numbers are in this book. At state parks and national parks you can often just pick up a map when you drive into the park entrance. If it costs a buck, pay it. Trails that are located in national forest lands are the only ones that may require a little advance planning. For these, send $4 per map to USDA Forest Service, Office of Information, 1323 Club Drive, Vallejo, CA 94592 and ask for a map of the national forest you'll be visiting. For more information, their phone number is (707) 562-8737.

We've drawn some trail maps in this book to help you find your way on more complicated loop trips and connecting trails, but they are no substitute for the real thing. Our maps may help you if you don't have a park map, but remember that trails change all the time, mostly because of weather problems but sometimes because park officials change the names or routes of trails. Get an updated park map whenever possible.

• *Extra clothing.* Being cold is right up there with being hungry or thirsty, in my opinion. It makes me downright crabby. On the trail, conditions can change at any time. Not only can the weather suddenly turn windy, foggy, or rainy, but your own body conditions also change: You'll perspire as you hike up a sunny hill and then get chilled at the top of a windy ridge or when you head into shade. My hiking companions have to put up with me alternately tying my jacket around my waist, then untying it to put it on, about a million times per hike. But hey, I'm cozy all the time. Bring a lightweight jacket or some pants with you. Put them in your daypack or tie them around your waist. Polar fleece clothing is best; it's warm and weighs almost nothing.

• *Sunglasses and sunscreen.* Of course you know the dangers of the sun. Wear both sunglasses and sunscreen. Put on your sunscreen 30 minutes before you go outdoors so it has time to take effect.

• *Flashlight.* Just in case your hike takes a little longer than you planned and it gets dark, bring a flashlight. Mini-flashlights are available everywhere, weigh almost nothing, and can save the day. Make sure the batteries work before you set out on the trail.

• *First aid kit.* Nothing major is required here unless you're fully trained in first aid, but a few large and small **band-aids** and **moleskin** for blisters and an **ace bandage** for minor emergencies can be valuable tools. Also, if anyone in your party is allergic to bee stings or anything else in the outdoors, carry their **medication.** I also like to carry a **pocket knife,** one with several blades, a can opener, and a scissors on it. I've never used it to perform first aid, but it does come in handy for picnics. Finally, it's a good idea to carry **matches in a waterproof container and a candle,** just in case you ever need to build a fire in a serious emergency. Outdoor stores sell these.

What About Snakes, Mountain Lions, and Bears?

All three of these creatures deserve your respect, and you should know a little bit about them. You may never see a mountain lion, but chances are good that you'll run into a snake or a bear somewhere.

Rattlesnakes—Rattlesnakes live in warm, low-elevation areas, even in fairly developed parks like those in Santa Rosa and Sonoma. The standard advice is to give them lots of room. If you're hiking on a warm day when they might be out sunning themselves, keep your eyes open so you don't step on one. They are not seen very often, though, as they tend to shy away from creatures with large hiking boots. If you should happen to get bitten by a rattlesnake, don't panic or run. Slowly walk back to your car, then drive yourself to the nearest hospital.

Answers to Questions

Most other Northern California snakes are completely harmless. Just give them some room to slither by.

Mountain lions—Mountain lions are almost everywhere in California, although they are rarely seen. When they do show themselves, they get a lot of media attention. If you're hiking in an area where mountain lions or their tracks have been spotted, remember to keep your children close to you on the trail and your dog leashed. If you see a mountain lion and it doesn't run away immediately, the standard advice is to make yourself appear as large as possible (raise your arms, open your jacket, wave a big stick) and speak loudly and firmly or shout. If you have children with you, pick them up off the ground, but try to do it without crouching down or leaning over. (Crouching makes you appear smaller and less aggressive, more like prey.) Don't turn your back on the cat or run from it, but rather back away slowly and deliberately, always retaining your aggressive pose and continuing to speak loudly.

I've hiked for two decades in mountain lion country and I've never seen one, except for the stuffed ones in some interpretive centers. Some of my hiking friends have seen them, however, and they tell me that in each encounter, the cat simply vanished into the forest at the first sign of nearby humans. They all agreed that seeing one, even for a fraction of a moment, was a special experience, a rare glimpse into a very private animal's life.

Bears—You'll only find bears in bear country (for the areas covered in this book, that would be the chapters on North Coast and The Redwoods; Redding, Shasta, and Lassen; Yosemite and Mammoth Lakes; and Gold Country, Tahoe, and Plumas). The only bears in California are black bears (even though they are usually brown in color). They can be a nuisance, and even though they almost never harm human beings, they can make your hair stand on end. There's only one important thing to remember about bears: They love snacks. Any time you see a bear, it's almost a given that he's looking for food, preferably something sweet. So keep your food packed away in bear-proof containers when you're camping, and get an update from the rangers in the park you're visiting about suitable bear precautions. It's less common to encounter a bear on the trail, although it happens occasionally. If you're hiking, bears will most likely hear you coming and avoid you. You're far more likely to see bears in campgrounds, looking for a little chow.

What About Ticks, Poison Oak, and Stinging Nettles?

Ticks, poison oak, and stinging nettles—I'd say these three are far worse than a whole convention of snakes, mountain lions, and bears.

But you can avoid them with a little common sense, and here's how:

Ticks—The easiest way to stay clear of ticks is to wear long pants and long sleeves, and to check your clothes when you take them off. If it's too hot to be covered up in long sleeves, just make sure you look yourself over thoroughly when you leave the trail and remove anything that's crawling on you. (A friend can be a good assistant in this pursuit.) Remember that if you find a tick on your skin, the larger brown ones are harmless. It's the tiny brown-black ones that are deer ticks and can possibly carry Lyme disease. If you find a very small tick on you and he's not crawling around, he's actually biting you, you should do the following: Remove the tick, put it in a plastic bag, and take it to your doctor for examination to see if it is carrying Lyme disease.

Rangers also warn people that if they've been in the outdoors, and then a few days or a week later start to experience headaches, fever, nausea, or rashes, they should see a doctor immediately and tell him or her that they are concerned about possible exposure to ticks and Lyme disease. Caught in its early stages, Lyme disease is easily treated with antibiotics.

If you stay on the trails when you hike, and if you perform tick checks faithfully after every trip outdoors, you should have no problem with ticks.

Poison oak—That old Boy Scout motto holds true: Leaves of three, let them be. If you can't readily identify poison oak, stay away from vine-like plants that have three leaves. Remember that in spring and summer poison oak looks a little like wild blackberry bushes and often has red colors in its leaves as well as green. In late fall and winter, poison oak goes dormant and loses its leaves, but it's still potent. Avoid poison oak by staying on the trail and wearing long pants and long sleeves if you're allergic to it. (Some people react more strongly to it than others.)

Stinging nettles—I had my first experience with this nasty plant in Point Reyes National Seashore, when I eagerly bounded off the trail to look at a pretty curve in the stream above Alamere Falls. All of a sudden, the skin on my calves and ankles was stinging like mad. Ouch! Nettles are bright green and rather pretty. When you brush against one it zaps you with its poison, which feels like a mild bee sting. The sting can last for up to 24 hours, but usually lasts less than an hour. Here's an important tip: Stinging nettles grow near creeks or streams, and they're usually found in tandem with deer ferns and sword ferns. If the nettles zing you, grab a nearby fern leaf and rub the underside of it against the stinging area. It sounds weird, I know, but it helps take the sting out.

What If Somebody Gets Lost?

If you're hiking with a family or group, make sure everybody knows to stay together. If anyone decides to split off from the group for any reason, make sure they have a trail map with them and know how to read it. Also, ensure that everyone in your group knows the rules regarding what to do if they get lost:

- Whistle or shout loudly at regular intervals.
- "Hug" a tree. Or a big rock or a bush. That means find a noticeable landmark, sit down next to it, and don't move. Continue to whistle or shout loudly. A lost person is easier to find if they stay in one place.

Protecting the Outdoors

Take good care of this beautiful land you're hiking on. The primary rules are to leave no trace of your visit, pack out all your trash, and try not to disturb animal or plant life. But you can go the extra mile, if you want. Pick up any litter that you see on the trail. Teach your children to do this as well. Carry an extra bag to hold picked-up litter until you get to a trash receptacle, or just keep an empty pocket for that purpose in your day pack or fanny sack.

I must confess that after years of hiking in parks located close to urban areas, I had begun to turn a blind eye to tiny bits of trash on trails and at picnic areas and campsites. Although I always took care never to add to the mess, I had gotten somewhat resigned to seeing other people's litter, even in pristine places. But then one day I hiked with a friend and watched as he stopped on the trail every time he saw the smallest piece of trash. Every single time, he'd stop, pick up the litter, and put it in his daypack. He told me that he had broken his ankle years ago, and doctors told him he wouldn't be able to walk again without a limp. So he made a deal with the Great Hiker in the Sky and said that if he could continue hiking long miles in beautiful places, he would pick up every piece of trash he saw. And so he does, and now I do, too, and hopefully you and your children will also.

If you have the extra time or energy, you can join a trail organization in your area or spend some time volunteering in your local park. Anything you do to help this beautiful planet will be repaid to you, many times over.

HOW TO USE THIS BOOK

This book is organized geographically, with each hike numbered from 1 to 110. Use the maps on pages 8 and 9 to locate trails in the areas of Northern California where you want to hike. Then find the trails' stories by using the table of contents, the index, or just by thumbing through the book. (The trails are arranged in numerical order.)

Or you can simply turn to the chapter covering the region where you'd like to hike and read all of the stories in that chapter.

Each hike also has one or a series of graphic icons listed with it, which denote which types of trail users can use the trail. If you wish to bring your horse, dog, or mountain bike with you, or if you wish to hike with someone in a wheelchair, look for these symbols:

Hikers	Wheelchairs	Horses	Dogs	Mountain Bikes

Remember that if you are going to bring a bicycle, dog, horse, or wheelchair with you on any of the trips in this book, you should call park officials for updates on trail rules and conditions.

Each of the hikes in this book is rated for trail distance and time required for hiking. While the mileages are as accurate as possible, the time required is more subjective and you may find that you take a longer or shorter time. Next to the distance and time rating, you'll see a note about the steepness of the trail. Trails are rated as "mostly level terrain" (the trail is almost flat), "rolling terrain" (there are some minor ups and downs on the trail), or "some steep terrain" (there are short sections of trail where you will be breathing hard). Even though all the trails in the book have been selected for easy hiking, there is some variation in their difficulty level.

At the end of most trail listings you'll find the feature "Make it easier" or "Make it more challenging." These are additional trail notes that give you some options for customizing your hike.

A word about timing: When you're hiking in Northern California, remember that weather and season will play an important part in the quality of your trip. While some high elevation mountain areas are clearly not suitable for winter hiking, other areas may have weather restrictions that aren't so obvious. For example, you'll probably want to avoid hiking in the hills of the East San Francisco Bay, Sonoma, or Napa during the heat of summer. Also, remember that waterfalls that flow forcefully in winter can completely dry up by late spring. Read each story for information about the best seasons to hike each trail.

BEST EASY HIKING LISTS

5 Easiest Hikes:
Simpson-Reed & Peterson Trails, *Jedediah Smith Redwoods State Park*, p. 20
Smithe Redwoods & Eel River Trail, *Smithe Redwoods State Reserve*, p. 40
Lily Lake & Fern Falls Trails, *Plumas National Forest*, p. 111
Sand Pond Interpretive Trail, *Tahoe National Forest*, p. 114
Lagoon Trail, *Golden Gate National Recreation Area*, p. 170

5 Most Difficult Hikes:
Lembert Dome Trail, *Yosemite National Park*, p. 226
Stevens Trail, *BLM Folsom Resource Area*, p. 99
Old Briones Road & Lagoon Trail Loop, *Briones Regional Park*, p. 176
Wild Plum Loop, *Tahoe National Forest*, p. 118
North Peak Trail to Prospectors Gap, *Mount Diablo State Park*, p. 181

5 Best Waterfall Hikes:
McCloud Falls Trail, *Shasta-Trinity National Forest*, p. 47
Headwaters & Pacific Crest Trails, *McArthur-Burney Falls Memorial State Park*, p. 52
Fern Canyon & Falls Loop Trails, *Russian Gulch State Park*, p. 78
Frazier Falls Trail, *Plumas National Forest*, p. 113
Horsetail Falls Trail, *Eldorado National Forest*, p. 129

5 Best View Hikes:
Rubicon Trail, *D. L. Bliss State Park*, p. 123
Coastal & Matt Davis Trails, *Mount Tamalpais State Park*, p. 165
Phyllis Ellman Trail, *Ring Mountain Preserve*, p. 158
Skyline Trail to Summit Rock, *Sanborn-Skyline County Park*, p. 201
Sentinel Dome Trail, *Yosemite National Park*, p. 230

5 Best Hikes with Dogs:
Cascade Falls Trail, *Tahoe National Forest*, p. 125
Horsetail Falls Trail, *Eldorado National Forest*, p. 129
Kehoe Beach Trail, *Point Reyes National Seashore*, p. 134
Clark Boas & Belgum Trail Loop, *Wildcat Canyon Regional Park*, p. 174
Old Briones Road & Lagoon Trail Loop, *Briones Regional Park*, p. 176

5 Best Hikes to See Wildlife:
Wetlands Walk, *Sacramento National Wildlife Refuge*, p. 98
Tomales Point Trail, *Point Reyes National Seashore*, p. 132
Bon Tempe Lake Loop, *Marin Municipal Water District*, p. 148
Sequoia Audubon Trail, *Pescadero Marsh Natural Preserve*, p. 205
Fern Canyon Trail, *Prairie Creek Redwoods State Park*, p. 25

5 Best Hikes to See Birds:

Hookton Slough Trail, *Humboldt Bay National Wildlife Refuge,* p. 37
Fern Canyon Nature Trail, *Point Reyes Bird Observatory,* p. 141
Kent, Griffin, & North Loop Trails, *Audubon Canyon Ranch,* p. 143
Palo Alto Baylands Nature Trail, *Palo Alto Baylands Preserve,* p. 193
Mark Twain Scenic Tufa Trail, *Mono Lake Tufa State Reserve,* p. 239

5 Best Coastal Hikes:

Yurok Loop & Coastal Trail, *Redwood National Park,* p. 23
Rim Trail: Wedding Rock to Rocky Point, *Patrick's Point State Park,* p. 34
Headlands & Devil's Punchbowl Trail, *Russian Gulch State Park,* p. 76
Bluff Trail, *Salt Point State Park,* p. 84
Old Landing Cove Trail, *Wilder Ranch State Park,* p. 209

5 Best Stream Hikes:

Fern Canyon Trail, *Prairie Creek Redwoods State Park,* p. 25
Kings Creek Falls Trail, *Lassen Volcanic National Park,* p. 60
Root Creek Trail, *Castle Crags State Park,* p. 50
Mill Creek Trail, *Whiskeytown National Recreation Area,* p. 57
Hat Creek Trail, *Shasta-Hat Creek County Park,* p. 54

5 Best Lake Hikes:

Castle Lake Trail, *Shasta-Trinity National Forest,* p. 45
Terrace, Shadow, & Cliff Lakes, *Lassen Volcanic National Park,* p. 62
Smith Lake Trail, *Plumas National Forest,* p. 109
Dog Lake Trail, *Yosemite National Park,* p. 223
Parker Lake Trail, *Inyo National Forest/Ansel Adams Wilderness,* p. 242

5 Best Wildflower Hikes:

Macdonald Trail, *Anthony Chabot Regional Park,* p. 179
North Peak Trail to Prospectors Gap, *Mount Diablo State Park,* p. 181
Hawk Ridge Trail Loop, *Russian Ridge Open Space Preserve,* p. 194
Peter's Creek Trail & Long Ridge Road, *Long Ridge Open Space Preserve,* p. 199
Coastal & Matt Davis Trails, *Mount Tamalpais State Park,* p. 165

5 Most Unusual Hikes:

Bumpass Hell Trail, *Lassen Volcanic National Park,* p. 64
Mark Twain Scenic Tufa Trail, *Mono Lake Tufa State Reserve,* p. 239
Devils Postpile & Rainbow Falls Trail, *Devils Postpile National Monument,* p. 244
Hot Creek Geothermal Area Trail, *Inyo National Forest,* p. 249
Taft Point Trail, *Yosemite National Park,* p. 233

North Coast &
The Redwoods

(For locations of trails, see map on page 8.)

1. SIMPSON-REED & PETERSON TRAILS
Jedediah Smith Redwoods State Park
Off U.S. 101 near Crescent City
0.75 mile round-trip – 30 minutes — mostly level terrain

If you haven't had much exposure to coast redwoods and their ecosystem, hiking in the forests of northwestern California can raise a lot of questions. The Simpson-Reed and Peterson trails can answer them, and provide a half hour of pleasant walking in the process. The Simpson-Reed Trail serves as an excellent introduction to the redwoods; the connecting Peterson Trail extends the trip by making a figure-eight loop.

Get out your notebooks and your number two pencils. Here's the kind of information you'll gather on the Simpson-Reed Trail: California has two species of native redwoods—the coast redwood and the Sierra redwood or Sequoia. Sequoias grow wider and bulkier, but coast redwoods grow taller—as tall as 360 feet. They are the tallest living things on earth. Coast redwoods like fog and rain, and grow best at less than 2,000 feet in elevation. These giants can live for more than 2,000 years.

A redwood forest is often considered to be a monosystem, but in fact many other plants live alongside the big trees, including ferns of all kinds, vine maples, huckleberries, salmonberries, and redwood sorrel. (Sorrel has distinctive, clover-like leaves with purple undersides, and pink flowers.) You'll notice these neighbors of the redwoods as you walk the Simpson-Reed Trail, and learn how to identify them.

Other trees may grow in a redwood forest, including Douglas firs and maples. One of the redwood's most interesting cohabitants can be seen on this trail; it's a special type of tree nicknamed the "octopus tree." These are western hemlocks that have sprouted on the tops of redwood stumps, then grown over and around them, clutching the stumps in their roots or "legs." When the fallen redwood has finally rotted away, the hemlock remains standing on its long, thick roots.

An old-growth forest doesn't support much wildlife, because there is little for animals to eat. But the huge stumps of redwoods make perfect nesting grounds for the spotted owl. I was lucky enough to see one in midday as I drove down the road to this trailhead. You'll also hear the sounds of busy woodpeckers, drilling holes in trees with the precision of miniature jackhammers.

The Simpson-Reed Trail shows visitors how redwood trees reproduce and grow. Unlike other conifers, redwoods can sprout additional trunks as well as reproduce by seed. Often you'll see a circle of baby redwoods, called "cathedral trees," surrounding an old redwood that has been fire-scarred or felled. The sprouts begin as dormant buds that are stored in burls, the large bumpy growths you see near the base of the redwood. The dormant buds, or sprout seeds, are released during forest fires or through the gradual decay of the tree.

Simpson-Reed Loop Trail

As you loop around to the east side of the Simpson-Reed Trail, be sure to take the connecting loop to the Peterson Trail. This quarter-mile path shows off a riparian area with impressive big-leaf maples, skunk cabbage, and many charming footbridges over cascading streams.

Make it more challenging: If you're seeking more big trees and a longer walk, head across the road to the trailhead for the Hatton Trail. Walk out and back for as far as you like.

Trip notes: A $6 state park day-use fee is charged by Jedediah Smith Redwoods State Park. An interpretive brochure is available at the trailhead for 25 cents. For more information, contact Jedediah Smith Redwoods State Park, 1375 Elk Valley Road, Crescent City, CA 95531; (707) 464-6101 or (707) 445-6547.

Directions: From Crescent City, drive about five miles north on U.S. 101, then turn east on U.S. 199. Drive just under three miles to mile marker 2.84. The Simpson-Reed Trailhead will be on your left. Park in the gravel pullout alongside the road.

2. ENDERTS BEACH TRAIL
Redwood National Park
Off U.S. 101 near Crescent City
1.8 miles round-trip — 1 hour — rolling terrain

The Enderts Beach Trail may be too short to be considered much of a hike, but it leads to a terrific stretch of beach with pristine sand and good tidepooling opportunities. A bonus is that the trail goes right past Nickel Creek Campground, an easy-to-reach backpacking camp that makes a great first-time overnight trip for families or couples.

The trail begins where Enderts Road ends near Crescent Beach Overlook, just a few miles south of Crescent City. It follows an old abandoned road that has partly collapsed into the sea. Just to show you that Mother Nature isn't finished yet, the trail passes by an impressive landslide, just a few yards from the parking area.

Most of the route is wide enough for hand-holding, and it's just a simple downhill walk of six-tenths of a mile to a three-way trail junction. To the left is a short nature trail along Nickel Creek, straight ahead is the Coastal Trail heading south, and to the right is the path to Nickel Creek Campground and Enderts Beach. Before you make a beeline for the beach, walk the quarter-mile Nickel Creek Nature Trail to your left. In its short stretch it leads to some truly remarkable fern-covered trees. The ferns are the licorice variety, which grow high off the ground on tree branches and trunks. Along Nickel Creek, they hang off tree limbs from every possible angle and look like massive, leafy burls on the trees.

The nature trail ends abruptly at a viewing bench by the creek. Have a seat and remind yourself that you're in the northwest corner of California; this short stretch of trail is like a walk in the Florida Everglades.

After exploring Nickel Creek, return to the junction and follow the opposite trail into Nickel Creek Campground. Check out its five campsites and make a plan for a future overnight trip, then take the right fork that leads uphill above the rest room. In a matter of minutes you reach a grassy bluff above a long, crescent-shaped beach. You can easily descend to the beach, or pick a high perch on the bluffs to survey the scene. Enderts Beach is rocky and driftwood-strewn, but it also has large sandy stretches where you can lay out your towels. We saw two families sprawled out on the sand, complete with beach umbrellas, coolers, and the like. One father and son were earnestly fishing for surf perch and sea trout.

If you like exploring tide pools, consult your tide chart before you visit. During low tides, Enderts Beach has some excellent pools at its southern end. At certain times of the year, park rangers lead visitors on guided tidepool walks. Check with the ranger station in Crescent City for information on current dates and times.

Make it more challenging: After visiting Enderts Beach, return to the junction before Nickel Creek Campground where the Coastal Trail heads south. Hike south on the Coastal Trail for as far as you like, then turn around and hike back to your car at Crescent Beach Overlook.

Trip notes: There is no fee. Free trail maps are available from park headquarters. For more information, contact Redwood National Park Headquarters, 1111 Second Street, Crescent City, CA 95531; (707) 464-6101.

Directions: From Crescent City, drive three miles south on U.S. 101 and turn right (south) on Enderts Beach Road. Drive 2.2 miles to the end of road. The trailhead parking lot is just beyond Crescent Beach Overlook.

---

3. YUROK LOOP & COASTAL TRAIL
Redwood National Park
Off U.S. 101 near Crescent City
2.25 miles round-trip — 1 hour — rolling terrain

Everybody likes to walk along the ocean at the end of the day and watch the waves come in and the sun dip into the water. But few enjoy facing the gale-force winds that attack the coast on most clear days in Northern California. That's what makes the semi-protected Yurok Loop a great little trail, especially when combined with a short section of the Coastal Trail that leads to spectacular Hidden Beach.

Begin hiking at the northwest end of the Lagoon Creek parking lot. You'll cross a bridge and then head north toward the ocean. The Yurok Loop is an interpretive trail with numbered posts keyed to its brochure, which is usually available from a box at the bridge. If you pick up a brochure, you'll learn about Yurok Indian culture and their many uses of the land in this area. The trail itself is an ancient Yurok pathway leading south along the sea bluffs. It alternates through an oak and alder forest and open, grassy areas. What captures your attention are the views of driftwood-laden False Klamath Cove to the north and

Coastal Trail's Hidden Beach

massive False Klamath Rock to the west. At 209 feet tall, this huge
rocky outcrop dwarfs all the other sea stacks in the area. The Yurok
Indians used to dig for the bulbs of brodiaea plants (called "Indian
potatoes") by this rock.

Stay to the right when the trail forks at the sign for the Coastal
Trail, saving the second part of the Yurok Loop for your return. Ramble
along the Coastal Trail, a forested, fern-lined route. In a half mile of
mostly level walking, you'll meet up with the spur trail to Hidden
Beach. Follow it to the right for 100 yards to reach a classic Northern
California stretch of sand, complete with jagged rocks, mighty waves,
and driftwood of all shapes and sizes. The beach is prime for sunset-
watching. Bring a flashlight in case it gets dark sooner than you expect.

After visiting Hidden Beach, head back the way you came on the
Coastal Trail. This time turn right and walk the other side of the Yurok
Loop, descending through a tunnel-like canopy of alders.

When you return to the parking lot, be sure to explore around the
freshwater pond on Lagoon Creek. It's covered with big yellow pond
lilies and happy water birds, including ducks, egrets, and herons. The
pond is also popular with trout fishermen.

Make it easier: Hike the Yurok Loop only for a one-mile round-trip.

Trip notes: There is no fee. Free trail maps are available from park
headquarters. For more information, contact Redwood National Park

Headquarters, 1111 Second Street, Crescent City, CA 95531; (707) 464-6101.

Directions: From Crescent City, drive south on U.S. 101 for approximately 14 miles. Turn right at the sign for Lagoon Creek Fishing Access. The trail begins on the west (ocean) side of the parking lot.

---

4. FERN CANYON TRAIL
Prairie Creek Redwoods State Park
Off U.S. 101 near Orick
0.75 mile round-trip — 30 minutes — mostly level terrain

🚶🚶

As I was driving down the road to Fern Canyon in Prairie Creek Redwoods State Park, I kept muttering to myself, "This better be worth it." Why was I fretting? Well, getting to the trailhead requires a seven-mile drive on a one-lane gravel road. If the road hasn't been graded recently, it can be slow going. But I soon found out that patience is a virtue with a payback. The trip to Fern Canyon is worth every minute it takes to reach the trailhead.

The drive itself is actually part of the adventure. The road runs through the middle of the Elk Prairie section of Prairie Creek Redwoods, home to a large herd of Roosevelt elk (named after president Teddy). You have numerous chances to see these enormous creatures, which have the distinction of being California's largest land animals. They can weigh as much as 1,000 pounds. As you drive, you may see at a distance a meadow full of 50 or 60 elk. Then moments later you may have a close encounter with a dozen more, as they contentedly munch the grasses alongside the road. Often the massive elk are close enough to touch. They ignored me completely, even as I leaned out the car window to take their picture and say, "Hi, Elkies." The elk are very docile, although you shouldn't mess with the bulls, especially during mating season.

Although your hiking destination is a secluded fern grotto, a hidden paradise of giant ferns growing on 50-foot rock walls, the road to the trailhead leads along a windswept ocean beach. As beautiful as it is, ignore the beach for now, and continue to the road's end at the Fern Canyon Trailhead.

When you get there, lace up your hiking boots. (These are required equipment unless the stream is running very low or you like having wet feet.) Then start walking up the streambed to your right.

The path changes course at different times of the year, and you may or may not have to do some rock-hopping to get across the stream. In summer, park rangers make the hike easy by installing small bridges in several places. In the rainy season, the creek runs with a fury, so the bridges are removed.

As you walk up the streambed, you'll notice the canyon walls growing taller and squeezing tighter. Dense ferns line the canyon walls like wallpaper. Home Creek gushes near your feet. Miniature waterfalls pour down the rock walls. Moss grows everywhere, and combined with the multitude of ferns, the canyon feels like a rainforest. The color green is the order of the day.

Watch for the frogs, salamanders, and newts that make their home in the canyon, including the rare Pacific giant salamander. If you're very lucky, you might spot the coastal cutthroat trout, which travels from the ocean in spring to lay its eggs in the gravel streambed. Practice your fern identification as you walk. An interpretive sign at the trailhead explains the identifying characteristics of various fern varieties, including sword, lady, five-finger, chain, and bracken ferns—up to eight different species, all waving delicately in the breeze.

Continue up the canyon for a half mile until you reach a signed trail on the left that climbs out of the canyon on wooden stairsteps and loops back through the forest to the parking lot. (This is a short section of the James Irvine Trail.) When you finish out the loop, you have the option of continuing your hike by crossing the access road near the parking area and walking down to pristine, windswept Gold Bluffs Beach. Wander the beach as far as you please. You can beachcomb or watch for more Roosevelt elk. Dogs are allowed on the beach, although they aren't allowed in Fern Canyon or on any state park trails. Be sure to keep your dog leashed if you see any elk.

Make it more challenging: To extend the trip, turn right on the James Irvine Trail after you climb out of Fern Canyon. A mile or two out-and-back on this densely forested trail can only be a fine addition to your day.

Trip notes: A $6 state park day-use fee is charged by Prairie Creek Redwoods State Park. A trail map is available at the entrance kiosk. For more information, contact Prairie Creek Redwoods State Park, Orick, CA 95555; (707) 464-6101 or (707) 445-6547.

Directions: From Eureka, drive north on U.S. 101 for 41 miles to Orick. Continue north for 2.5 more miles to Davison Road, then turn left (west) and drive seven miles to the Fern Canyon Trailhead. The access road is gravel and may be rough; no trailers or motor homes are permitted.

5. BROWN CREEK TRAIL
Prairie Creek Redwoods State Park
Off U.S. 101 near Orick
2.8 miles round-trip — 1.25 hours — rolling terrain

Prairie Creek Redwoods State Park is such a great place that you can close your eyes, point your finger to any trail on its map, hike that trail, and have a great time. The park is criss-crossed with miles of beautiful paths; each is well-signed and easy to follow. As you drive the well-named Scenic Parkway that runs through the park, you continually pass little signs that read, "Trailhead parking 750 feet." You park in a pullout or a parking area, lock up your car, and go. What could be simpler?

In addition, the redwoods are big here, real big. You like your trees tall and wide? They've got 'em. People routinely walk around Prairie Creek Redwoods State Park with necks craned, looking up toward the sky. They're not checking for rain or gawking at skyscrapers—just looking at trees.

Big redwoods on the Brown Creek Trail

The only problem at this park, aside from trying not to get a neck-ache, is choosing which big tree trail to take. Here's my recommendation: Start at mileage marker 129, the trailhead for the Brown Creek Trail. Although the trail marker at the parking area announces the South Fork Trail, follow it anyway. You'll take the Foothill Trail/South Fork Trail for one-tenth of a mile toward the Brown Creek Trail. Stay on the South Fork Trail, heading toward the Rhododendron Trail, for another 100 yards to the trail marker that puts you on the Brown Creek Trail. Ignore the right turn to the Big Tree Trail. Sounds confusing? It's really not. Best of all, in about five minutes of walking, you've made enough trail switches to leave the crowds behind. Once you're on Brown Creek Trail, follow it all the way to its intersection with the Rhododendron Trail, then retrace your steps.

Now for the good part: The Brown Creek Trail traces through a pristine redwood forest complete with virgin groves of old growth trees, and it meanders along a perfectly charming stream. Just follow the creek for the entire distance. If you like, take some of the short spur trails to see various memorial groves and trees. As you walk, you'll find yourself being gradually immersed in the whisper-still solitude and the magic of the big redwoods.

The size of the trees along Brown Creek is truly humbling. Often the ones that leave you the most awestruck are the fallen giants lying on the ground, toppled by centuries of weather. Their huge root balls look like intricate sculpted knots, and their horizontal trunks serve as natural planters for entire microcosms of ferns, moss, mushrooms, and sorrel. Some of these tree trunks make such perfect garden boxes that you'll wonder if Mother Nature doesn't hire elfin landscape architects to help her do her work.

The Brown Creek Trail continues beyond its intersection with the Rhododendron Trail, but a turnaround at this junction makes an easy round-trip of just under three miles.

Make it more challenging: Where the Brown Creek Trail junctions with the Rhododendron Trail, turn right on the latter to make a loop. The trail climbs a bit steeply, then curves across the hillside, with views back down into the canyon. In a little over a mile, you'll meet up with the South Fork Trail. Turn right and finish out the loop with a switchbacking descent. When you reach the Brown Creek Trail again, turn left and follow the South Fork Trail for two-tenths of a mile back to your car.

Trip notes: A $6 state park day-use fee is charged by Prairie Creek Redwoods State Park. A trail map is available at the entrance kiosk. For more information, contact Prairie Creek Redwoods State Park, Orick, CA 95555; (707) 464-6101 or (707) 445-6547.

Directions: From Eureka, drive north on U.S. 101 for 41 miles to Orick. Continue north for approximately five more miles, then take the Newton B. Drury Scenic Parkway exit and turn left. Drive 2.5 miles to the parking pullout near mileage marker 129. The trail is signed "South Fork Trail."

6. SKUNK CABBAGE & COASTAL TRAIL
Redwood National Park
Off U.S. 101 near Orick
6 miles round-trip – 2.5 hours — rolling terrain

👫

Sometimes it takes a while for the obvious to become apparent. My hiking partner and I were walking on the Skunk Cabbage Trail, marveling at the dense forest and especially the huge, leafy plants that grew on the ground near every stream or spring. But we kept shaking our heads, puzzled by the plants' identification. Neither one of us had a clue about what the large-leafed foliage could be. It took almost three miles of hiking before the light bulb in my brain turned on. "Hey! I bet these big leafy plants are the trail's namesake—skunk cabbages!"

Indeed they were. The Skunk Cabbage Trail is a section of the Coastal Trail in Redwood National Park. It leads deep into a lush, jungle-like alder and spruce forest—so dense with foliage that you may think you've walked onto the set of *Jurassic Park*. Then, without any advance notice, the trail suddenly opens out to a wide stretch of coast at Gold Bluffs Beach.

The out-and-back trail is three miles each way, but with very little elevation change. The scenery will capture your imagination, particularly from about a half-mile in where the trail begins to follow Skunk Cabbage Creek. Here you'll find the largest numbers of skunk cabbages growing near the stream. They are vibrant green and as large as five feet across, with individual leaves growing a foot wide. The plants look something like cabbage heads on steroids, but they are actually a relative of the corn lily. Spring is the best time to see them.

The skunk cabbages grow in dense clusters under a canopy of alders, Sitka spruce, and occasional big redwoods. The white bark of the alders shines bright white in the dimly lit forest. Where you don't see skunk cabbages, you'll see massive clumps of sword ferns and redwood sorrel. Your trail weaves among all this foliage, crossing and recrossing Skunk Cabbage Creek on wooden footbridges.

After two delightful miles, the trail ceases its mostly level meandering and suddenly starts to climb. Leaving the creek behind, you continue up a ridge through a dense alder forest. (We saw probable bear evidence here in one stand of trees, where the bark on several alders had been torn to shreds as high as eight feet off the ground.) At 2.7 miles out, you round a curve in the trail, and—surprise—you're high on a

Skunk Cabbage Trail

bluff overlooking the ocean. It's quite startling to see the dense, terrarium-like forest end so abruptly at a broad expanse of open coastline.

Here, at a trail junction, you must make a choice: right is the continuation of the Coastal Trail that eventually leads to Gold Bluffs Beach, and left is a spur trail that beckons you to the beach directly below. And just a few yards west of this junction is a fine view of the coast, and perhaps a spot to sit and have lunch. Take your pick. If you want to hike farther, left is the best option. A descent of about 300 feet over a quarter-mile of moderate switchbacks will take you to the dune-like stretch of sand below. Once there, what will you find? Mussel Point, a rocky outcrop, lies about three-quarters of a mile to the south. Other than that, there's plenty of driftwood, sand verbena, and precious solitude.

Make it easier: The only way to make this one easier is to cut it short. Turn around before the trail starts to climb, which is about 45 minutes or two miles down the path. You'll still have an incredible jungle-like walk.

Trip notes: There is no fee. Free trail maps are available from park headquarters. For more information, contact Redwood National Park Headquarters, 1111 Second Street, Crescent City, CA 95531; (707) 464-6101.

Directions: From Eureka, travel north on U.S. 101 for 41 miles to Orick, then continue north for one more mile. Just past the cutoff for Bald Hills

Road, take the left turnoff that is signed for the Skunk Cabbage Section of the Coastal Trail. Drive a half mile down the road to the parking area and trailhead.

7. LADY BIRD JOHNSON GROVE
Redwood National Park
Off U.S. 101 near Orick
1 mile round-trip – 30 minutes — mostly level terrain

It was on the Lady Bird Johnson Grove that I first had "The Redwood Experience." In case you've never felt it, it happens something like this: You are wandering among ancient redwood trees that are hundreds of feet tall. Perhaps the fog has moved in, casting eerie filtered shadows in the forest. Your footsteps begin to slow. You find yourself noticing the most minute details, like the dewdrops on the pink petals of a rhododendron, or the bark pattern on one square inch of a 300-foot-tall redwood tree. Your voice drops to a whisper; you walk very softly, almost on tiptoe. The redwood forest has wrapped you in its embrace, and you may never want to leave.

That's "The Redwood Experience." It has happened to many hikers on many trails in Redwood National Park. It's this kind of feeling that makes visitors return to the redwoods, year after year. The Lady Bird Johnson Grove is one of the easiest places to get a taste of it.

From the trailhead parking area, cross the sturdy bridge over Bald Hills Road to access the trail. The 300-acre Lady Bird Johnson Grove was named for President Lyndon Johnson's wife, who dedicated the park in 1969. President Johnson signed the bill that created Redwood National Park in 1968, protecting these trees for generations to come.

The trail through the redwoods is only one mile round-trip, but you may find it takes you a while to hike it. You'll want to stop to read the interpretive signs, which explain about the history of white men in the redwood region. Jedediah Smith first explored this area in 1828, and Josiah Greg took the first recorded measurements of the redwood trees in 1849. Not surprisingly, the logging industry moved in next, although the loggers did not touch this particular grove.

In the understory of the redwoods, you'll see salmonberry, huckleberry, salal, and rhododendron. Sword ferns and sorrel grace the forest floor. If you picked up an interpretive brochure at the trailhead, you'll learn to identify "goose pens" (hollowed out redwood trunks that early settlers used for keeping poultry) and "sprout trees" or "cathedral trees" (redwoods that have sprouted additional trunks instead of reproducing by seed).

On the return half of the loop, you'll notice more Douglas fir and western hemlock trees in addition to the coast redwoods. The trail is short and simple, but it's likely to leave you feeling different from when you started. In the words of Lady Bird Johnson: "One of my most unforgettable memories of the past years is walking through the redwoods last November, seeing the lovely shafts of light filtering through the trees so far above, feeling the majesty and silence of that forest, and watching a salmon rise in one of those swift streams. All our problems seemed to fall into perspective and I think every one of us walked out more serene and happier."

Make it more challenging: Combine this walk with a hike on the Skunk Cabbage Section of the Coastal Trail, detailed in the previous story. The trailheads are only a three-mile drive apart.

Trip notes: There is no fee. Free trail maps are available from park headquarters. For more information, contact Redwood National Park Headquarters, 1111 Second Street, Crescent City, CA 95531; (707) 464-6101.

Directions: From Eureka, drive north on U.S. 101 for 41 miles to Orick, then continue north for one mile. Turn right on Bald Hills Road and drive 2.7 miles to the trailhead parking area on the right.

8. TALL TREES GROVE
Redwood National Park
Off U.S. 101 near Orick
3 miles round-trip — 1.5 hours — some steep terrain

It might sound like too much trouble to go to the Redwood Information Center, pick up a permit and a gate combination for the Tall Trees Access Road, then drive 16 miles to the trailhead—just to hike a trail that features big redwoods. After all, there are plenty of other redwood trails in the area that don't require a permit. But these aren't your average big redwoods; the Tall Trees Grove features the world's tallest tree at 367 feet high, as well as the third and sixth tallest trees in the world.

Of course, if there weren't plaques on the ground identifying the first, third, and sixth tallest tree, you'd never know which was which. Every redwood in this grove is immense. It's impossible to see all the way to their skyscraping summits.

The permit system is necessary because the Tall Trees Access Road (also called C-Line Road) is narrow and winding; too many cars at once would surely result in accidents. But the side benefit of the permit system is that it limits the number of hikers in the grove and adds to the serenity of the experience. (Only 50 cars are given a permit each day, but that limit is rarely reached except on peak summer weekends. If you are concerned about getting a permit on a particular day, just show up at the visitor center when it opens in the morning—don't wait until later in the day.)

At the Tall Trees Trailhead, pick up an interpretive brochure at the kiosk and head downhill. You'll pass a junction with the Emerald Ridge Trail in the first 100 yards; stay right. The first stretch of trail leads gently downhill through a mixed forest with myriad rhododendrons— no big redwoods yet. At 1.2 miles, you pass a rest room, which seems oddly out of place in the natural beauty of the forest. Just beyond it, the trail bottoms out and you reach the start of the loop trail through the grove. Follow the trail clockwise (to the left). Take the left spur trail to see Redwood Creek; in summer a bridge spans the creek to connect hikers to the Redwood Creek Trail. In winter and spring the creek is wide and powerful—more on the order of a river. (If the summer bridge is in place, walk across it. The best view of the world's tallest tree is from the far side of the creek.) The rich soils from Redwood Creek's stream bed, combined with the coastal climate, cause the redwoods to grow to their enormous size.

Tall Trees Grove

Back on the main trail, you'll reach the base of the world's tallest tree in short order. But don't turn around here, because this trail isn't about numbers, or about any one specific tree. The entire grove is remarkable. There are so many mammoth-sized trees in such close proximity that humans feel ant-sized in comparison. Even the rhododendrons grow extra large—as tall as 15 feet. They display flashy pink blooms among the dark shadows of the redwoods.

The trail continues past more huge redwoods to the north end of the loop, where it leads through a quarter-mile stretch of big leaf maples and California bays—a distinct contrast to the giant redwoods. This area is beautiful in its own way, especially in autumn when the maples turn colors. The loop heads back into the big trees, passing the sixth tallest and third tallest trees in the world. Finally, the loop rejoins the main trail to head back uphill. Linger a while among the giants before you go.

Make it more challenging: If the summer bridge is in place across Redwood Creek, cross it and hike for as far as you like on the opposite side of the stream. You'll pass 44 Camp, a small backpacker's camp and a good picnic spot.

Trip notes: There is no fee. Free trail maps are available from park headquarters. For more information, contact Redwood National Park Headquarters, 1111 Second Street, Crescent City, CA 95531; (707) 464-6101.

Directions: From Eureka, drive north on U.S. 101 for 40 miles to the Redwood Information Center on the west side of the highway. (It's two miles south of the town of Orick.) At the visitor center, pick up a Tall Trees Grove permit and the gate combination for the access road. Then drive north on U.S. 101 for three miles and turn right on Bald Hills Road. Drive seven miles on Bald Hills Road to the Tall Trees Access Road on the right (just past Redwood Creek Overlook). Turn right, stop at the gate, use your combination to open it, then drive through. Close and lock the gate behind you. Drive six miles on the Tall Trees Access Road (also called C-Line Road) to the trailhead parking lot.

9. RIM TRAIL: WEDDING ROCK to ROCKY POINT
Patrick's Point State Park
Off U.S. 101 near Trinidad
1 to 4 miles round-trip — 30 minutes to 2 hours — mostly level terrain

𝄡 ♿

Although I had heard the phrase "sea stack" before, I never knew exactly what it meant until I came to Patrick's Point State Park. Thousands of years ago, the main part of the seaside park was once entirely submerged in the ocean. When the water receded, tall sea stacks—precipitously balanced, 100-foot-tall, cliff-like outcrops—were left standing high and dry. Today the park shows off numerous examples of sea stack geology.

Two of these sea stacks, dubbed Ceremonial Rock and Lookout Rock, are a part of the main land mass of Patrick's Point State Park. They have many isolated rocky cousins just off the coast. On land and on sea, the sea stacks provide prime coastside drama for hikers. The best way to see them is on a short trek on the park's Rim Trail.

The complete trail is two miles in length, making it four miles round-trip, which is just fine if you feel ambitious. If you don't, you can taste the park's highlights by hiking only a section of the Rim Trail and then adding on the short spur trails that connect to three ocean overlooks—Wedding Rock, Patrick's Point, and Rocky Point.

If you start at the parking lot near Wedding Rock, you can take the connector trail from the Rim Trail to Wedding Rock, a majestic, castle-like rock terrace. From there, you can head left (southwest) on

Rim Trail—Wedding Rock to Rocky Point

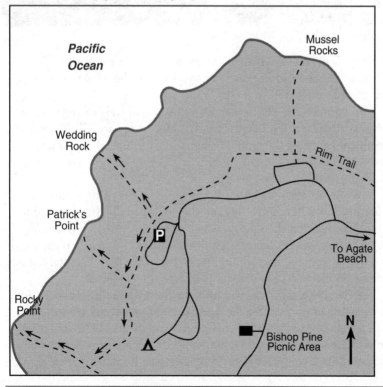

Looking out to sea from Wedding Rock

the Rim Trail and take the wheelchair-accessible cutoff to Patrick's Point, and then head further southwest on the Rim Trail to your final destination, the cutoff to Rocky Point.

In between the three overlook points, you'll walk through a mixed forest of Sitka spruce, Douglas fir, red alder, and pine. Wildflowers are abundant in spring, including Douglas iris, trillium, rhododendron, and salal. In spring and fall, be sure to scan the ocean horizon for migrating California gray whales.

While the Rim Trail itself is fairly level, the cutoff trails to the three overlooks have some ups and downs, especially the spur trail to Rocky Point. Even though you won't walk many miles on this route, you'll feel like you are getting a bit of a workout, especially if the wind is howling, which it does about 99 percent of the time. Coastal fog can also be problematic, especially if you came for the views.

If the day is mild and you have the energy for a longer walk, drive your car a half mile east to the Agate Campground parking area, then take a walk on the Agate Beach Trail to Agate Beach. (The trailhead is on the east side of the parking lot.) This is the only large sand beach in the park. Rock collectors flock to Agate Beach for its semiprecious agates, which are best found right at the surf line.

Note that the trail descends somewhat steeply to the beach, so be sure to save some energy for your climb back up. The round-trip to Agate Beach is just over a mile.

Make it easier: Skip the extra trip to Agate Beach and the descent from the Rim Trail to Rocky Point. You can enjoy roughly the same views at Patrick's Point and Wedding Rock, but without the return climb.

Trip notes: A $6 state park day-use fee is charged by Patrick's Point State Park. A trail map/brochure is available for 75 cents at the entrance station. For more information, contact Patrick's Point State Park, 4150 Patrick's Point Drive, Trinidad, CA 95570; (707) 677-3570 or (707) 445-6547.

Directions: From Eureka, drive north on U.S. 101 for 25 miles, past the town of Trinidad, and take the Patrick's Point Drive exit. Follow the signs to the entrance station for Patrick's Point State Park, then continue through it and past the Bishop Pine Group Picnic Area. Turn left and park at the paved parking lot near Wedding Rock and Patrick's Point.

---

10. HOOKTON SLOUGH TRAIL
Humboldt Bay National Wildlife Refuge
Off U.S. 101 near Eureka
3 miles round-trip — 1 hour — mostly level terrain

The Hookton Slough Trail is a flat, wide, and easy trail that gives you a guarantee of seeing wildlife as you walk. You want to see birds? No problem. Waterfowl, raptors, shorebirds—the Hookton Slough Trail has 'em all. You want a chance to see harbor seals basking in the mud? Your chances are good if the tide is high; that's when the seals swim up the slough from Humboldt Bay in search of a meal. Sand dabs, leopard sharks, and salmon also migrate through this estuary.

The key to all this wildlife diversity is the eelgrass, mudflats, and wetlands that provide habitat for thousands of living creatures—from tiny invertebrates to crabs and clams, from more than 200 species of birds to migratory fish and mammals like the harbor seals.

In one trip here, I saw dozens of white egrets soaring like small elegant swans, plus several species of ducks and gulls. Huge flocks of western sandpipers clustered by the edge of the bay, racing back and forth within inches of the water but never getting wet. Every 100 feet or so on the trail, I encountered giant goose eggs that had been cracked open, their contents either given over to predators or hatched to life.

Hookton Slough Trail, Humboldt Bay National Wildlife Refuge

September through March is the main bird viewing season, but the most interesting show comes from mid-March to late April, when black brants (also called sea geese) pass through town on their way from Alaska to Baja. Humboldt Bay is an important resting stop for them, because it provides the largest beds of eelgrass south of Washington.

The hike is simple: Begin at the parking lot, walk 1.5 miles out to the end of the trail (clearly marked at a boundary), and then walk back. On the return trip, when I took my eyes off the mudflats and looked ahead to the farms and hillsides in the west, I noticed large white spots in the tops of the trees. The "spots" were actually a few dozen white egrets, nesting in the tallest treetops.

Make it easier: Just shorten your walk.

Trip notes: There is no fee. Free trail maps/brochures are available at the trailhead. The Hookton Slough Trail is open every day from sunrise to sunset. The refuge office is open on weekdays from 7 a.m. to 4 p.m. For more information, contact Humboldt Bay National Wildlife Refuge, 1020 Ranch Road, Loleta, CA 95551; (707) 733-5406.

Directions: From Eureka, travel 10 miles south on U.S. 101. Take the Hookton Road exit and drive 1.2 miles west on Hookton Road to the Hookton Slough parking area. (The refuge office is located off the same exit but on Ranch Road. It's not necessary to go to the refuge office; you can drive directly to Hookton Slough.)

11. BIG TREE AREA: BULL CREEK FLATS TRAIL
Humboldt Redwoods State Park
Off U.S. 101 near Garberville
2.5 miles round-trip — 1.5 hours — mostly level terrain

🀉

Humboldt Redwoods State Park encompasses more than 51,000 acres, making it one of the largest state parks in California. This results in it having seven separate exits off the freeway and an overflowing abundance of trails to choose from. A first-time visit here can seem daunting. The trick, of course, is to know where to go.

If you're an avid fan of gargantuan *Sequoia sempervirens* and pretty streamside walks, the park's Big Tree Area is your ticket. Just driving to the trailhead on Bull Creek Flats/Mattole Road is a thrill. The road is winding, shaded, and narrow, with big trees so close that you can touch them by leaning out your car window.

From the parking area, walk straight ahead across the long, narrow footbridge, which rises 20 feet above Bull Creek. Turn left on the trail to see the Giant Tree, which is recognized by the American Forestry Association as the National Champion Coast Redwood. It's a colossal 363 feet tall and 53.2 feet in circumference. Next, follow the trail signs back to the Flatiron Tree, a huge fallen tree that is flat on one side, appearing nearly triangular in shape instead of round.

Big Tree Area, Bull Creek Flats Trail

To find more big trees, retrace your steps across the bridge to the parking area, walk across the lot, and locate the trail to the Tall Tree. How tall, you ask? It's a whopping 359.3 feet, and a pleasant little loop trail travels around it.

If you've had your fill of trees named every possible synonym for "big," continue from the Tall Tree, heading west on the Bull Creek Flats Trail and paralleling Bull Creek. You can take the trail from the Tall Tree all the way to Albee Creek Campground, a distance of just under one mile. The trail travels along the creek, where you'll find plenty of horsetails and Douglas irises in the spring. When you come to Bull Creek Flats/Mattole Road and the access road for the camp, turn around and head back to your car.

Make it easier: Just tour the feature trees near the parking lot—this takes only about a half mile of walking—and skip the Bull Creek Flats Trail to Albee Creek.

Trip notes: There is no fee. For more information and a $1 park map, contact Humboldt Redwoods State Park, P.O. Box 100, Weott, CA 95571; (707) 946-2409 or (707) 445-6547.

Directions: From Garberville, travel north on U.S. 101 for about 20 miles, heading into Humboldt Redwoods State Park. Take the Founder's Grove/ Rockefeller Forest exit and drive approximately four miles on Bull Creek Flats Road/Mattole Road to the Big Tree Area of Rockefeller Forest. Turn left at the Big Tree Area and park in the lot. The trail begins from the south side of the lot, at the bridge over Bull Creek.

---

12. SMITHE REDWOODS & EEL RIVER TRAIL
Smithe Redwoods State Reserve
Off U.S. 101 near Leggett
0.5 mile round-trip — 30 minutes — mostly level terrain

👫

For many Californians, the mention of "U.S. 101" brings to mind visions of rush-hour traffic jams—the Ventura Highway going from the San Fernando Valley into Los Angeles, or the rat race in the Bay Area going from the Peninsula to San Francisco. So what a treat it is to point your car north and head for the upper left-hand corner of the state, where U.S. 101 becomes a winding two-lane road piercing through miles and miles of forest. All of a sudden, it feels like you're driving on a country road instead of a major highway. Plus, once you get this far north, U.S. 101 is lined with one redwood park after another—perfect places to pull off the road, get out of the car, and take a stroll.

Smithe Redwoods State Reserve is one of the first redwood parks you reach as you drive northward. In the 1920s, the reserve's grounds were a popular resort named Lane's Redwood Flat, complete with a museum, restaurant, and 18 cabins. The resort met its fate in a forest fire and eventually the California State Park system obtained the land. Although Smithe Redwoods is small compared to other redwood parks further north, an easy walk and a picnic here is the perfect antidote for too much time spent in the car.

Dora Falls

As you pull in, you'll notice that all the parking spots have one-hour parking signs, which seems strange for a state park. But one hour is just about the right amount of time to enjoy this little reserve. Start by hiking around the big redwood trees; a short trail leads off to your left. Then take any of the cutoff trails that lead down to the South Fork of the Eel River. You can walk alongside the river for quite a distance, sometimes on dirt paths and sometimes on the rocky bed of its shoreline.

Part of the beauty of this park is that you can just plop down anywhere and have a picnic. I saw an older couple using one of the picnic tables among the big trees, and a family with two young boys sitting on the rocks by the Eel River, eating sandwiches. The kids were throwing stones into the river, having the time of their lives.

There's one more short walk to take at Smithe Redwoods, and it gets missed by many people because it isn't obvious. On the north side of the parking lot near the rest rooms you'll find Dora Creek, which runs through the reserve and empties into the Eel River. If you stand right next to the creek and look back across the highway, you'll see a decent-sized waterfall flowing down the hillside in winter and spring.

You can walk right up to the waterfall's base: Look both ways several times, cross U.S. 101 with caution, then walk behind the guard rail and head up a dirt path for about 100 yards.

The waterfall is often overlooked because it's across the road from the rest of the reserve and has no sign pointing to it. Dora Falls was once twice its size—60 feet tall instead of 30 feet—but a landslide in 1978 covered its bottom half with mud and dirt. Still, the waterfall is worth seeing, especially after winter rains.

Make it easier: It doesn't get much easier than this. You might want to skip the walk across the highway to see the falls, especially if you have children with you. You can still get a peek at the falls by standing near the creek and looking back across the highway.

Trip notes: There is no fee. Smithe Redwoods State Reserve is administered by rangers from Richardson Grove State Park, (707) 247-3319, and Standish-Hickey State Recreation Area, (707) 925-6482.

Directions: From Willitts, drive north on U.S. 101 for 47 miles. Smithe Redwoods State Reserve is 2.4 miles north of Standish-Hickey State Recreation Area. It comes up quickly on your left as you are traveling north on U.S. 101.

Redding, Shasta, & Lassen

(For locations of trails, see map on page 8.)

13. SACRAMENTO RIVER & CANTARA LOOP TRAIL
Shasta-Trinity National Forest
Off Interstate 5 near Dunsmuir
1.5 miles round-trip — 45 minutes — mostly level terrain

John Muir once said that "Nature is always lovely, invincible, glad, whatever is done and suffered by her creatures. All scars she heals, whether in rocks or water or sky or hearts." Few places is Nature's healing more evident than on the Cantara Loop Trail along the Sacramento River.

The Cantara Loop is a stretch of horseshoe-shaped railroad track that bridges the Sacramento River upstream of the town of Dunsmuir. In July of 1991, California's worst inland toxic spill occurred on this stretch of track when an improperly loaded Southern Pacific freight train derailed. It dumped 19,000 gallons of metam sodium, an inert plant and insect killer, into the river. The poison, when mixed with water, did exactly what it was manufactured to do: It killed every living organism within its reach, and also sickened people and animals in nearby Dunsmuir.

That terrible event happened not many years ago, and yet when you hike the Cantara Loop today, it seems as if you're in one of the most pristine places on earth. The river runs strong and clear, the streambeds and shorelines are teeming with plants and birdlife, and even the fishing has returned to its pre-disaster status. If you didn't know about the toxic spill, you would never guess it had occurred.

Begin your hike at the Cantara Loop by walking on the trail that parallels the river, heading downstream. Just after crossing the train tracks, you'll gain a good view of the Cantara Bridge. You can see how the train route curves through the valley, making a perfect "U" at the bridge. This tight turn is where the train derailed.

When the trail splits, head away from the water and through lovely meadows filled with daisies and Canada thistle. Then follow the trail back down toward the river again. The path eventually disappears in thick brush, forcing you to turn around and retrace your steps.

While hiking the Cantara Loop Trail, your peaceful meandering may be interrupted by the sound of an oncoming train. It happened to me on my trip: A long, 100-plus-car freight train rolled through the loop, its cars continuing in an seemingly endless chain after the engine had passed, screeching through the tight curve around the bridge. The sight and sound of it made me hold my breath. I watched as the conductor of this freighter, who was surely accustomed to the routine, leaned out the engine window and kept his eye on the bridge tracks. I wondered if he was crossing his fingers.

Make it more challenging: If you want to extend your walk, you can also take this trail in the other direction from the parking area, heading upstream along the river.

Trip notes: There is no fee. For more information, contact Shasta-Trinity National Forest, Mt. Shasta Ranger District, 204 West Alma Street, Mt. Shasta, CA 96067; (530) 926-4511.

Directions: From Redding, drive north on Interstate 5 for 65 miles to the town of Mt. Shasta, then take the Central Mt. Shasta exit. At the stop sign, turn left, cross the overpass, and continue for half a mile to South Old Stage Road. Turn left on South Old Stage Road and drive two-tenths of a mile to a Y in the road, where you bear left and continue on South Old Stage Road for 2.1 miles to Azalea Road. Turn right at Azalea, drive over the train tracks, and continue for a half mile to Cantara Road. Turn right on Cantara Road and drive eight-tenths of a mile to the parking area along the Sacramento River. The trailhead is on the left; head downstream.

---

14. CASTLE LAKE TRAIL
Shasta-Trinity National Forest
Off Interstate 5 near Dunsmuir
2 miles round-trip — 1 hour — rolling terrain

While national and state parks always seem to be bustling with visitors, fewer travelers make it to the lesser-known national and state forests, a 20-million-acre wonderland in California. Maybe that's because the Forest Service people don't exactly string up neon lights and shout from a megaphone, alerting everyone to their presence. So if it's solitude you seek, a trip to the Forest Service lands in Shasta-Trinity National Forest might suit you well. A hiking trip at Castle Lake is a perfect start; it offers an easy trail to a spectacular lookout high above a granite-lined lake.

When you pull into the parking area by Castle Lake's edge, you may gasp in surprise—this lake is really pretty. Set in a glacial bowl at 5,450 feet in elevation, the lake is backed by a high rock cliff and views of Mount Shasta on clear days.

The trail starts at the parking lot, where a small but popular campground is located. The first 200 feet of trail are the trickiest: You have to boulder-hop across a stream, which ranges from two feet wide in

Castle Lake, Shasta-Trinity National Forest

summer to 25 feet wide after winter snow and rain. The trail laterals around the lake, climbing gradually through a sparse conifer forest. Your views keep getting more spectacular all the time. When you reach the ridge above the lake, in about a mile of hiking, you're at 5,900 feet in elevation. Have a seat on a rock, pull out your picnic, and stay a while.

Hikers looking for more adventure can continue over the ridge to two smaller lakes—Little Castle Lake and Heart Lake. Less ambitious hikers will find that their ridgetop view of Castle Lake offers plenty to satisfy. The crystal clear lake has 47 surface acres of water and a depth of 120 feet against its back granite wall. Some people claim the lake has rejuvenative powers; they swear that swimming in Castle Lake is like being dipped in magic water. I'd say it's more like being dipped in ice cubes, because the lake's water is mostly snowmelt from Mount Shasta.

The Shasta and Wintu Indians called Castle Lake "Castle of the Devil." They believed an evil spirit lived in the lake and made the eery echoing noises often heard in winter. The sound is actually just the movement of ice—and maybe the grumbles and moans of people who come here in winter to ice-fish. (They don't catch much, unfortunately.) Ice skating is also popular in winter.

Make it more challenging: You can add on a hike from Castle Lake's ridge to Little Castle Lake and Heart Lake. Little Castle Lake is a 15-minute hike just over the ridge, with a 300-foot drop down to the lake (really a pond). Farther up the ridge, accessible via a faint trail, is Heart Lake. Obtain a Forest Service map from the address below for more details.

Trip notes: There is no fee. For more information, contact Shasta-Trinity National Forest, Mt. Shasta Ranger District, 204 West Alma Street, Mt. Shasta, CA 96067; (530) 926-4511.

Directions: From Redding, drive north on Interstate 5 for 65 miles to the town of Mt. Shasta, then take the Central Mt. Shasta exit. At the stop sign, turn left, cross the overpass, and continue for one-half mile to South Old Stage Road. Turn left on South Old Stage Road and drive two-tenths of a mile to a Y in the road, where you bear right and continue on W. A. Barr Road. Travel 2.2 miles on W. A. Barr Road, crossing over the dam at Lake Siskiyou; then turn left on Castle Lake Road and drive 7.2 miles to where the road dead-ends at the parking area for Castle Lake. The trailhead is at the edge of the parking lot to the left of the lake.

---

15. McCLOUD FALLS TRAIL
Shasta-Trinity National Forest
Off Highway 89 near McCloud
3.5 miles round-trip — 30 minutes — rolling terrain

It's surprising that the Forest Service hasn't put up a big sign and pay-as-you-enter kiosk at spectacular Middle McCloud Falls. The small, easy-to-miss Forest Service sign on Highway 89 says simply "River Access," giving no indication of the impressive waterfall nearby.

Middle McCloud Falls and its siblings Lower and Upper falls are located by Fowler's Camp in the town of McCloud. Of the three waterfalls on the McCloud River, Middle McCloud Falls is the show-stopper. All three falls are easily visited via a 3.5-mile round-trip trail.

Lower McCloud Falls is the easiest to access; you can drive right up to it. It's a popular put-in spot for kayakers heading down the McCloud, and for swimmers who want to jump in and cool off in summer. Start your trip with a visit to Lower Falls (follow the signs along the camp road). This will get you in the waterfall mood. Then follow the paved trail along the river into the campground, where the McCloud Falls trail begins.

For the next half-mile, you'll walk on a flat, pine-needle-strewn route along the McCloud River, with pretty water views the whole way. Soon you'll hear a furious rush of water, and then suddenly Middle Falls appears—tall, wide, and majestic. The gushing water drops about 75 feet over a cliff, forms a deep pool at its base, then continues on its way downstream.

After the record winter rains of 1995 and 1998, the usually serene

Middle Falls looked downright dangerous. Water was not falling but rocketing over the cliff, hitting the pool below with such force and fury that it created a tremendous upsurge. The barreling falls evoked a perilous feeling, as if Mother Nature was saying, "Hey, don't forget what I'm capable of."

From Middle McCloud Falls, you can follow the trail uphill and through a few switchbacks to an overlook of Upper McCloud Falls. The upper fall is the hardest of the three waterfalls to get a good look at, but from several points on the trail you can catch sight of its narrow funnel of water plunging into a rocky bowl.

Here's a tip for your visit: Locals and campers who know about Middle McCloud Falls are most likely to be here in summer, when the air and water temperatures heat up. But the best time to see the falls is in late winter and spring, when the water is running hard and fewer people are around. If you plan your trip for April or early May, you'll have a good chance of having the waterfalls all to yourself.

Make it easier: Visit Lower Falls only, which is accessible even for wheelchair users.

Trip notes: There is no fee. For more information, contact Shasta-Trinity National Forest, McCloud Ranger District, P.O. Box 1620, McCloud, CA 96057; (530) 964-2184.

Directions: From Redding, drive 65 miles north on Interstate 5. Take the Highway 89/McCloud/Reno exit and drive east on Highway 89. Pass the town of McCloud in nine miles, then continue 4.5 miles further east to a small Forest Service sign on the right for "River Access." Turn right and follow the signs to the McCloud River Picnic Area and Lower McCloud Falls. (Bear right at the road forks, driving past Fowlers Camp.) Park in the day-use area.

16. HEDGE CREEK FALLS TRAIL
City of Dunsmuir
Off Interstate 5 in Dunsmuir
0.4 mile round-trip — 20 minutes — rolling terrain

Imagine you're hightailing it up I-5 with the kids on the way to visit Grandma in Portland. They're going berserk from being locked in the car for hours, and you're about to lose it if you see any more concrete, guard rails, or fast-food chains. But then you reach the town of Dunsmuir, 57 miles north of Redding, and you remember a freeway antidote: the Hedge Creek Falls Trail.

Get off the freeway and head to Dunsmuir Avenue. Park in the small parking lot, and maybe have a snack in the tiny park where the waterfall trail begins. Then take an easy hike down the path. Blink and you'll miss it—not the waterfall but the walk to it, because you'll reach the falls in about five minutes of downhill cruising.

Impressive Hedge Creek Falls drops 30 feet over a vertical granite slab into a shallow pool and a pretty babbling stream. The rock face that forms the fall is so sheer that it makes the water chute appear much

Hedge Creek Falls, Dunsmuir

grander in size than it is. A large indentation in the bottom of the cliff, near where the fall hits the pool, creates a small cave behind the falls. When the water flow is diminished in summer, you can crawl into the cave and pretend you are a water ouzel, that funny bird that makes its home behind waterfalls.

Prolong your visit to this little paradise just off the freeway by settling in on the bench by the falls. More benches are positioned up and down the trail, which may come in handy on the return climb. When you hike back uphill, be sure to turn around a few times for parting glances at the falling water. At a few points, about 20 to 30 feet from the fall, you can peer through the lush canopy of leaves and see another waterfall directly above this one, set farther back in the canyon.

Make it easier: As short as this trail is, it does involve a steep climb on your return. Anyone in your party who doesn't want to climb should wait in the pretty city garden at the Hedge Creek Falls trailhead.

Trip notes: There is no fee. For more information, contact the city of Dunsmuir at (530) 235-4822.

Directions: From Redding, drive 57 miles north on Interstate 5 to Dunsmuir and take the Central Dunsmuir/Siskiyou Avenue exit. Turn left at the stop sign and cross under the freeway, then turn right on Dunsmuir Avenue, travel about 20 yards, and turn left into the small parking area.

Traveling south on Interstate 5 near Dunsmuir, take the Dunsmuir Avenue/Siskiyou Avenue exit. Turn right at the stop sign. Turn right again immediately on Dunsmuir Avenue, travel about 20 yards, and turn left into the small parking area.

---

17. ROOT CREEK TRAIL
Castle Crags State Park
Off Interstate 5 north of Lake Shasta
2 miles round-trip — 1 hour — mostly level terrain

🚶🚶

How many times have you driven up Interstate 5, gaping at mammoth Mount Shasta up ahead, and then suddenly looked over your left shoulder and seen those big, gray, craggy rocks looming over you—the unmistakable jagged outline of the ancient granite spires of Castle Crags?

Admiring the crags from afar is good, but getting closer is even better. The problem is that the spires of Castle Crags go straight up, jutting abruptly into the stratosphere at 6,500 feet in elevation. The trails to reach them are steep with a capital *S*. Although some people climb the Crags Trail all the way to Castle Dome's base—gaining 2,300 feet in nearly three miles, a prodigious climb—let's dispense with our summit illusions and go for something more manageable.

Starting from the vista point parking lot, the first trip you should take is the short walk uphill to the vista point. You'll get an eyeful of Castle Crags and, on a clear day, Mount Shasta to your right and Grey Rocks to your left. Conical Mount Shasta at 14,162 feet is obviously a volcano, albeit one that's not currently in service. But Castle Crags is a completely different type of geological formation, made of a granite material (granodiorite) that was formed below the earth's surface millions of years ago and then slowly forced upward. Grey Rocks looks vastly different from either Mount Shasta or Castle Crags and is of yet another geologic type. It's greenstone and slate metamorphic rock, thrust upward and sideways from the earth and weathered by the centuries.

Retrace your steps from the vista point, cross the parking lot, and head down the access road for about 40 yards to the trailhead for the

Root Creek Trail. Root Creek Trail is mostly level, and it travels through a conifer and hardwood forest all the way to Root Creek. At trail's end you get a surprising look straight up at Castle Dome, the big, smooth, rounded rock formation that leads the parade of crags.

At different times of the year you may spot the crags from other points along the trail, not just at the end, depending on the thickness of the forest canopy. But views or no views, the walk is terrific, with pine needles at your feet and five-finger and deer

Root Creek, Castle Crags State Park

ferns leading the way. Root Creek is a quick and cool stream, bubbling over rounded rocks, with plentiful elephant ears growing along its banks. Also called Indian rhubarb, elephant ears are the foot-high, huge-leafed green plants you see growing along many streams in Northern California. It's easy to understand where they got their moniker.

When you reach the trail's end at Root Creek, hang around for a while (there's a wooden bench for that purpose) and then backtrack to the parking area.

A great sidetrip after visiting the park is to drive northwest from the park entrance on Castle Creek Road. In only a few minutes, you'll gain elevation and reach some spectacular overlooks of Castle Crags.

Make it more challenging: The Root Creek Trail connects with both the Crags Trail and the Pacific Crest Trail. You can add on an out-and-back hike on either of these trails. The Pacific Crest Trail has an easier grade.

Trip notes: A $5 day-use fee is charged by Castle Crags State Park. A trail map is available from the ranger kiosk for $1. For more information, contact Castle Crags State Park, P.O. Box 80, Castella, CA 96017-0080; (530) 235-2684.

Directions: From Redding, drive 50 miles north on Interstate 5 and take the Castle Crags State Park exit, which is four miles south of the town of Dunsmuir. Turn west and follow the signs to the park entrance. After paying at the kiosk, turn right and follow the road to its end at the Vista Point parking area. The trailhead for the vista point is at the parking lot; the trailhead for Root Creek Trail is about 40 yards downhill from the parking lot.

18. HEADWATERS & PACIFIC CREST TRAILS
McArthur-Burney Falls Memorial State Park
Off Highway 89 near Burney
1 mile round-trip — 30 minutes — rolling terrain

Plenty of people drive to McArthur-Burney Falls Memorial State Park each spring and summer, park in the main lot, get out of their cars, and look over the railing at the falls. Maybe they even walk 50 yards or so to get a little closer to the huge surge of plunging water and mist. Then they take a few pictures, jump back in their cars, drive home, and brag to all their friends about how they ventured into the wilderness.

Burney Falls

Sure, Burney Falls is worth the trip—even if all you do is sightsee. Watching a hundred million gallons of water pour over the cliffs, rain or shine, is a breathtaking experience. President Theodore Roosevelt, a devout nature-lover, went so far as to call Burney Falls the eighth wonder of the world. But if you want to spend a little more time in this beautiful state park, you can leave the crowds behind and take a lovely loop hike to the waterfall.

To make the trip, park your car in the small lot to the left of the entrance kiosk (not the main lot to the right), and then begin walking on the Headwaters Trail, heading upstream and away from the falls. The woods are filled with conifers, including ponderosa pines (the trees with the clearly delineated, jigsaw puzzle bark) and huge Douglas firs, plus hardwoods such as white oaks and black oaks. If you visit in spring or early summer, you may notice the lovely sweet scent of mountain misery, a small shrub with tiny light blue or white flowers.

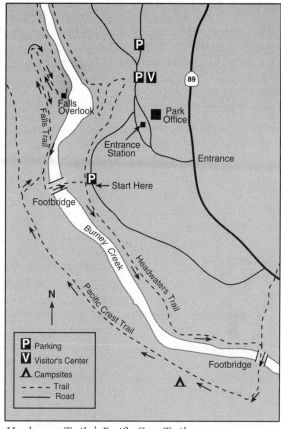

Headwaters Trail & Pacific Crest Trail

In a half mile, you'll reach a long footbridge over Burney Creek and an intersection with the Pacific Crest Trail. Cross the bridge and follow this small section of Pacific Crest Trail, heading downstream toward the falls on the other side of the creek. In another half-mile, exit the Pacific Crest Trail and turn right on the Falls Trail.

In a couple minutes of switchbacking down the trail, you'll come to a placard for the Burney Falls lookout and a small clearing through the woods, where the rushing cataract is framed by trees. It could be argued that the waterfall view from this angle is prettier than from the other, more photographed side of the creek.

At 129 feet, Burney Falls is not the highest waterfall in California, but what makes it unusual is that it flows at basically the same rate all year long, with no change in the dry season. This is because the water for Burney Creek comes mostly from underground springs and stored snowmelt in the basalt rock layers that make up the falls. If you look closely, you can see that much of the water actually pours out of the face of the cliff, rather than running over the top of the cliff. Due to its underground water source, the water temperature below the falls, even on warm summer days, is a chilly 42 degrees Fahrenheit.

As you hike, keep your eyes open for two unusual bird species who frequent this park: Migratory black swifts, who build their nests on the sheer cliffs of the waterfall in early summer (you can seeing them flitting in and out of the gushing water); and bald eagles, who nest at nearby Lake Britton.

To return to the parking area, backtrack up the Falls Trail for a few hundred yards and then turn left onto another footbridge.

Make it easier: Instead of starting out on the Headwaters Trail, take the Falls Trail from the same parking lot, cross the footbridge, and turn right to get to the viewing spot for the falls. (This is the reverse of the return trip for the hike in the story.)

Trip notes: A $5 day-use fee is charged by McArthur-Burney Falls State Park. A trail map is available from the ranger kiosk for $1. For more information, contact McArthur-Burney Falls Memorial State Park, 24898 Highway 89, Burney, CA 96013; (530) 335-2777.

Directions: From Burney, drive approximately four miles east on Highway 299 to the intersection of Highways 89 and 299. Turn left and drive north on Highway 89 for approximately six miles to the main entrance to the park. Pay at the kiosk, then drive past it and to the left. (The visitor center and main parking area is to the right.) Park in the small parking area a few hundred yards to the left of the kiosk. The trailhead for the Headwaters Trail is on the left side of the parking lot.

19. HAT CREEK TRAIL
Shasta-Hat Creek County Park
Off Highway 299 between Burney and Fall River Mills
4 miles round-trip — 2 hours — mostly level terrain

There's nothing quite as nice as watching a big stream roll by, unless of course you're watching two big streams roll by. That's what you can do on this hike along Hat Creek and the Pit River. It's a perfect walk to do with a loved one or ones, because the trail is flat and easy, and wide enough so that you can walk side by side.

Your hike is an easy stroll down an old dirt road that soon diminishes to a trail. The Pit River flows by on your right and Hat Creek on your left. You walk smack in between the two waterways for most of the trip, in a big meadow filled with wildflowers and birdlife and bordered by black oaks and white oaks. After a mile or so, the trail brings you closer to the Pit River side, and then curves around to your left to the confluence of the Pit River and Hat Creek. On your return, you stay closer to the Hat Creek side for a few hundred yards until you are led back to the main trail.

The faint spur trails you'll see along the way are mostly used by fishermen. You can take any or all of them without fear of getting lost, because the two waterways always keep you on track.

The broad open fields and oak woodlands that divide the Pit River and Hat Creek seem to naturally encourage good conversation, and the intersection where the two waters meet is the perfect place to lay out a blanket and have a picnic. As you wander, watch for birds. This type of meadow and woodland environment attracts numerous songbirds and birds of prey. Look for stellar's jays, robins, meadowlarks, blackbirds, red-tailed hawks, and Cooper's hawks. A local birding group has put up nesting boxes along the river in the hope of attracting more songbirds.

On your return hike along Hat Creek, you'll notice a small dam

Family hiking along the Hat Creek Trail

and a five-foot waterfall marked by orange buoys floating across the creek, just before the confluence of the two streams. These are signals to kayakers and canoeists not to float further downstream.

You may see anglers along Hat Creek, particularly at the stretch by the county park where you parked. The stream is famous for its wild trout and is popular with flyfishers. It's rare that you see anyone catch anything, though, because the fish are smart and the water is crystal clear. People travel from all over to fish at Hat Creek, which is catch-and-release only in this section. You won't see any frying pans.

Make it easier: Just cut your trip short, turning around when you wish.

Trip notes: There is no fee. For more information, contact Shasta County Public Works at (530) 225-5661.

Directions: From Burney, drive 7.5 miles east on Highway 299, past the intersection of Highways 89 and 299, to just before the highway bridge over Hat Creek. Turn left into Shasta-Hat Creek County Park just before the bridge; park and then walk back to the road and across the bridge. The trailhead is a dirt road about 20 feet from the east end of the bridge.

---

20. LAKE SHASTA OVERLOOK TRAIL
Shasta-Trinity National Forest
Off Interstate 5 north of Redding
1.6 miles round-trip – 1 hour — rolling terrain

What more can anyone say about Lake Shasta? It's the largest man-made reservoir in California, with statistics that rank with some of the greatest recreation lakes in America—370 miles of shoreline, more than 1,000 campsites, 29,000-plus acres of water, and nearly two dozen boat ramps. Anglers, boaters, water-skiers, houseboaters, sun-worshippers—everybody loves Lake Shasta.

But for some reason I never thought of it as a place to hike. With so many recreation enthusiasts out on the lake, I couldn't imagine it as a place to find solitude in the woods. Guess I was missing the boat, so to speak.

The best way to hike at Lake Shasta is to climb above it all to get the big picture, or a good piece of it. The Lake Shasta Overlook Trail is just the ticket. It ascends gently through a mixed conifer and hardwood forest, with the sound of a running creek serenading you as you walk. From the trailhead, you climb just under a mile, slowly switchbacking up a ridge. At the top, you reach the first lake overlook point, which comes supplied with a wooden bench for enjoying the view. The trees have grown quite large here, framing the water vista.

But this overlook is only a preview, so don't use up all your film taking pictures. Just 50 more yards farther is the *real* overlook, with a wide-angle look at Packers Bay leading into the main body of the lake.

The Overlook Trail makes a tiny loop around some huge manzanita bushes and then heads back downhill. If you want to hike further, go back to the parking area and pick up Waters Gulch Trail, which is another out-and-back trail but is about twice as long.

Make it easier: Hike on the out-and-back Waters Gulch Trail instead, which doesn't climb as much. You won't get the lake views as soon on this trail, but you will get a pretty, mostly flat forest/stream walk.

Trip notes: There is no fee. For more information, contact Shasta-Trinity National Forest, Shasta Lake Ranger District, 14225 Holiday Road, Redding, CA 96003; (530) 275-1587.

Directions: From Interstate 5 at Redding, drive north for 15 miles to Lake Shasta and take the Packers Bay exit. Drive southwest on Packers Bay Road for one mile to the trailhead, a dirt parking area on the right. (If you come to the boat ramp, you've gone too far.) There are two trailheads located here: Overlook Trail and Waters Gulch Trail.

---

21. MILL CREEK TRAIL
Whiskeytown National Recreation Area
Off Highway 299 west of Redding
4 miles round-trip — 2 hours — rolling terrain

The Mill Creek Trail is for people who prefer the ferris wheel to the roller coaster at amusement parks. Going on the ferris wheel makes you feel like you're having an adventure, when in fact you know you're perfectly safe. You can have all the fun you want without having to worry. Riding the roller coaster feels like an adventure, too, but you can't relax until it's over and you've survived. Somehow, that's not as much fun.

This out-and-back trail in the Whiskeytown National Recreation Area is for people who want to have an adventure—hiking in a dense forest, boulder-hopping across a stream more than two dozen times, taking a dip in a swimming hole—without having any worries. The trail bounces back and forth across startlingly clear Mill Creek, but because the creek is rarely more than five feet wide and eight inches deep, a misstep or a fall is no big deal. Even small children can walk this trail, and those I saw were having a ball.

Hiking the entire length of the Mill Creek Trail is not for everybody, however. It continues for 2.5 miles one-way, ending in a climb to a dirt fire road, and looping back isn't possible. The trail also becomes more narrow and indistinct, and the stream crossings grow progressively more difficult. But you can simply travel as far as you like, weaving your way through the thick pine and fir forest and rock-hopping across Mill Creek, then turn around and head back. In summer, when the water level is low, most people will hike about two miles out for a four-mile round-trip. You'll know it's time to head back when you start thinking, "Jeez, do I have to cross this creek *again?*"

The trail begins at the El Dorado Mine, which was built in the 1880s and was still in operation as late as 1967. Over the years, El Dorado and other mines in this area produced substantial gold profits. Recreational gold panning continues in the park to this day. After you've taken a look at the mine shaft and the remaining mine buildings, continue past the mine on the marked trail, which heads up the creek. At the first few trail intersections, you can choose to stay where you are or cross to the other side of the creek. Either direction is fine, as long as you keep heading upstream. (Don't take the trail intersection on the east side of the creek that connects to the Clear Creek Vista Trail or you'll be heading downstream.) Soon the junctions cease to exist and only one trail skips back and forth across Mill Creek, crossing some 20 times on the way out and 20 more on the return trip.

Depending on the season, the trail can be somewhat indistinct in places, but the stream always keeps you on track. Be sure to pause for a rest break on a granite boulder, cool your feet in the stream, and notice the flora and fauna in this riparian habitat. You'll see elephant ears (the big leafy plants alongside the stream), as well as vine maples growing underneath the shade of incense cedars and Ponderosa pines. The music of songbirds fills the air and, because this is a rock-hopping stream, frogs are ubiquitous.

Make it easier: For a much shorter and easier walk, head out to the El Dorado Mine and then return via a loop trail on a dirt road.

Trip notes: There is no fee. For more information and a free trail map, contact Whiskeytown National Recreation Area, P.O. Box 188, Whiskeytown, CA 96095; (530) 246-1225 or (530) 241-6584.

Directions: From Interstate 5 at Redding, take Highway 299 west for 16.5 miles, passing Whiskeytown Lake and turning left at the sign for "Towerhouse Historic District." Park in the lot, walk down the paved path, cross a wooden bridge, walk through a white picket gate, and cross a second bridge. A dirt road leads past a park residence to the El Dorado Mine and the trailhead.

22. CHAOS CRAGS & CRAGS LAKE
Lassen Volcanic National Park
Off Highway 44 east of Redding
3.6 miles round-trip — 2 hours — some steep terrain

🚶🚶

When most of Lassen Volcanic National Park is still buried in snow, it can feel like summer in the Manzanita Lake area of the park. This early season is an excellent time to hike uphill to Crags Lake, and perhaps take a bracing swim before the long days of sunshine dry up the snow-fed lake. Crags Lake is a beauty, and the trail to reach it is an easy ascent of only 1.7 miles, followed by a short but steep drop to the water's edge.

Chaos Crags and Crags Lake

Initially, the path climbs very gently through pine and fir forest. Many of the trees are stunted from the poor volcanic soil they grow in; some have a healthy quantity of bright green staghorn lichen coloring their trunks. The forest is situated along the edge of Chaos Jumbles, a two-mile-square rockslide caused by volcanic activity sometime around the year 1700.

The trees hide much of your view of the rockslide, but as you climb, you'll see other evidence of volcanism. A group of six plug domes called the Chaos Crags rise above the upper reaches of the trail. The Chaos Crags were formed by thick, viscous lava. The lava was so thick that it didn't flow outward; rather it squeezed upward through vents in the earth and then hardened in place. The Crags are estimated to be about 1,000 years old—much older than the Chaos Jumbles. A depression or small crater at the base of the Crags is what forms Crags Lake each year as the snow melts.

As you proceed uphill, the forest cover starts to thin and your views get wider. A few switchbacks take you up to the crest of a ridge—the high point on this trail. You are rewarded with a dramatic view of the Chaos Crags towering hundreds of feet above you. Below you is the steep bowl in which blue-green Crags Lake lies, and far off in the distance are the Chaos Jumbles and forested Hat Creek Valley.

Many people turn around at this point, but it's only a short descent of about 100 yards down to the lake's edge. If you go swimming, you'll find that the water temperature is comfortable near the shore, but it drops dramatically the deeper you go. If you don't want to swim, you can find a spot along the water's edge and have a picnic, admiring the ephemeral lake. By about September, its snow-fed waters will have dried up under the Lassen sun.

Make it easier: Skip the descent to the lake's edge. Just admire the view from the trail above the lake.

Trip notes: A $10 entrance fee is charged by Lassen Volcanic National Park (good for seven days). Free park maps are available at the entrance stations. For more information, contact Lassen Volcanic National Park, P.O. Box 100, Mineral, CA 96063; (530) 595-4444.

Directions: From Redding, drive east on Highway 44 for 46 miles. Turn right on Highway 89 and drive a half mile to the park's northwest entrance station. Continue southeast on Highway 89 for a half mile to the right turnoff for Manzanita Lake Campground (just beyond the Loomis Museum). Turn right and drive 100 yards to the trailhead on the left.

23. KINGS CREEK FALLS TRAIL
Lassen Volcanic National Park
Off Highway 36 east of Red Bluff
2.4 miles round-trip — 1.5 hours — some steep terrain

The waterfall on Kings Creek is pretty, not spectacular, but the beauty of the trail to reach it makes Kings Creek Falls one of the most visited attractions in Lassen Volcanic National Park. The hike is a downhill trek along Kings Creek, starting from a nondescript pullout along the park road. On weekdays, a yellow school bus is often parked in this pullout; Kings Creek Falls is a popular destination for visiting school classes.

The first part of the trail meanders under the shade of big fir trees, but at a quarter mile out, the trail leaves the forest for a pleasant traverse along the edge of Lower Meadow. The meadow is dark green and teeming with ebullient corn lilies in spring and early summer. It makes a perfect place to rest on the uphill hike back.

Beyond the meadow, you reach a fork and have two options: the Foot Trail or the Horse Trail. The Foot Trail is the most scenic choice. It leads steeply downhill for a half-mile on stair-steps cut into the rock, just inches away from an area of Kings Creek called The Cascades. Hikers who have trekked the world-famous Mist Trail in Yosemite will find a kinship between that trail and the granite walkway to Kings Creek Falls, although the latter has much less of a grade.

Just before you step down the granite staircase, take a look ahead at the far-off valley vista. Once you're on the stair-steps, you must keep your eyes on your feet and their placement, because you're hiking only a few inches from the rushing cascade of white water. Some hikers mistake these cascades for Kings Creek Falls, and they unknowingly turn around before they reach the real thing. Keep going until you come to a fenced overlook area.

Kings Creek Falls are about 50 feet high and split by a rock out-crop into two main cascades, which make a steep and narrow drop into the canyon. The fence surrounding the waterfall keeps hikers out of trouble on the unstable canyon slopes. If you want to take pictures, arrive here in the morning, when the cataract is evenly lit.

For your return trip, you can retrace your steps on the spectacular Foot Trail back uphill along Kings Creek, or you can take the easier Horse Trail, which connects back with the main trail near Lower Meadow.

Make it more challenging: You can add on a side trip to Sifford Lakes and then loop back to the trailhead for a total round-trip of 5.2 miles. Look for the right turnoff to Sifford Lakes about 100 yards before the waterfall overlook. Make sure you carry a trail map with you; there are several junctions to negotiate in order to stay on the loop.

Trip notes: A $10 entrance fee is charged by Lassen Volcanic National Park (good for seven days). Free park maps are available at the entrance stations. For more information, contact Lassen Volcanic National Park, P.O. Box 100, Mineral, CA 96063; (530) 595-4444.

Directions: From Red Bluff on Interstate 5, turn east on Highway 36 and drive 45 miles. Turn north on Highway 89 and drive 4.5 miles to the park's Southwest entrance station. Continue north on Highway 89 for 12 miles to the Kings Creek Falls pullout area on both sides of the road. The trail begins on the right side of the road.

24. TERRACE, SHADOW, & CLIFF LAKES

Lassen Volcanic National Park
Off Highway 36 east of Red Bluff
3.4 miles round-trip — 2 hours — some steep terrain

🥾🥾

There are many, many lakes in Lassen Volcanic National Park, and they spawn a fair amount of debate about which one is the best, the prettiest, and/or the most suitable for swimming. It's hard to make a definitive choice on the matter, but certainly this hike to Terrace, Shadow, and Cliff Lakes takes you to three lakes that qualify for the park's Top 10 list. Surprisingly, all three are remarkably different, although they lie only one mile apart.

Although some hikers trek to the lakes the long way, starting from Hat Lake in the north part of the park, the more common route is a short downhill hike from the park road two miles east of the Lassen Peak Trailhead. Following this path, you'll reach Terrace Lake in a half mile, Shadow Lake in eight-tenths of a mile, and Cliff Lake in 1.7 miles. Of the three lakes, Shadow Lake is the largest and is best for swimming. If you hike only to Shadow Lake, you'll have a mere 1.6-mile round-trip. Remember that no matter how far you go, it's downhill on the way in, and uphill on the return.

Although many lakes in Lassen are a disappointment for swimmers, due to shallow waters, forested or grassy shorelines, and too many tree snags in the water, these three lakes are exceptions. You'll reach the first lake, Terrace, in about 15 minutes of hiking. Terrace Lake is long and narrow, with a cliff forming its back wall and trees and rocks surrounding the rest of it. The trail leads closely along its south side. At the far end of the lake, you can look back and see the tip of Mount Lassen peeking up. Hike a few yards farther on the trail and you'll peer down on Shadow Lake, remarkably close by.

The trail drops to Shadow Lake, which is huge and round—at least double the size of Terrace Lake. Like Terrace, it has a rocky shoreline and some trees, but overall it is much more open and exposed. Conveniently, the trail clings to the lake's southeast shore, so at any

Shadow Lake

point, you can kick off your shoes and wade in. It takes another 10 minutes to hike to the far side of Shadow Lake, but when you get there, look back over your shoulder for a fine view of Mount Lassen in the background.

Shadow Lake makes a fine destination by itself, but it would be a shame to turn around here, because the trail just keeps getting more scenic. It descends again, then crosses a stream and passes a small pond in a meadow. Again, look over your shoulder for admirable views of Lassen Peak—the best of the entire trip. The trail then re-enters the forest. Watch for a fork and a spur leading to the right; this is the path to Cliff Lake. Hike through the trees to the small lake, which does indeed have a cliff, plus an impressive talus rockslide of white rocks on its southwest perimeter. Reading Peak rises to the south; the rockslide began on its slopes.

Cliff Lake's waters are shallow, clear, and green. The lake's most intriguing element is a small, tree-lined island on the west end. Walk to your right along the shoreline until you reach the lake's inlet, where you'll find an abundance of wildflowers, including wandering daisies, lupine, heather, and corn lilies.

Make it easier: Hike only to Shadow Lake and back for a 1.6-mile round-trip and an easier return climb.

Trip notes: A $10 entrance fee is charged by Lassen Volcanic National

Park (good for seven days). Free park maps are available at the entrance stations. For more information, contact Lassen Volcanic National Park, P.O. Box 100, Mineral, CA 96063; (530) 595-4444.

Directions: From Red Bluff on Interstate 5, turn east on Highway 36 and drive 45 miles. Turn north on Highway 89 and drive 4.5 miles to the park's Southwest entrance station. Continue north on Highway 89 for 8.8 miles to the pullout area on the left. A small trail sign indicates the path to Terrace, Shadow, and Cliff Lakes.

---

25. BUMPASS HELL TRAIL
Lassen Volcanic National Park
Off Highway 36 east of Red Bluff
3 miles round-trip — 1.5 hours — mostly level terrain

🏃🏃

If you travel Lassen Volcanic National Park with children, you will quickly learn that Bumpass Hell is their favorite trail destination because it has the distinction of having not one but two foul words in its name. When you explain that "Bumpass" was the name of the man who discovered this strange geologic area, this distinction may be lessened somewhat, but then again, maybe not.

The "Hell" in Bumpass Hell is easy to recognize. Bumpass Hell is an active hydrothermal area, part of the Lassen Geothermal System, which encompasses Bumpass Hell, Sulphur Works, Boiling Springs Lake, Little Hot Springs Valley, Morgan Springs, and Terminal Geyser. Bumpass Hell is geology in action—16 acres of boiling springs, hissing steam vents, noisy fumaroles, and bubbling mud pots.

This geologic commotion is the result of crack-like fissures in the earth that penetrate deeply enough to tap into volcanic heat (or with a little imagination, into the searing hot landscape of Hades). Surface water from rain and snowmelt seeps into these fissures and travels downward until it touches volcanically heated rock. This creates steam, which rises back up to the surface. As a result, pools of water in the Bumpass Hell area can reach temperatures of 250 degrees. Kendall Vonbook Bumpass, who discovered Bumpass Hell in the 1860s, lost one of his legs when he stepped into one of these boiling thermal pools.

Fortunately, today hikers have a trail to follow in Bumpass Hell, and a plethora of signs to remind us to stay on the boardwalk and off the unstable soil. The hike is an easy stroll with a gradual elevation change, and it's a popular route for families. Visitors seeking a longer walk can trek 1.5 miles to Bumpass Hell, then another 1.5 miles to

Bumpass Hell Trail

Cold Boiling Lake. Most people simply explore Bumpass Hell, take few pictures of the strange volcanic landscape, and then return.

In addition to its fascinating geology, the Bumpass Hell Trail features wide views of surrounding peaks in its first mile. A half-mile in, between interpretive posts 10 and 11, is a short spur on the right leading to an overlook of Mount Conard, Diamond Peak, Brokeoff Mountain, Mount Diller, and Pilot Pinnacle. All of these mountains are a part of the ancient volcano Mount Tehama, which once stood on this spot. Long since collapsed and eroded, Mount Tehama once soared to an elevation of 11,500 feet. Lassen Peak was formed from lava that flowed from Mount Tehama.

As you round a curve and reach the highest point in the trail, you find an interpretive sign explaining the wonders of Bumpass Hell, which is now directly below you. You also hear the strange ruckus caused by all the hydrothermal activity—sounds variously described as steam engines, trucks speeding by, or turbine motors. The smell of sulphur is ubiquitous. A short descent takes you into the hydrothermal area, and boardwalks lead you over and around the various hot pools, steam vents, and mudpots. Even the stream that flows through Bumpass Hell is odd looking—its water is milky gray instead of clear. Most of the hot pools in the area are also gray, except for the large pool at the end of the boardwalk, which is a marvelous turquoise blue.

Make it more challenging: From Bumpass Hell, you can continue another 1.5 miles to Cold Boiling Lake, then turn around and retrace your steps for a six-mile round-trip.

Trip notes: A $10 entrance fee is charged by Lassen Volcanic National Park (good for seven days). Free park maps are available at the entrance stations. For more information, contact Lassen Volcanic National Park, P.O. Box 100, Mineral, CA 96063; (530) 595-4444.

Directions: From Red Bluff on Interstate 5, turn east on Highway 36 and drive 45 miles. Turn north on Highway 89 and drive 4.5 miles to the park's Southwest entrance station. Continue north on Highway 89 for 5.8 miles to the Bumpass Hell Trailhead on the right.

Mendocino, Sonoma, & Napa

(For locations of trails, see map on page 8.)

26. LA LAGUNA TRAIL

Lake Cleone, MacKerricher State Park

Off Highway 1 near Fort Bragg
1.1 mile round-trip — 45 minutes — mostly level terrain

MacKerricher State Park is a rare find in the California state park system for two reasons: It's free, and its trails have excellent wheelchair-accessibility. In addition, MacKerricher is a coastal park with a fresh-water lake just a few hundred yards from the ocean, with a great easy hiking trail on the lake's perimeter.

It comes as a bit of a shock not to hand over five bucks as you drive through the state park entrance station. Apparently, the guy who donated all this land to the California State Parks system insisted that day-use at MacKerricher must always be free. Just wave and smile at the park rangers and they'll even give you a free map as you drive in. Then head for the parking area by Cleone Lake, a striking circle of freshwater blue just a short walk from the ocean beach.

Free access can translate into lots of visitors and packed parking lots. But when we visited on a sunny Saturday afternoon in August, during peak season, we had no trouble finding a parking space. Even better, because most folks come to MacKerricher for its spectacular beaches and tidepools, we only encountered a couple of people on the La Laguna Trail around Cleone Lake.

Start this walk on the ocean side of the parking lot, where you'll find rest rooms and a billboard describing the birds you may see on the lake. Follow the dirt path parallel to the paved access road for about 75 yards, until you come to a trail marker for the La Laguna Trail on your left. The trail leads away from the road and into thick vegetation along the southwest side of the lake. You'll feel as if you've entered another world, more quiet and peaceful than the rest of the park. The only distraction is the faint sound of Highway 1, which fades away as you walk along the smooth dirt trail through the dense thicket surrounding the lake. A couple of cutoff trails lead to campgrounds, the ranger's residence, and the camp headquarters, but just stay on the main trail as it circles all the way around the lake, sometimes straying a bit from its edge but always returning.

Bird viewing is excellent on this trail, even for novices. We saw a great blue heron and a huge great egret, as well as several species of smaller birds. We were close enough to see the egret catch a small fish and swallow it, leaving a telltale lump in its long neck. Other

La Laguna Trail, Lake Cleone

birds to watch for are mallards, surf scooters, sanderlings, and avocets.

The Department of Fish and Game stocks the lake with trout every few weeks in summer, so you're likely to see a few anglers trying their luck from shore or on the lake from small rafts and kayaks. Even very young anglers seem to have a good time of it.

At the east end of the lake, where the route traverses a marsh, the trail is set on a raised wooden walkway, serving the dual purpose of making this part of the path completely wheelchair-accessible and also keeping foot traffic off the fragile wetlands. The total length of the walkway trail section is half a mile.

As you finish the loop on the north side of Lake Cleone, you'll leave the marsh and come close to the lake's edge again, where the shoreline is bordered by big Monterey cypress trees, poised to withstand the coastal winds. Picnic tables are located at the end of the trail, near the boat ramp, although my choice for a picnic would be right along the trail on the more secluded south side of the lake.

Make it easier: Wheelchair users can access the wheelchair-accessible portion of the trail near the park entrance kiosk. Ask a ranger at the entrance kiosk about the best place to park.

Trip notes: There is no fee. A free trail map/brochure is available at the entrance station. For more information, contact MacKerricher State Park, P.O. Box 440, Mendocino, CA 95460; (707) 937-5804.

Directions: From Mendocino, drive 11.7 miles north on Highway 1 to the signed entrance to MacKerricher State Park on the left (three miles north of Fort Bragg). Turn left into the park, drive past the ranger kiosk, and turn left again, heading toward the camping areas. In half a mile, you'll see Lake Cleone on your left. Park in the parking lot right next to the lake, and begin hiking from the trail near the rest rooms.

27. HEADLANDS TRAIL
MacKerricher State Park
Off Highway 1 near Fort Bragg
1 mile round-trip — 30 minutes — mostly level terrain

The Headlands Trail at MacKerricher State Park offers something for everybody. Families can take their kids to explore the tidepools along the shore, lovers can hike off on side trails to secluded bluffs where they can hold hands and gaze out to sea, and everyone, including wheelchair-users, can make the trip to the Laguna Point Seal Watching Station to watch those beloved sea mammals sunbathe on the rocks.

Although the trail is only one mile in length, the sights along the way are sure to slow you down. The trail is on a raised, wheelchair-accessible boardwalk that loops around Laguna Point, a small peninsula on the headlands overlooking a rocky stretch of Mendocino coast.

Laguna Point was the site of a Pomo Indian village for thousands of years until the early 20th century, when it saw duty as a loading chute for big schooners sailing in to load lumber. Today, Laguna Point is inhabited by a 200-plus resident population of harbor seals, along with the thousands of visitors who come to see them.

A number of dirt trails break off from the main wooden walkway and explore around the neighboring bluffs and rocky tidepools. If you take your children tidepooling, be sure to explain to them that all the sea animals and plants in the tidepool areas are protected by law and should not be taken from their native habitat.

The best way to hike the Headlands Trail is to start on the left side of the loop, which cuts across the center of Laguna Point's land mass and leads directly to the seal-watching station a half-mile away. There you can see dozens of seals and sea lions snoozing on offshore rocks. It is biology and not slothfulness that drives the pinnipeds' languid behavior: While body fat keeps most of the seal's body warm in the frigid ocean water, its flippers have little body fat and must be exposed to the sun for hours a day to retain heat.

Tidepool exploring on the Headlands Trail at MacKerricher State Park

From the overlook, most people climb down from the boardwalk to get a closer look at the rocky tidepools just below. You can explore this area for hours, finding sea anemones, starfish, limpets, and the usual cabal of tidepool creatures. Birdwatching is also excellent here, with ocean birds such as seagulls and scooters hanging around in hope of finding a good catch.

If it's privacy you seek, take any of the dirt cutoff trails to the left of the seal-watching station and its boardwalk. These informal paths crisscross over the blufftops for more ocean vistas. It's a little quieter out on this side of the point, although you may meet up with equestrians. Most of these dirt trails were built for horseback riding, a popular activity at MacKerricher.

The return loop on the boardwalk from the Laguna Point Seal Watching Station back to the parking area takes you along the edge of the bluffs, past more tidepools and offshore rocks, where you might see abalone divers taking the plunge. The hike ends at the wide sandy beach that fronts the trailhead parking lot, which makes an excellent picnic destination.

Make it easier: Just walk out to the seal-watching station and back, ignoring the loop and the side trails.

Trip notes: There is no fee. A free trail map/brochure is available at the entrance station. For more information, contact MacKerricher State Park, P.O. Box 440, Mendocino, CA 95460; (707) 937-5804.

Directions: From Mendocino, drive 11.7 miles north on Highway 1 to the signed entrance to MacKerricher State Park on the left (three miles north of Fort Bragg). Turn left into the park, drive past the ranger kiosk, and turn left again, heading toward the camping areas. Drive a half-mile past Lake Cleone and turn right, heading two-tenths of a mile further to the parking lot at the beach near Laguna Point. Begin hiking at the wooden walkway which leads from the west side of the parking lot out to the headlands.

---

28. CHAMBERLAIN CREEK FALLS
Jackson State Forest
Off Highway 20 east of Fort Bragg
0.5 mile round-trip — 30 minutes — rolling terrain

A trip to Mendocino means seeing spectacular ocean vistas, visiting hidden, rocky coves laden with fascinating tidepools, and watching the sun set over the ocean whenever the fog rolls out to sea. Mendocino is the quintessential place for a Northern California coastal experience, and everyone should come here at least once to partake in it.

But there's another, lesser-known face to the Mendocino landscape, and a short drive inland unveils it. Jackson State Forest, approximately 20 miles northeast of Mendocino off Highway 20, stretches over thousand of acres thick with mixed conifers. The forest plays a crucial role in the local timber industry, and provides space for recreation as well. A trip down the logging roads in Jackson State Forest reveals not only old-growth trees but also a surprising waterfall, accessible via an easy hike.

The drive to the waterfall trailhead includes four miles of narrow, unpaved road, with the possibility of logging trucks bearing down on you at any time, so go slowly. In good weather, passenger cars can make the trip without a problem, but when the roads are wet and muddy, four-wheel-drive is more appropriate.

Winter is the best time to view Chamberlain Creek Falls, although even in summer a steady, thin stream of water pours off the 50-foot rock face that forms the fall. After parking your car alongside the road at the trailhead, walk down a series of wooden steps that descend into a steep canyon, then continue downhill on the dirt trail, switchbacking deeper into the canyon. If the weather is wet when you visit, be careful both on the steps and the trail, as the fallen tanoak leaves underfoot can be very slippery.

The canyon is dense with foliage, including old-growth Douglas firs, redwoods, ferns, and sorrel. After 10 to 15 minutes of descending through the forest canopy, you'll catch your first glimpse of Chamberlain Creek Falls and then walk right to its base. The waterfall's setting is stunningly simple—just a huge piece of black rock jutting out of the forest wall, forcing Chamberlain Creek to tumble over its bulk before the stream can continue on its way. In winter, the entire rock face is covered with rushing water, while in summer, the stream is reduced to less than a foot wide. In July and August, the water is usually warm and tame enough for you to stand beneath its spray and take a shower.

After visiting the waterfall, keep hiking a little further on the trail. Only a few more footsteps reveal a pristine stand of virgin forest, with tall Douglas firs and redwoods untouched by the logger's saw. It's a magical grove, with an ambience much like that of the ancient redwood forests further north.

Just beyond the old-growth grove, the trail begins to climb steadily back out of the canyon. Turn around and retrace your steps when you wish. The return trip is short but quite steep, so be sure to take your time and tread carefully.

Make it more challenging: You can continue hiking past the waterfall as far as you wish. Get a map from the address below before you go.

Trip notes: There is no fee. A free trail map is available by writing to Jackson State Forest. For more information, contact Jackson State Forest, 802 North Main Street, Fort Bragg, CA 95437; (707) 964-5674.

Directions: From Fort Bragg, drive south on Highway 1 for one mile to the turnoff for Highway 20. Turn east on Highway 20 and drive 17 miles. Turn left on Road 200, an unsigned dirt road immediately after the Chamberlain Creek bridge (just past the sign for the Chamberlain Creek Conservation Corps camp). Drive one mile on Road 200 until it forks, then bear left and drive for three more miles. At the three-mile mark, you'll see a wooden railing on the left side of the road; this marks the trailhead where steps lead down into the canyon. Park alongside the road, pulling off as far as possible to allow logging trucks to pass.

29. ECOLOGICAL STAIRCASE NATURE TRAIL
Jug Handle State Reserve
Off Highway 1 near Mendocino
5 miles round-trip — 2 hours — rolling terrain

The Ecological Staircase Nature Trail is a great five-mile round-trip hike, with all kinds of interesting natural phenomena ranging from rocky ocean coastline to dry grasslands to dense green forest. But the name is just a little misleading. It's like a staircase only in theory, not in practice, so don't start envisioning a continually elevating trail that climbs to some final destination. It's not. In fact, the trail climbs only 200 feet the whole way, and it does so almost imperceptibly, making for a gentle walk through a variety of natural terrain.

So why call it the Ecological Staircase? Jug Handle State Reserve consists of a series of marine terraces, carved by ocean waves and other forces of nature over the course of half a million years or more. Each terrace is 100 feet higher in elevation and 100,000 years older than the one below, with very different and distinct soil and plant life. The geological evolution continues to this day, with future terraces still under water. While marine terraces are common along the California coast, they are rarely as well-preserved and distinguishable as these.

The trail starts off with stunning scenery as it heads out from the parking area for a short half-mile walk around the Jug Handle Bay headlands, with access to and views of beautiful white sand beaches. April through June are the best wildflower months along this stretch of coast, with the coastal bluff plants showing their vivid colors, including golden poppies, Indian paintbrush, coastal lupine, seaside daisies, and

Beach view from the Ecological Staircase Nature Trail

wild strawberries. Summer is occasionally blessed with fog-free days, when beach life here is as good as anywhere on the California coast.

After walking the blufftops, head inland underneath the freeway bridge and along the streambed of Jug Handle Creek. You'll have to tolerate a certain amount of road noise for about 15 minutes while you walk up the creek canyon, but it will fade away as you enter the first terrace, a grassland environment peppered with bishop and Monterey pines. Although the bishop pines are natives to the area, the Monterey pines are not, and removal efforts are underway.

Another three-quarters of a mile of hiking brings you to the second terrace, a mixed conifer forest of bishop pine, Douglas fir, Sitka spruce, and western hemlock. The Sitka spruce, found along the Pacific coast all the way to Alaska, are at the far south end of their range here in Mendocino. Further along the trail on the second terrace is a combination redwood and Douglas fir grove. These tall trees tower over the shade-loving ferns and sorrel growing at their base.

The third terrace, nearly two miles in (and an hour into the hike), is composed of hardpan soil, sand dunes, and pygmy trees. Soil and drainage are so poor here that trees and shrubs grow only in stunted sizes. If you pay close attention, you can see the warning signs of the approaching third terrace as you come close to it: The tall trees of the conifer forest begin to thin out and diminish in size. The soil in the pygmy forest is 300 feet higher in elevation than at the ocean beach you viewed from the blufftops, but 300,000 years older.

The trail, which is now a logging road, makes a loop around the pygmy forest. At this point you've officially left Jug Handle State Reserve and are now in Jackson State Forest. You can choose to either walk the entire loop or hike a short way in and out of the pygmy forest. (I did the latter since the dusty logging road seemed unappealing after hiking on the beautiful forested trail.) When you're ready to return to the trailhead, reenter the conifer forest and hike back downhill.

Several spur trails cut off from the Ecological Staircase Nature Trail; most are marked with branches across them to keep you on the main path. But if you find yourself confused at any point, just watch for numbers along the trail. The Ecological Staircase Nature Trail is an interpretive walk with 32 trail numbers corresponding to its brochure, so if you stop coming across numbered signs, you've taken a wrong turn. If you like, you can pick up a trail brochure at the building near the parking lot before starting your hike.

Make it easier: Just walk on the headlands trail and spend some time exploring the beaches, or hike only to the first or second terraces.

Trip notes: There is no fee. A map and trail guide is available for 50 cents outside of the building on the southwest side of the parking lot. For more information, contact Jug Handle State Reserve, P.O. Box 440, Mendocino, CA 95460; (707) 937-5804.

Directions: From Mendocino, drive four miles north on Highway 1 to the signed entrance to Jug Handle State Reserve on the left. Turn left and park in the parking area. The Ecological Staircase Nature Trail begins on the southwest side of the parking lot. A more direct trail, which bypasses the coastal headlands, begins on the northwest side of the parking lot.

---

30. HEADLANDS & DEVIL'S PUNCHBOWL TRAILS
Russian Gulch State Park
Off Highway 1 near Mendocino
1 mile round-trip — 30 minutes — mostly level terrain

There's something so dramatic and spectacular about the Mendocino coast that it draws thousands of visitors every year. Many of them are hoping for little more than the chance to walk on a romantic, uncrowded coastal bluff and watch the sun go down. One of the best places to do just that is at Russian Gulch State Park, on the small stretch of the park west of Highway 1 and east of the ocean breakers.

The trail on the ocean side of the park is so informal that it doesn't even have a proper name, but everyone knows it as the place to see the Devil's Punchbowl. That's the rather imaginative name for a "blowhole" in the headlands, a geyser-like hole in the middle of soft bedrock, where ocean waves push up underneath the rock and then burst, spouting and splashing, through the top of the hole. The Devil's Punchbowl is one of the Mendocino coast's most famous blowholes.

At first glance, the Devil's Punchbowl looks like little more than a large hole in the ground, which park rangers have surrounded by a wooden fence to keep people from falling in. A closer look at the hole—which is more than 100 feet in diameter and 60 feet deep—reveals that its bottom is a tidepool, with the rhythm of ocean waves continually moving water in and out. That means the land you're standing on, which seems firm and sturdy enough, is actually "land" for only about 30 feet down—its base is carved out by the pounding of the sea. You are actually standing on a ledge, the roof of a giant sea cave.

Although the Devil's Punchbowl is "geyser-like," don't come here expecting to see something like Old Faithful. The blowhole is so large and wide-open that the geyser effect is greatly diminished, except during big storms and very high tides. Most of the time, waves just roll in through the sea cave, then retreat back to sea.

Keep your eyes and ears out for big spouts and splashes, however, although not necessarily from the Devil's Punchbowl. Friendly gray

View from the headlands at Russian Gulch State Park

whales frequent this area all year long, most prevalent from December until April. We saw one about 200 yards offshore from this trail in late summer, spouting and flopping around like he was having a fine time.

From the parking area, the hike begins at the wooden fence, by a signboard explaining how erosion creates the sea caves and other formations. You can start hiking from either of two trails; the trail on the right takes you more directly to the fenced-in Devil's Punchbowl. After that, you're on your own. A series of paths cut across the blufftop, and all of them lead to the bluff's edge to view the dramatic rocky shoreline and azure blue ocean. If you keep heading to your right along the bluffs and then circle back along the coast to your left, you can make a loop out of the trip.

The best times to take this walk are in the early morning or just about sunset, when the coastal wind diminishes. Always bring a jacket and be prepared for either heavy fog or brilliant sunshine and wind.

Make it easier: Just hike straight out to the Devil's Punchbowl and back.

Trip notes: A $5 day-use fee is charged by Russian Gulch State Park. A free map is available at the entrance kiosk. For more information, contact Russian Gulch State Park, P.O. Box 440, Mendocino, CA 95460; (707) 937-5804.

Directions: From Mendocino, drive two miles north on Highway 1 to the entrance sign for Russian Gulch State Park on the left. Turn left and then left again immediately to reach the entrance kiosk at the park. After paying, drive past the kiosk and turn right at the sign for the picnic area. Drive past the picnic area to where the road ends at the parking area for the Blowhole and Devil's Punchbowl. The trailhead is at the fence directly in front of you.

31. FERN CANYON & FALLS LOOP TRAILS
Russian Gulch State Park
Off Highway 1 near Mendocino
4.6 miles round-trip — 2 hours — rolling terrain

There comes a time when you just have to stretch the rules a little. For me, this occurred when I hiked the Fern Canyon Trail to the waterfall at Russian Gulch State Park. My rule was "never hike on pavement," and it was one I tend to be adamant about. But the lure of a pretty waterfall in a fern-filled canyon was too much for me, even though it required walking on an old paved trail for two-thirds of the total 4.6-mile round-trip.

What I found out was that this trail is too good to pass up, paved or not. To hike it, you simply take the Fern Canyon Trail to its intersection with the Falls Loop Trail, where the pavement ends and bikers must park their bikes. Then take the left side of the Falls Loop Trail (now on dirt) for the shortest route to the waterfall, a stunning 36-foot cascade that pours over a huge slab of rock.

Purists can get around the pavement problem, if they wish, by using the alternate, unpaved North Trail. For hikers only, it connects to the Falls Loop Trail but adds two miles to your hike, making for a 6.6-mile round-trip.

The Fern Canyon Trail may not be completely *au naturel,* but it is rutted, cracked, and covered with leaves and pine needles. It's also so secluded and beautifully framed by forest and stream that even anti-pavement types like me will almost forget that it's not dirt. The route is almost completely level, making for a gentle and easy hike accompanied by the sound of water from Russian Gulch, which runs alongside the trail the whole way. A thick forest, filled with second-growth redwoods, hemlocks, Douglas firs, big leaf maples, alders, and tons of ferns, borders the trail on both sides. In late summer, trailside blackberry bushes provide nourishment for hungry hikers. Stinging nettles and poison oak are also prevalent, so watch where you tread if you stray off the pavement.

When you reach the intersection with the Falls Loop Trail, you'll see a few picnic tables and a bike rack, as well as the intersection with the North Trail for those who hiked the longer path. The Falls Loop Trail gives you the choice of going left or right; both paths eventually join at the waterfall, but the left trail is much shorter (seven-tenths of a mile to the waterfall versus 2.3 miles). The path is soft dirt, and it has a few more ups and downs than the paved trail, including some wooden stairsteps. In seven-tenths of a mile, a glimpse of Russian Gulch Falls comes into view just before the trail heads downhill to its base.

The falls at Russian Gulch prove the adage that when it comes to waterfalls, setting rather than size is what counts. At a mere 36 feet, Russian Gulch Falls is no record-setter, but it drops into a verdant grotto so beautiful that it makes a lasting impression. In winter, the waterfall can be a rushing torrent that spills over the huge boulder at its base, while in summer, it's reduced to one main cascade and a smaller, thinner stream that pours down the left side of the rock.

Several broken tree trunks and branches are jammed around the base of the falls, having fallen and tumbled over its lip. Some of these trunks have been there so long that plants are growing out of them, creating a lush green frame for the falling water. One tree trunk, leaning vertically against the waterfall's boulder, is completely lined with dense thriving ferns.

Make it easier: Ride your bike on the paved trail, then park and lock it at the bike rack where the paved trail intersects the Falls Loop Trail. From here, follow the Falls Loop Trail seven-tenths of a mile to the waterfall.

Trip notes: A $5 day-use fee is charged by Russian Gulch State Park. A free map is available at the entrance kiosk. For more information, contact Russian Gulch State Park, P.O. Box 440, Mendocino, CA 95460; (707) 937-5804.

Directions: From Mendocino, drive two miles north on Highway 1 to the entrance sign for Russian Gulch State Park on the left. Turn left and then immediately left again to reach the entrance kiosk. After paying, drive past the kiosk and continue straight, crossing back under the highway, to the eastern side of the park. Drive past the recreation hall and all of the campsites to the parking area for the Fern Canyon Trail. Start hiking from the trailhead at the east side of the parking area.

32. BIG HENDY GROVE & HERMIT HUT TRAILS
Hendy Woods State Park
Off Highway 128 near Philo
2 miles round-trip — 1 hour — rolling terrain

As you drive on Highway 128 from Cloverdale to Mendocino, you notice from your car windows as the landscape changes from dry oak grasslands to dense, deep redwood forest. Would-be hikers may be tempted by the sight of hiking paths leading from the roadside into the redwoods. Who could resist a walk among big trees paralleling the Navarro River?

But if you pull over you may be disappointed. None of these trails go farther than a few hundred yards, stopping at a few good swimming and fishing holes. If it's a real hike in the redwoods that you want, the best place in the neighborhood is just off the road at Hendy Woods State Park, a little visited preserve that features many beautiful trees, plus an unusual twist—a story that will add an unexpected dimension to your trip.

From the park's day-use parking area, start off hiking on the wheelchair-accessible All-Access Trail, turning left and following the trail signs for the Discovery Trail and Big Hendy Grove. You'll pass tall standing redwoods as well as several downed trees, where children love to play on the huge horizontal trunks and gnarled root balls. The farther you walk from the parking area, the more peaceful and quiet this old forest becomes. Patches of sorrel form soft green clouds on the ground. Black-tailed deer can be seen munching on the plants of the forest floor. Sunlight filters through the tall trees, softly illuminating the scene.

If you compare this redwood grove to many others along the California's north coast, one quality stands out: The folks at Hendy Woods didn't put up plaques on all the trees, giving them goofy names like "Gentle Giant" and "Fallen Emperor." They let the trees speak for themselves, giving them the air of respectability they deserve.

After making the loop and returning from the Big Hendy Grove, walk a little farther south on the All-Access Trail (away from the parking area) until you come to the trail marker for the Hermit Hut Trail on your left. Hermit Hut Trail climbs steadily up from the redwood valley floor through a drier forest of oaks and madrones. You'll feel the temperature rise a bit as you ascend out of the dense shade of the redwoods. After crossing a fire road, climb another 100 yards until you reach an unmarked trail intersection. Continue straight ahead to a trail billboard displaying newspaper clippings about the Hermit Hut Trail's hermit—a Russian immigrant named Petrov who lived for 18 years in these woods, building huts out of branches and tree stumps.

The display is a sad memorial to Petrov, who died in the early 1980s. He lived out his days eating food he gathered from the forest and from neighboring gardens, wearing patched-together, discarded

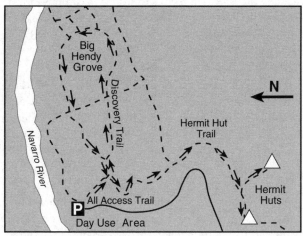

Big Hendy Grove/Hermit Hut Trails

clothing from campers and other park visitors, and living in the huts that still stand on these trails. One is located right behind the billboard. A ramshackle batch of branches serves as a roof over a large, hollowed-out tree stump. To see another of Petrov's huts, head back down the trail to the unmarked intersection, then take the right fork for a short distance.

Make it easier: The Hermit Hut Trail climbs, but the Discovery Trail/Big Hendy Grove Trail is basically level, so stick to the latter.

Trip notes: A $5 day-use fee is charged by Hendy Woods State Park. A free map is available at the entrance station. For more information, contact Hendy Woods State Park, P.O. Box 440, Mendocino, CA 95460; (707) 937-5804.

Directions: From Mendocino, drive south on Highway 1 for approximately 10 miles to the Highway 128 turnoff. Head east on Highway 128 for 18 miles until you see the sign for Hendy Woods State Park at Greenwood Road. Turn right on Greenwood Road and drive to the park entrance. Drive through the park to where the road ends at the day-use parking area. The trailhead is on the east (right) side of the parking area.

---

33. CHINESE GULCH & PHILLIPS GULCH TRAILS
Kruse Rhododendron State Reserve
Off Highway 1 near Jenner
3 miles round-trip — 1 hour — rolling terrain

You've made the long trip to the Sonoma Coast on Memorial Day weekend, and the beaches and parks are packed with people. On top of that, the sun hasn't shown itself for days, so you're not exactly enjoying stellar coastal views. Well, cheer up, because here's a peaceful coastal hike that's enjoyable even in the densest fog.

The Chinese Gulch and Phillips Gulch trails in Kruse Rhododendron State Reserve join together to provide a three-mile redwood, fir, and oak forest hike with a chance to see plenty of the park's featured species—the coast rhododendron *(rhododendron macrophylum)*. These showy plants can be anywhere from three to fourteen feet tall, with large clusters of pinkish-purple flowers blooming from April to June. Each cluster is about the size of a nosegay or small bouquet.

The rhododendrons thrive because of a fire that burned through this area many years ago, causing a succession of plant regeneration that will eventually lead to a completely reforested second-growth redwood

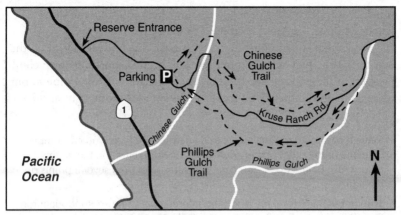

Chinese Gulch & Phillips Gulch Trails

and fir grove. The rhododendrons are slowly losing their hold in the forest as the trees grow up and around them, blocking out their light.

If it's the regal rhododendron that you've come to see, you might want to follow the quarter-mile Rhododendron Trail Loop that starts right at the parking lot. That's where you'll find the most flowers. But the longer Chinese Gulch and Phillips Gulch trails offer charms of their own, including plentiful ferns and a thick redwood and fir forest, with tiny grasses and wildflowers growing up and out of dying redwood stumps—new life literally springing from the old. The trail climbs and descends a fair amount, but redwood logs along the way make comfortable benches. This is a trail for taking your time, and stopping to enjoy the forest as you go.

Both Chinese and Phillips gulches are good-sized streams flowing under rustic wooden bridges. The bridges are whimsically built of rough-hewn logs with branches for railings; some even have large mushrooms growing on them.

The map at the trailhead sign shows the two gulch trails totalling 2.2 miles, but I'd say their combined distance is closer to three miles. The route is well marked. At several points, the trail junctions with paths that lead to "County Road" (the dirt and gravel road you drove in on), but stay on the gulch trails unless you want to take a shortcut back. At about 1.5 miles, you cross the road to transfer from the Chinese Gulch Trail to the Phillips Gulch Trail.

The hiking is generally easier on the Phillips Gulch Trail, which is the second half of your loop. I startled two young deer on this stretch. They bounded off down a ravine and up and over a hill, behaving as if they weren't used to human visitors. Indeed, the reserve doesn't get much foot traffic. Most people who come here just hike the short Rhododendron Trail and head back to their cars.

Your final stream crossing is at Chinese Gulch, which flows all the way to the Pacific Ocean. From there you begin a short but steep climb back up to the parking lot. It's less than a quarter mile of climbing, but it's just enough to make you feel like you got a workout right at the end of the trip.

Make it easier: If you don't want to hike the entire loop, you can simply hike one or the other of the gulch trails and then return on the county road, Kruse Ranch Road. You can access this road from several points on the trail.

Trip notes: There is no fee. For more information on Kruse Rhododendron State Reserve, contact Salt Point State Park, 25050 Coast Highway 1, Jenner, CA 95450; (707) 847-3221.

Directions: From U.S. 101 at Santa Rosa, drive west on Highway 116 for 33 miles, through Sebastopol and Guerneville, to Highway 116's intersection with Highway 1 near Jenner. Continue north on Highway 1 for 24 miles, passing several Salt Point State Park entrances. Turn right on Kruse Ranch Road, one-tenth of a mile north of the Fisk Mill Cove parking area. Drive a half-mile on Kruse Ranch Road to the small dirt parking area at the trailhead. Begin hiking on the north side of the parking lot, at the wooden steps on the left that lead to Chinese Gulch.

---

34. BLUFF TRAIL
Salt Point State Park
Off Highway 1 near Jenner
1.75 miles round-trip — 1 hour — rolling terrain

You may have heard of the Stump Beach Trail at Salt Point State Park. It's the park's premier hiking trail, which climbs 700 feet in a little over a mile from the ocean to the hills high above. Unfortunately, everyone else has heard of it, too, and the trail is often crowded with hikers on summer weekends. If you'd like an easier, quieter, and less populated walk at Salt Point State Park, head for the Fisk Mill Cove parking lot and take a hike on the Bluff Trail.

As you start down the dirt path, you'll see a trail marker that points you to the left to South Cove (one-tenth of a mile away), or to the right to Sentinel Rock and Fisk Mill Cove. If you're visiting in winter or early spring, this signpost is a good place to get a view of a small waterfall that plunges from the bluffs down to the sea.

The trail directions are simple: Begin your hike by heading left to South Cove, ending up right on top of this seasonal waterfall. Continue a short distance to the bluffs beyond the cove, where the trail ends at a brushy area. Then simply turn around and hike back, keeping the ocean on your left. When you reach the trail sign again, continue past it toward Sentinel Rock and Fisk Mill Cove. After you've admired these destinations, just double back to your car.

This is not a hike where you'll mind retracing your steps. While you wander on the Bluff Trail, you're never more than 50 feet from the bluff's edge and the ocean (and often tantalizingly closer). You walk on a nearly level, pine needle-strewn path through a forest of ferns, rhododendrons, and stands of cypress and bishop pines. You're offered peek-a-boo views of rocky, pocket beaches with crashing waves, playful seals, and abalone divers, while you're ensconced in the shade of this peaceful pine forest. You cross three charming wooden footbridges, spanning streams that carry runoff from the hills down to the ocean, and pass a large sandstone formation with tiny hollowed caves begging for exploration. Perhaps most enticing is a lovely trailside meadow, protected from the wind on three sides. During our late April visit, the meadow was completely covered with purple Douglas irises.

The Bluff Trail is fairly level, with many short spurs that lead you to vistas of the ocean and coves below. The spurs either dead-end or rejoin the main trail, so it's impossible to stray too far. The Bluff Trail's

Seals and sea lions at Salt Point State Park

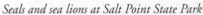

only ascent is on the stairstepped path to the viewing platform on top of Sentinel Rock. The climb is worth the effort; from Sentinel Rock you get that I'm-on-top-of-the-world-and-it's-gorgeous feeling. Have a seat on the bench and enjoy the ambience.

After descending from Sentinel Rock, take the short path that leads down to rocky Fisk Mill Cove, a picturesque beach and a popular spot for abalone diving. Then make the one-mile return trip to your car. Picnic tables and fire grills are situated right at the trailhead, so you might cap off your hike with a spot of lunch.

Make it easier: The best way to make this one easier is to skip the side trip up the path to Sentinel Rock. You might also want to bypass the drop down to Fisk Mill Cove, because you'll have to climb back up to return.

Trip notes: A $3 state park day-use fee is charged at Fisk Mill Cove. At the main park entrance, the day-use fee is $5. At Fisk Mill Cove, you pay at the "iron ranger," a metal box where you deposit your money and keep a receipt. Trail maps are available at the ranger kiosk or visitor center for 50 cents. For more information, contact Salt Point State Park, 25050 Coast Highway 1, Jenner, CA 95450; (707) 847-3221.

Directions: From U.S. 101 at Santa Rosa, drive west on Highway 116 for 33 miles, through Sebastopol and Guerneville, to Highway 116's intersection with Highway 1 near Jenner. Continue north on Highway 1 for approximately 24 miles. Bypass the main Salt Point State Park entrance at Gerstle Cove and turn left at the Fisk Mill Cove parking area, located 2.6 miles north of Gerstle Cove. When you enter, pay the entrance fee at the "iron ranger." You have a choice of turning left or right into two separate parking areas; park in the left parking lot, then find the trailhead on the ocean side of the lot. The trail is not marked, but it is the only trail, with picnic tables and fire grills nearby.

35. FORT ROSS COVE TRAIL
Fort Ross State Historic Park
Off Highway 1 near Jenner
2 miles round-trip — 1 hour — rolling terrain

If it's a sunny day on the Sonoma Coast, put on a jacket and take this hike at Fort Ross State Historic Park. Not only will you have the chance to learn a little history and explore an old Russian colonial fort, but you'll also get to stroll along the scenic Sonoma coastline.

The Fort Ross Cove Trail is not an official designated trail, but rather a wander-as-you-wish meander through Fort Ross' stockade walls and then along steep bluffs that drop hundreds of feet into the sea. You can choose your own route, stopping to enjoy the scenery or the history as you please.

The huge old fort begs for exploration. It includes a huge barracks area and two-story blockhouses with impressive cannons. Fort Ross was built in 1812 in only a few weeks by Russian colonists who were eager for eastern expansion. It was occupied until 1841. The smell of the wood in the old buildings evokes images of those earlier times, when colonists tried to develop an economy here based first on sea otter pelts and later on agriculture. Neither led to great profits.

When you've seen enough of the fort, follow the gravel road that leads out the main gate toward the ocean. The road circles down into Fort Ross Cove, which was once the first shipyard in California, established by the Russians for their pelt-trading business. Today you'll find a few picnic tables here.

Explore the tiny cove if you wish. It is covered with odd-shaped driftwood and wave-smoothed rocks. A small, shallow stream must be crossed in springtime—a little strategic foot placement on rocks should work, although I prefer the leap-and-pray method of stream crossing. After crossing, look for the closest point on the bluffs across from you. Here, about thirty yards from the stream, you'll find an indistinct trail that leads up the bluffs.

Follow the trail to the blufftops. Here, you get a true taste of what the Sonoma Coast is all about. If it's a clear day, the wind will likely blow with near-gale force. In spring, you'll see the usual cabal of coastal wildflowers—lupine, paintbrush, and Douglas irises. Hawks and gulls soar overhead. You can peek over the edge of the bluffs to watch the waves crashing against the rocky shoreline. Often you'll see abalone divers plying their trade at the base of the cliffs.

The trail soon descends to a gravel road where there are rest rooms and a primitive, 20-site campground. A path leads off to the right, down to the beach. Two tiny streams come together here on their way to the ocean, and horsetail ferns grow along their banks. Pick your way among the rocks down to the beach, but beware of stinging nettles.

The way back is easy; you return facing the old fort, which you can see from almost everywhere. When you reach the gravel road that leads out of Fort Ross Cove and back into the fort, you have a little bit of climbing to do and then you're home.

Make it easier: There's only one way to make this trail easier—make it shorter. Skip the stream crossing and the bluff walk, and just walk down to Fort Ross Cove and back.

Trip notes: A $5 state park day-use fee is charged by Fort Ross State Historic Park. A park brochure is available at the visitor center for $1.25. For more information, contact Fort Ross State Historic Park, 19005 Coast Highway 1, Jenner, CA 95450; (707) 847-3286.

Directions: From U.S. 101 at Santa Rosa, drive west on Highway 116 for 33 miles, through Sebastopol and Guerneville, to Highway 116's intersection with Highway 1 near Jenner. Continue north on Highway 1 for approximately 15 miles through an inland detour, then when the detour ends and you are back at the coast on Highway 1, turn left and drive south to the entrance to Fort Ross State Historic Park.

---

36. WOODLAND RIDGE TRAIL
Lake Sonoma Recreation Area
Off U.S. 101 near Geyserville
1 mile round-trip — 30 minutes — rolling terrain

Lake Sonoma Recreation Area is a place with a great reputation for all the recreation options it provides. You can bring the whole family here—even your dog—and then spend the weekend doing any or all of the following: Hiking, camping, boating, fishing, wildlife watching, horseback riding, mountain biking, or even checking out all the natural history exhibits at the visitor center and fish hatchery.

Easy hikers will want to head for the Woodland Ridge Trail. The trail is a loop; take the left fork on your way out. The first few hundred yards will wake up your heart and lungs as you climb dozens of steps and then continue uphill to where the trail tops out near a road. You're in a mixed forest for most of the climb. Madrones, bays, and firs provide shade, a critical element in the Sonoma hills. If it's winter or spring—the best times to visit—you'll see tiny, bright green growth spurts shooting out from the fir branches. The new growth looks like Christmas ornaments decorating the tips of the limbs. Every year, a few more inches grow.

Once you hit the ridge, you're surrounded by oak grasslands, with four different kinds of oaks and plenty of wildflowers in spring. But the best is saved for last on this trail, because the downhill side of the loop is even prettier. The madrone forest is very dense and colorful. Madrones are easily identified by their bark, which peels off in thin layers, leaving their surfaces very smooth and shiny, with colors from light green to dark red. The madrones look especially pretty when wet from fog or rain. This dense grove produces such a shady, cool environment

Peeling bark of a madrone tree on the Woodland Ridge Trail

that even ferns can grow under their protection.

On the way downhill, take the spur trail on the left signed for "vista point," where you can see Lake Sonoma's dam (an engineer's dream) and part of the lake. In the opposite direction, away from the dam, are the more appealing views—of the Sonoma wine country hills and the Alexander Valley.

Watch for birds as you hike. We saw several songbird species, as well as hawks and other raptors. You'll spot them soaring overhead as you descend, on an even steeper path than on the way up, all the way back to the parking area.

Make it easier: If the initial climb is too steep, walk a small portion of the return loop (it begins on the right side of the trailhead). Although this climb is also steep, you don't have to hike as far to experience the beauty of the woodlands.

Trip notes: There is no fee. For more information, contact the U.S. Army Corps of Engineers, Lake Sonoma, 3333 Skaggs Springs Road, Geyserville, CA 95441-9644; (707) 433-9483.

Directions: From Santa Rosa, drive 12 miles north on U.S. 101 to the town of Healdsburg. Take the Dry Creek Road exit and turn left (west). Follow Dry Creek Road for 11.5 miles to the park visitor center and fish hatchery. The Woodland Ridge trailhead is along the road shortly beyond the visitor center. Park alongside the road in the gravel pullout or at the far end of the visitor center parking lot.

37. RITCHEY CANYON & REDWOOD TRAILS
Bothe-Napa Valley State Park
Off Highway 128/29 near St. Helena
2.5 miles round-trip — 1 hour — rolling terrain

🚶🚶

Even the most devoted and enthusiastic wine-tasters in the Napa Valley eventually tire of their task. If it's a hot summer day, perhaps they start daydreaming of a shady redwood forest where they could walk for a while or sit by a stream. Such a daydream might seem preposterous. Where in the midst of the hot and dusty vineyards could a redwood tree possibly grow?

At Bothe-Napa Valley State Park, that's where. The Ritchey Canyon and Redwood trails take you through a lovely stand of them, one of the most eastern groves of coastal redwoods in California. It's a 2.5-mile loop trip that will leave you even more intoxicated with this Napa Valley wine country.

Joining the redwoods are plenty of Douglas firs, plus buckeyes and bigleaf maples growing near Ritchey Creek, and ferns galore. Look carefully among the branches of the trees: five different kinds of woodpeckers live within the park's borders. My hiking partner and I saw the largest of these, the pileated woodpecker, on a tree right by the picnic area. He was working his way up and down a big Douglas fir like a

Ritchey Creek

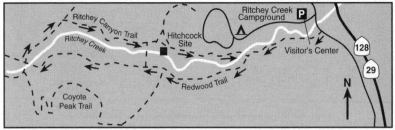

Ritchey Canyon and Redwood Trails

telephone lineman on triple overtime. Who can blame the hardworking woodpeckers, with all these big, meaty trees around to peck?

Start the hike by heading up the creekside path on Redwood Trail from the small bridge near the visitor center. The first half-mile, which parallels the campground on the far side of the creek, can be somewhat noisy, but soon the forest grows thicker and you leave civilization behind. Ferns, wild grape, and blackberry bushes line the trail. Keep walking upstream, staying on Redwood Trail as you pass its intersection with Coyote Peak Trail. Redwood Trail climbs gently to its end at 1.5 miles and a creek crossing, where you join Ritchey Canyon Trail and begin your return.

Ritchey Canyon Trail offers more of the same forested hiking, although this side of the creek is a little drier, with fewer redwoods and more firs. You'll pass the old Hitchcock home site right beside Ritchey Creek, where Lillie Hitchcock Coit and her parents lived in the 1870s. Coit is probably best known for lending her name and money to Coit Tower on Telegraph Hill in San Francisco, but she also threw some grand parties for the San Francisco elite here at the Hitchcock estate.

Spring is the best season to hike at Bothe-Napa, preferably in April or May when the buckeyes are in fragrant bloom and the creek is running strong. Wildflowers, including solomon's seal and redwood orchids, bloom in the cool shade. The park visitor center runs a small native plant garden near the start of this trail for those who want to brush up on plant identification before or after the trip.

Make it easier: Cross the stream on a seasonal bridge just past the intersection of Redwood Trail and Coyote Peak Trail and return on the Ritchey Canyon Trail from there, cutting the hike in half.

Trip notes: A $5 state park day-use fee is charged by Bothe-Napa Valley State Park. Trail maps are available at the ranger kiosk for $1. For more information, contact Bothe-Napa Valley State Park, 3801 St. Helena Highway North, Calistoga, CA 94515; (707) 942-4575 or (707) 938-1519.

Directions: From the city of Napa, drive north on Highway 29 through

Yountville, Oakville, and Rutherford to St. Helena. Continue past St. Helena on Highway 128/29 for five more miles (passing the entrance to Bale Grist Mill State Park) to the entrance to Bothe-Napa Valley State Park on the left side of the road. Drive through the entrance kiosk, then go straight, and park near the visitor center. The trail begins on the south side of the small bridge over Ritchey Creek, near the visitor center.

38. HISTORY TRAIL to BALE GRIST MILL
Bothe-Napa Valley State Park
Off Highway 128/29 near St. Helena
2.4 miles round-trip — 1.5 hours — rolling terrain

Perhaps you've seen the sign for Bale Grist Mill while driving through the Napa wine country and wondered what the heck it was, but never found the time to check it out. (After all, a trip to a historical monument is a hard sell in Napa, considering all of the area's other attractions and diversions.)

Well, the best way to learn about the history of the Bale Grist Mill is to hike there from neighboring Bothe-Napa Valley State Park, following the History Trail. The trail begins at a small pioneer cemetery near the highway, then slowly starts to climb, heading up a ridge. A canopy of hardwoods provides much-needed shade on hot days. Madrone trees with their shiny red trunks and peeling bark pepper the forest. In spring, the woodland wildflowers put on a show, including waxy yellow fairy lanterns and purple, vine-like spring vetch. Also in spring, the buckeye trees blossom, exhibiting their banana-shaped flower clusters and giving off a sweet lilac aroma. Although non-native in Northern California, the buckeye tends to grow in places formerly inhabited by Native Americans, who apparently carried the buckeye seeds with them to plant. (The seeds are too heavy to be carried on the wind and aren't eaten by animals, so they weren't transported through animal scat.)

The History Trail is best walked on cool spring days, before Napa's summer temperatures heat up. Avoid midday walks when it's warm, because the trail climbs a few hundred feet before dropping into Bale Grist Mill State Park.

The scenery changes as you near the Bale Grist Mill. In contrast to the dry, wooded slopes you've been walking on, the terrain here includes a stream and water—enough to drive the big water wheel that ran Edward Bale's flour mill in the 1840s and 1850s.

Still in operating condition, Bale Grist Mill's water wheel is 36 feet tall and has several large millstones, which were used to convert grains grown in the Napa Valley to usable flour. Water was diverted from Mill Creek into a mill pond and several ditches, where it was transported to the top of the waterwheel via a wooden flume. The water turned the wheel and generated power, which in turn ran the millstones which ground the grains.

After your visit to the grist mill and perhaps a picnic near

Bale Grist Mill, Bale Grist Mill State Park

the stream, simply retrace your steps back to your car.

Make it easier: You can drive to Bale Grist Mill State Park and walk around the mill area from the parking lot. The entrance to Bale Grist Mill State Park is 1.5 miles south of Bothe-Napa Valley State Park on Highway 29/128.

Trip notes: A $5 state park day-use fee is charged by Bothe-Napa Valley State Park. Trail maps are available at the ranger kiosk for $1. For more information, contact Bothe-Napa Valley State Park, 3801 St. Helena Highway North, Calistoga, CA 94515; (707) 942-4575 or (707) 938-1519.

Directions: From the city of Napa, drive north on Highway 29 through Yountville, Oakville, and Rutherford to St. Helena. Continue past St. Helena on Highway 128/29 for five more miles (passing the entrance to Bale Grist Mill State Park) to the entrance to Bothe-Napa Valley State Park on the left side of the road. Drive through the entrance kiosk, then go straight past the swimming pool and rest rooms, until the road ends at the picnic area and trailhead for the History Trail.

39. CANYON TRAIL
Sugarloaf Ridge State Park
Off Highway 12 near Kenwood
1 mile round-trip — 45 minutes — rolling terrain

🚶🚶

You want a short, pretty trail in the forest? You got it. You want to see a 25-foot waterfall in winter and spring? Here it is. You want to go downhill all the way? No problem. You want to climb uphill all the way back to your car? Sorry, but that's part of the bargain, too.

But the return climb is a small price to pay for what you get on the Canyon Trail. The path is short enough so that almost anyone, even very small children, can hike it. And the trail is such a lovely shaded route that you'll find plenty of reason to go slow, enjoying the sound of gurgling Sonoma Creek, as well as the many trees, plants, and mossy rocks along the way.

You start at 1,100 feet in elevation and descend 300 feet through a forest of hardwoods—oak, bay, madrone, alder, and sycamore. When you reach the falls (after about a 15-minute walk), you're welcomed by a lush, wet canyon that is piled with huge, rounded, moss-covered boulders. Many of them are more slippery than they look, so be careful. The trail is routed by the edge of the creek, and you can climb around the rocks and get close to the base of the falls.

Notice the bigleaf maple trees that are thriving along this shady stream. (You can easily identify them because their leaves look like the classic maple leaf on the Canadian flag, but the trees grow small, looking more like vines or bushes.) Just downstream of the falls the maples are crowded out by tall redwood trees. Redwoods? In Sonoma? Yes, a very fine grove of them.

If it suits you better, you can reach the waterfall by an even shorter route. After paying the day-

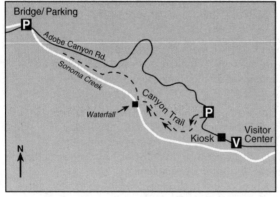

Canyon Trail, Sugarloaf Ridge State Park

use fee at the park entrance kiosk, turn around and drive back down Adobe Canyon Road for 1.1 miles, where you'll find a small parking area just west of a bridge. Park in the lot, cross the bridge, and walk uphill on the road (east, toward the park) for a quarter mile. Take the Canyon Trail from the trail marker on your right. This way your walk to the falls will be mostly level, except for the short uphill stretch on the paved road. Plus, you'll have

On top of the waterfall on Sonoma Creek

the chance to meander through the redwood grove that lies downstream of the falls.

A caveat: It gets hot at this park in summer, with temperatures in the 90s almost every day, so Sonoma Creek often dwindles by June or July. The best time to see the waterfall is shortly after winter and early spring rains.

Make it more challenging: After visiting the waterfall, you can add on a loop hike on the Pony Gate Trail and Stern Trail. The trailhead is located near where you parked your car. This loop will add another mile to your trip; see a park map for details.

Trip notes: A $5 state park entrance fee is charged. A trail map is available from the ranger kiosk for 75 cents. For more information, contact Sugarloaf Ridge State Park, 2605 Adobe Canyon Road, Kenwood, CA 95452-9004;

(707) 833-5712 or (707) 938-1519.

Directions: From U.S. 101 in Santa Rosa, turn east on Highway 12 and continue for 11 miles to Adobe Canyon Road. Turn left and drive 3.5 miles to the park entrance kiosk. Pay the entrance fee, then turn around and head back down the road for about 100 yards to the gravel parking area on your right and the trailhead for the Pony Gate Trail. (Don't park anywhere in the park without a permit from the kiosk.) Cross the street to reach the trailhead for the Canyon Trail.

Gold Country, Tahoe, & Plumas

(For locations of trails, see map on page 8.)

40. WETLANDS WALK
Sacramento National Wildlife Refuge
Off Interstate 5 near Willows
2 miles round-trip — 1 hour — mostly level terrain

🚶🚶

Here's a trail that may require a leap of faith to get you hiking on it. Not because it's steep or dangerous or patrolled by a pack of hungry wolves, but because this peaceful little trail in Sacramento National Wildlife Refuge is situated smack in the middle of the Central Valley, only about a mile from the endless noise and exhaust of Interstate 5. This place probably would win the award for Least Likely Place for a Nature Preserve. Or maybe Most Likely Place to Experience Car Fumes.

But don't let the miles of asphalt highway fool you. The area surrounding this part of I-5 is prime farmland, mostly for rice and other grains. That's why the Sacramento National Wildlife Refuge had to be positioned here. Long before modern farmers moved in to the area, the Central Valley was a key stop for birds on the Pacific Flyway. Even today, an estimated 60 percent of all ducks, geese, swans, and other birds on the Flyway spend part of their year in the Central Valley.

It turns out the birds and the farmers all like the same thing—the valley's huge expanses of marshes and wetlands, which are created by seasonal flooding of the Sacramento River. The problem is, when man and birds compete, man usually wins. In the Central Valley and most of California, agricultural needs combined with the encroachment of urbanization and industry have led to the destruction of more than 90 percent of the wetlands—prime bird territory—that once existed.

But the birds don't give up. In the Central Valley, they tried using the farm fields for their habitat, much to the chagrin of the farmers. So as early as the 1950s, the federal government smartened up and opened three wildlife refuges in the Central Valley. Now, the birds are happy, the farmers are happy, and people who love easy wildlife walks are especially happy.

When you visit, first you have to overcome a little culture shock: Moments ago you were passing trucks going 70 miles per hour on the freeway, but now you are walking through peaceful seasonal marshes, gazing at ponds and vernal pools, and seeing an incredible amount of wildlife. I saw more jackrabbits along the refuge's two-mile loop trail than I saw collectively in a year of hiking. You may also see raccoons, deer, squirrels, frogs, and lizards, plus more birds than you can imagine.

Be on the lookout for migrating ducks and geese, plus resident great blue herons, great egrets, pheasants, hawks, harriers, coots, avocets, sandpipers, owls, woodpeckers, and songbirds.

The trail is a breeze to follow. It's completely level and ludicrously well-signed. From the parking area, the path crosses the entrance road, then makes two connected loops, like a figure-eight. Winter is the prime season to see wildlife (particularly migratory waterbirds). But even in June, there is plenty of life in these marshes. Time your trip so that you arrive in the morning or late afternoon—the best times for wildlife watching.

Make it easier: Take the shortcut from the halfway point. When your loop takes you across the access road for the refuge, you can walk straight back to your car rather than hiking the longer loop.

Trip notes: There is no fee. A free trail map/brochure is available at the trailhead or refuge visitor center. For more information, contact the Sacramento National Wildlife Refuge, Route 1, Box 311, Willows, CA 95988; (916) 934-2801. The street address is 752 County Road 99W.

Directions: Traveling north on Interstate 5 from Sacramento, take the Norman Road/Princeton exit, which is 18 miles north of Williams and Highway 20. (It is signed for the Sacramento National Wildlife Refuge.) At the first intersection, turn left on County Road 99W and drive for one mile, then turn right into the refuge. Park in the parking area. The trail begins from the parking area, and you can take the loop in either direction. (If you're driving south on Interstate 5, the wildlife refuge exit is seven miles south of Willows.)

---

41. STEVENS TRAIL
BLM—Folsom Resource Area
Off Interstate 80 in Colfax
3 miles round-trip — 1.5 hours — some steep terrain

Most people need a darn good reason to get out of their air-conditioned cars when driving east of Sacramento on I-80 in the summertime. Like maybe because a UFO has landed on the freeway in front of them, or Elvis is selling lemonade and signing autographs at a rest stop.

The Stevens Trail, managed by the Bureau of Land Management, is another good reason to pull off the road and challenge the heat. The BLM? Aren't those the guys that manage all that cattle grazing and strip mining land? Aren't all trails on BLM land simply fire roads that are hot, dry, dusty, and steep? Well, yes and sometimes. The Stevens Trail is

Waterfall along the Stevens Trail

an exception to the stereotypical BLM trail, which is often better suited for equestrians, mountain bikers, or off-roaders than for those traveling on two feet. The Stevens Trail is steep, but manageably so. It heads through some lovely forest with abundant wildflowers, crossing several streams and leading you past a waterfall to spectacular views of the South Fork of the American River.

Just remember these tips: Don't hike here in the middle of the day, and try to time your trip for sometime between January and June. By midsummer, things get hot and dry out here. The waterfall disappears, the wildflowers choke on the heat, and you'll want to throw this book far into the canyon as you pant your way back uphill to your car. Of course, some people are less sensitive to hot weather. Just check in with your personal heat-o-meter before you visit.

I first hiked the Stevens Trail on a hot day at the end of June. I was on my way to Tahoe and looking for a way to break up the long drive. The Stevens Trail was easy to get to and only five minutes out of my way, right off Interstate 80. At the trailhead, I could hear the near-deafening sound of cars whizzing by on the freeway. But in 10 minutes of walking, I had dropped down into the canyon and was completely free of the road noise.

The delights of the Stevens Trail are a pleasant surprise. The path cuts through a tranquil oak, pine, fir, and dogwood woodland. It is loaded with pretty wildflowers in spring and early summer, including poppies, lupine, and monkeyflower. Small streams cross the trail in several places. After about 15 minutes of downhill walking through this shady forest, you reach a dirt road where you turn left and head out into the sunlight. Shortly thereafter, you reach an intersection of four dirt roads and turn right. The trail is well-signed the entire way, but the vegetation is so lush that it sometimes obscures the signs.

After a quarter-mile stretch on open road bordered by numerous buckeye trees and a coursing stream, you'll head back into dense wood-land again on your final descent to the waterfall. The entire Stevens Trail is a total 4.5 miles (nine miles round-trip), leading all the way to the edge of the American River's South Fork. But because your return trip is almost all uphill, I recommend you go only as far as the trailside waterfall. This requires about a 35-minute walk downhill to your desti-nation, and then about a 45-minute walk back uphill to your car.

The waterfall, too, comes as a surprise. It's hard to believe how much water runs through here in the spring. The trail crosses the stream on granite slabs by the fall. There are two cascades, one that you walk right over and one that is about 30 yards upstream, hidden by thick vines and branches. In June, the crossing was easy, because the lower cascade was dry. But I took the short spur trail upstream a few yards and was amazed at how much water still poured down the larger cascade. With a little scrambling over rocks, you can find a few shallow pools to dunk your feet in.

Be sure to cool off before heading back uphill to your car. Oh, and when you get back, I hope Elvis is around somewhere selling lemonade, because it sure tastes good after hiking on a hot day.

Make it easier: Take the trail through the woodland to the first fire road and turn around there. Although you'll miss seeing the waterfall, you'll still get to experience the flora along the trail, and your climb back to the car will be much shorter.

Trip notes: There is no fee. For more information, contact the Bureau of Land Management, Folsom Resource Area, 63 Natoma Street, Folsom, CA 95630; (916) 985-4474.

Directions: From Sacramento, drive east on Interstate 80 for approximately 50 miles to Colfax. Take the Colfax exit, turn left at the stop sign, and drive east on the frontage road (North Canyon Way) for seven-tenths of a mile to the trailhead. The trail and parking area are clearly marked.

---

42. SOUTH YUBA INDEPENDENCE TRAIL
South Yuba River Project
Off Highway 49 near Nevada City
2 miles round-trip — 1 hour — mostly level terrain

The problem with most wheelchair-accessible trails is this: They're paved. Although pavement may seem practical for wheelchair travel, trail users often state that the pavement takes away from the experience of being in the outdoors. In fact, most people head outdoors to get away from materials like pavement.

So for wheelchair-users, the South Yuba Independence Trail is a stroke of genius and a blessing. It's the first identified wheelchair wilderness trail in the United States, and it isn't paved. It leads a total of six miles on hard-packed dirt and wooden flumes along the Yuba River canyon.

Everything about this trail has been done right. A nonprofit group called Sequoya Challenge looks after the trail in partnership with California State Parks. The path was originally built in 1859, not as a hiking trail but as a canal to carry water from the South Yuba River to a hydraulic mining site in Smartville, 25 miles downstream. Consisting of rock-lined ditches with adjacent paths for ditch tenders, plus wooden flumes (bridges) allowing passage over creeks, the canal followed a nearly level contour along the steep hillsides above the South Yuba River.

Since 1970, the abandoned water canal has undergone a transformation. The old flumes were upgraded and rebuilt and new sections of trail were opened up for all-access hiking. In many places, two trails run parallel, one for wheelchairs and one for hiking legs. Outhouses built for wheelchair users are positioned along the trail, as well as accessible platforms for picnicking and fishing on Rush Creek.

At the trailhead, you have a choice of hiking east or west. (The trail does not loop; if you want to walk the whole route, you must go out-and-back in both directions.) To see one of the trail's main highlights, a waterfall on Rush Creek, head to the right (west) for one mile. In the first 100 yards from the parking area, you must duck your head and pass through a tunnel under Highway 49. Beyond it, you walk through a densely wooded area and pass a roofed platform with a scenic overlook of the South Yuba River.

In short order you leave the forest and come out to an amazing cliff-hanging flume, its wooden boards making a horseshoe-shaped turn around the back of a canyon. Above and below it, Rush Creek Falls flows in multiple tiers over polished granite. The best place to see its lower cascades is from the eastern edge of the flume, before you reach the creek itself. The flume forms a bridge just above the tallest drop of the falls, a double tier that's 50 feet tall.

This portion of trail is called the Rush Creek Ramp at Flume 28. Volunteers built an intricate wooden ramp that circles down from the flume to the edge of Rush Creek, above the main drop of the fall. Several smaller cascades tumble upstream of the ramp, near a picnicking and fishing platform that's in place in summer months.

Make it more challenging: If you wish to continue beyond the falls, you can go another mile to Jones Bar Road, then turn around and hike back, making a four-mile round-trip. You can also hike the eastern section of trail from the parking area, a five-mile round-trip that includes more flumes, views of the river and foothills, and springtime wildflowers.

Trip notes: There is no fee. For more information and a map/brochure, contact South Yuba River Project, Bridgeport Ranger Station; (530) 432-2546.

Directions: From Interstate 80 at Auburn, drive north on Highway 49 for 27 miles to Nevada City. Continue on Highway 49 for eight miles past Nevada City to the trailhead parking area along the highway (just before the South Yuba River bridge). Park at the large paved pullout—it's well-signed but comes up fast.

43. GRASS LAKE TRAIL
Plumas-Eureka State Park
Off Highway 89 near Graeagle
3.5 miles round-trip — 2 hours — some steep terrain

For some reason, Grass Lake just doesn't get the respect it deserves. When I asked around about it, everyone told me to pass it by and head for the lakes beyond it: Rock, Jamison, and Wades lakes. Luckily, I paid no attention. Now that I've been there, I have plenty of respect for Grass Lake. For one thing, getting to it requires a healthy climb. When you reach it, you may be happy not to go any farther. Plus, Grass Lake has some great little trail camps, perfect places for a first-time back-packing trip. The lakeside destination is equally fine for day-hikers.

You pick up the trail at the old Jamison Mine buildings in Plumas-Eureka State Park. The Jamison Mine was in operation from 1887 until 1919, producing gold for the Sierra Buttes Mining Company. Evidence of mining operations can be seen here and elsewhere along Jamison Creek.

Unlike on most state park trails, you don't have to pay a day-use fee to take this hike. Just park in the lot and set off on the trail. The trailhead is marked with mileages to Grass Lake, Jamison Lake, Wades Lake, Rock Lake, and Smith Lake. Although the trail begins in the state park, the lakes are located outside the border of the state park in national forest land.

The trail is well signed and easy to follow. After a left turn at the Jamison Mine buildings, you'll climb up, up, and up on a steep and rocky path until you reach the left cutoff for Smith Lake. If you're smart, you won't take the Smith Lake spur (like I did), because it climbs even more and then makes a mean descent to Smith Lake. (A much easier route to Smith Lake begins at the Gray Eagle trailhead; see page 109.) Continue straight to Grass Lake instead, now a level half-mile away. You'll exit the state park at the marked boundary and enter Plumas National Forest. As soon as you enter the national forest you'll notice felled trees and stumps, which tells you something about the different mandates of a state park and a national forest.

A few hundred feet beyond the state park boundary, you'll hear the sound of roaring water. A trail spur on the right leads you to Little Jamison Creek's edge and an overlook of 40-foot-high Jamison Falls. After snowmelt in spring, the cascade is quite impressive.

Five more minutes of level walking brings you to Grass Lake, elevation 5,842 feet, a pretty alpine lake surrounded by Jeffrey pine and red fir. Look for the gnawed-off trees that are evidence of beavers living near Grass Lake. Although beavers are rarely seen in the daytime, they make their whereabouts known by leaving chewed stumps wherever they go.

The trail continues along the east side of Grass Lake before heading farther to Rock, Wades, and Jamison lakes. Circle around to the west side of Grass Lake for the best view of

Hiking the perimeter of Grass Lake

the day: The stunning backdrop of craggy granite mountains on the lake's east side. You'll notice that backpackers set up camp on the west side of the lake, not just to get away from the busy trail but also to wake up to striking views.

Make it easier: Because this trail is steep from the start, it's not for anyone who doesn't want to climb. However, a separate, level trail leads from the same parking lot through the forest and along Little Jamison Creek to the state park campground.

Trip notes: There is no fee. A trail map is available at the state park museum and office for $1. For more information, contact Plumas-Eureka State Park, 310 Johnsville Road, Blairsden, CA 96103; (530) 836-2380 or (530) 525-7232. The Plumas-Eureka State Park museum and office is half a mile past the trailhead access road on County Road A-14.

Directions: From Truckee, drive north on Highway 89 for about 50 miles to Graeagle. At Graeagle, turn west on County Road A-14 and drive 4.5 miles to the Jamison Mine/Grass Lake access road on the left. Turn left and follow the unpaved access road for one mile, past Camp Lisa, to the trailhead parking area. The trailhead is at the far side of the parking lot, clearly marked with a sign for Grass, Smith, Rock, Wades, and Jamison lakes. (Another trail leads from this lot to the state park campground.)

---

44. MADORA LAKE TRAIL
Plumas-Eureka State Park
Off Highway 89 near Graeagle
1.5 miles round-trip — 45 minutes — mostly level terrain

Even though hiking on this state park trail doesn't require a day-use fee, I'd be willing to plunk down some change just to experience what I can only describe as the "primordial" environment of the place. That word kept running through my mind as I circled around the marshy pond that is Madora Lake. Then my hiking partner said it out loud: "Doesn't this place feel *primordial?*" echoing my thoughts exactly.

Madora Lake, Plumas-Eureka State Park

The Madora Lake Trail transports you to a more primitive time when the earth was young and life was just beginning to emerge from the ooze. Hike the trail in the quiet of the morning or evening and you'll see what I mean. The small lake is remarkably still and peaceful, and its surrounding area is abundant with wildlife.

This completely level trail begins conventionally enough near some picnic tables and rest rooms at the trailhead. A few hundred yards of walking takes you to a stream and the beginning of the trail loop. Set out along the streamside trail, make a left turn at the footbridge, and head through the thick conifer forest. The stream provides the ideal soggy environment for a veritable forest of ferns. Towering above them, pines and firs line the soft dirt trail.

Soon you'll see what looks like a stagnant pond on your right. It may seem disappointing if you were expecting Madora Lake to be a big, dramatic alpine lake. But don't judge too quickly. As you continue hiking, you'll come closer to the lake and begin to see that this body of water is teeming with life. Water birds—ducks, coots, and geese—as well as land birds such as pileated woodpeckers, hummingbirds, and saw-whet owls live on and around the lake. Gregarious bullfrogs call to each other from across the water.

A picnic table on the far side of the lake provides the perfect spot to view and contemplate a cluster of dead tree snags protruding from the water. The snags look like an eery ghost forest, but they provide important habitat for birds and other creatures.

A couple of dirt roads intersect the Madora Lake Trail, but stay on the main path until you circle all the way around the lake. You'll wind up back at the short connector trail to the parking lot.

Make it easier: Hike as far as you like and then backtrack, rather than making the loop around the lake.

Trip notes: There is no fee. A trail map is available at the state park museum and office for $1. For more information, contact Plumas-Eureka State Park, 310 Johnsville Road, Blairsden, CA 96103; (530) 836-2380 or (530) 525-7232. The Plumas-Eureka State Park museum and office is 2.3 miles farther up the road from the trailhead.

Directions: From Truckee, drive north on Highway 89 for about 50 miles to Graeagle. At Graeagle, turn west on County Road A-14 and drive three miles to the Madora Lake Trailhead on the right.

---

45. HALSEY FALLS TRAIL
Plumas National Forest
Off Highway 89 near Graeagle
2 miles round-trip — 1 hour — rolling terrain

People who stay at Gray Eagle Lodge in the Lakes Basin have a sweet deal. Like all the lodges in the Lakes Basin area, Gray Eagle has cozy cabins, a good restaurant, and access to all the hiking and fishing that anybody could want to do. But day visitors who don't have a reser-

Halsey Falls, Plumas National Forest

vation to stay at Gray Eagle Lodge can get a piece of the action by accessing the Forest Service trailhead located just a quarter-mile away. From this one trailhead in the Lakes Basin, you can hike to several lakes, a mountain summit, and two waterfalls.

Of the many hiking options from the Gray Eagle trailhead, the easiest and perhaps the most rewarding trail is the one-mile path to Halsey Falls. Anybody can make the trip, because it's nearly level and easy to walk. All you have to do is pour on the bug spray and go. (That's the only drawback to the Lakes Basin area: All the standing water in the numerous lakes means there are tons of mosquitoes in summer, kind of like a miniature Minnesota.)

Besides the mosquitoes, the only other thing to be wary of are the trails signs, which tend to disagree with each other about mileage and make oblique references to trails that don't exist. No need to fret, however; the trail markers are almost superfluous if you're walking to Halsey Falls. The path follows the creek for the entire route; your ears guide you to the sound of rushing water at the end.

Along the way, shady forest alternates with open areas and views of surrounding ridgelines. One brief ascent takes you to the top of a low ridge directly behind Gray Eagle Lodge, but the rest of the hike is level. You'll cross two small streams that feed into Gray Eagle Creek, the source of flow for Halsey Falls.

The roar of water gets louder and the air gets cooler as you approach Halsey Falls. Standing near the foot of the waterfall at its peak flow, you can feel the breeze from the wide, 20-foot-high cascade. If you want to cool off, climb on rocks and fallen trees until you're right underneath the spray.

Make it more challenging: Intrepid hikers can continue from Halsey Falls for another mile southeast to Grassy Lake or west to the northern edge of Long Lake. Both are good trout fishing lakes, but their routes are only passable in good weather and well after the thaw.

Trip notes: There is no fee. For more information, contact Plumas National Forest, Beckwourth Ranger District, P.O. Box 7, Blairsden, CA 96103; (530) 836-2575.

Directions: From Truckee, drive north on Highway 89 for about 50 miles to Forest Service Road 24 (Gold Lake Highway), and turn left. (Forest Service Road 24 is 1.3 miles south of the town of Graeagle on Highway 89). Drive five miles south on Road 24 until you see the sign for Gray Eagle Lodge. Turn right and drive three-tenths of a mile to the trailhead for Smith Lake and Halsey Falls (a quarter mile before the lodge). The trailhead for Halsey Falls is on the left side of the parking lot.

---

46. SMITH LAKE TRAIL
Plumas National Forest
Off Highway 89 near Graeagle
2 miles round-trip — 1 hour — some steep terrain

Smith Lake beckoned, and I followed its call. The only problem was that I followed it in the most difficult way possible, and when I arrived I was so tuckered out that I had to take a nap. It's impossible to fully appreciate a gorgeous alpine lake with your eyes closed, so I vowed to return another time. Luckily, on my second trip, I took a much tamer trail, which left me with plenty of enthusiasm to explore Smith Lake and take in its many offerings.

"Tamer" is a relative term, of course, and in this case, it still requires a good ascent, lateraling a dry ridge covered with manzanita. But it's worth the effort to reach this classic mountain lake, which is set just above 6,000 feet in a glacial rock bowl with a rough and jagged shoreline. You might even want to carry your fishing tackle.

The climb starts right from the parking area and it's completely exposed, with no shade. But the ridge above looks more difficult to conquer than it actually is, thanks to a path that's more horizontal than vertical. In 15 minutes or so, you'll be at the top, looking down over the valley below and the parallel ridge to your right and marveling at how high you've climbed.

Smith Lake Trail, Plumas National Forest

Another reward on the ridgetop is a shady pine and fir forest. The trail tunnels through the conifers before descending to a lush meadow and stream area, then crossing a creek. Here you'll find a trail marker pointing left to Smith Lake in a quarter mile. In short order you'll arrive at the lake, which is surrounded by an incredible old-growth fir forest. The trees are so big, there is almost no undergrowth at all. Staghorn moss covers the firs' trunks. A few fallen giants lay prone, reminiscent of the old-growth redwood forests of northwest California. The landscape seems oddly barren except for these big, imposing trees.

Walk the trail to the left around the lakeshore, and you'll see that Smith Lake is really two lakes (one very small) that merge during spring runoff. A creek separates the lakes the rest of the year. Follow the trail as far as you like along the water's edge. You'll probably want to turn around when the path begins to climb out of the lake bowl and up a steep ridge, heading back into the border of Plumas-Eureka State Park.

Parts of the trail around the lake's southern edge of the lake are submerged by water after snowmelt, so only go as far as you can without getting soaked feet. The trail doesn't make a complete circle around the lake, because the northern edge is a steep wall of granite. Retrace your steps when you're ready to return.

Make it easier: The tough part of this hike is the first part, the hike up the ridge, so if you want to make it easier, you'll have to be satisfied with walking only part way and taking in the views from somewhere on the ridge, but not going to the lake.

Trip notes: There is no fee. For more information, contact Plumas National Forest, Beckwourth Ranger District, P.O. Box 7, Blairsden, CA 96103; (530) 836-2575.

Directions: From Truckee, drive north on Highway 89 for about 50 miles to Forest Service Road 24 (Gold Lake Highway), and turn left. (Forest Service Road 24 is 1.3 miles south of the town of Graeagle on Highway 89). Drive five miles south on Road 24 until you see the sign for Gray Eagle Lodge. Turn right and drive three-tenths of a mile to the trailhead for Smith Lake and Halsey Falls (a quarter-mile before the lodge). The trailhead for Smith Lake is on the right side of the parking lot.

47. LILY LAKE & FERN FALLS TRAILS
Plumas National Forest
Off Highway 89 near Graeagle
1 mile round-trip — 30 minutes — mostly level terrain

The trail to Lily Lake may be the shortest walk in the entire Lakes Basin that takes you to a pristine alpine lake. You park your car at the trailhead, walk for 10 minutes, and you're there. If wandering around the lake, having a picnic on a rock or dropping a line in the water isn't enough to maintain your interest, you can get back in the car, drive a half mile up the road, and hike the trail to Fern Falls, which may be the shortest walk in the entire Lakes Basin that takes you to a waterfall overlook.

Get the picture? Two short walks, together totalling about one mile in length, combined with a two-minute drive from trailhead to trailhead, gives you access to a pretty little lake and a pretty little waterfall, two perfect settings for a family outing.

If you're in the mood for a little more exercise, you can walk halfway around Lily Lake and take the trail that leads to the Gray Eagle trailhead, from which you can hike to Halsey Falls (see the story on page 107). That would add another three miles to your round-trip.

But for many, Lily Lake at 5,920 feet in elevation is satisfying enough. The lake has a secluded feel to it, even though you are remarkably close to the highway. It's a fine place for a picnic.

The origin of Lily Lake's name remains a question. One friend told me the lake is completely covered with water lilies in the summer. I saw no lilies in June, however, and was told by somebody else that the lake's namesake was a pioneer gal named Lily, who made her way in these parts by participating in the world's oldest profession.

You can debate that little mystery on the half-mile drive to the Fern Falls pullout, which is marked with a large sign that reads "Fern Falls Picnic Area and Vista Trail."

With a drop of just 15 feet, Fern Falls seems more like a heavy flowing creek with some big boulders than a real waterfall, but the sight and sound of cascading water is satisfying nonetheless. The quarter-mile trail from the road takes you across a footbridge and up to the overlook, where you can climb on smooth granite rocks to get close to the stream.

If you plan to spend any time hanging around Lily Lake or Fern Falls, be sure to lather on the bug spray. The mosquitoes will generally leave you alone if you keep moving, but they flock to a sitting target.

Make it easier: Choose one half-mile hike or the other. Lily Lake would be my pick, since Fern Falls is a little more developed and popular.

Trip notes: There is no fee. For more information, contact Plumas National Forest, Beckwourth Ranger District, P.O. Box 7, Blairsden, CA 96103; (530) 836-2575.

Directions: From Truckee, head north on Highway 89 for about 50 miles to Forest Service Road 24 (Gold Lake Highway), and turn left. (Forest Service Road 24 is 1.3 miles south of the town of Graeagle on Highway 89). Drive 5.5 miles south on Road 24 to a pullout along the road marked for Lily Lake (it's a half mile south of the turnoff for Gray Eagle Lodge). The pullout for Fern Falls is a half mile farther south of Lily Lake on Road 24.

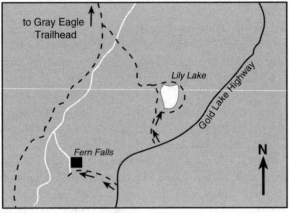

Lily Lake/Fern Falls Trails

48. FRAZIER FALLS TRAIL
Plumas National Forest
Off Highway 89 near Graeagle
1 mile round-trip — 30 minutes — mostly level terrain

Many people will go pretty far to see a good waterfall, but with Frazier Falls located right off the road in the Gold Lakes Basin, you don't have to tromp for miles just to see cascading water. With an easy 1.5-mile drive on a dirt road and a flat, half-mile walk, you can be at the lookout gazing at 200 feet of falling water in hardly any time at all.

And Frazier Falls is no disappointment in the falling water department. Consider these impressive statistics: Located 1.9 miles below Gold Lake at 6,000 feet in elevation, the falls are 176 feet high, with a total cascade length of 248 feet (this number takes into account the lower areas of white water that aren't technically part of the waterfall's freefall). In springtime, millions of gallons of water hurtle over the rocky ledge of the falls, producing a convincing display of the power of melting snow.

The hike consists of a half-mile walk from the parking area to a fenced-in overlook about 200 yards across from the falls—a safe distance for viewing a waterfall of this size. The overlook also gives you the best possible view of the entire cascade.

Is it impressive? You bet. Even with all the waterfalls in this part of the state, Frazier Falls stands out. A visitor's register at the overlook encourages waterfall viewers to write their comments. On the day I visited, someone summed up Frazier Falls with these two Batman-esque words: "Holy snowmelt."

Frazier Falls is not only a worthy destination, but it also has a great trail. The path is completely level until the very end, where it ascends only a bit. It is surrounded by large, polished granite rocks, ponderosa pines and firs, and mountain wildflowers, including light purple lupine and orange paintbrush. The trail features fine views of surrounding mountain ridges.

A small clearing, located 30 yards before you reach the official fenced-in waterfall overlook, offers a preview of what is to come. This is a good place to take pictures if your camera lens won't fit through the overlook's fence.

Although you probably won't recognize it until your return trip, at one point on the path to Frazier Falls you cross a footbridge over Frazier

Creek that is only 50 yards upstream of the waterfall. You can't hear the falls from this bridge, only the running water of the creek. But if you look closely, you can see the water downstream disappear over the edge of a cliff—this is the top of the waterfall.

One warning: Because Frazier Falls is so easy to reach and so dramatic, you can bet on having plenty of company at the waterfall overlook. The best way to see the falls is to visit early in the morning or late in the day, when the crowds are down and the sunlight on the rocks and ridges is spectacular.

Make it easier: Those who don't want to make the trip to the falls overlook can hang out at the picnic area at the trailhead.

Trip notes: There is no fee. For more information, contact Plumas National Forest, Beckwourth Ranger District, P.O. Box 7, Blairsden, CA 96103; (530) 836-2575.

Directions: From Truckee, head north on Highway 89 for about 50 miles to Forest Service Road 24 (Gold Lake Highway), and turn left. (Forest Service Road 24 is 1.3 miles south of the town of Graeagle on Highway 89). Drive 8.4 miles south on Road 24 and turn left at the sign for Frazier Falls (on Old Gold Lake Road, directly across Road 24 from Gold Lake). Drive 1.5 miles north on the dirt road to reach the trailhead parking for Frazier Falls.

---

49. SAND POND INTERPRETIVE TRAIL
Tahoe National Forest
Off Highway 49 near Bassetts
1 mile round-trip — 30 minutes — mostly level terrain

For people who are fascinated by furry mammals, especially furry mammals that slap their tails in the water and mow down trees for a living, the Sand Pond Interpretive Trail is a must-see. In half an hour of hiking you'll see so much beaver evidence that it will be impossible not to imagine seeing the little tree-chewers everywhere you go.

Of course, "evidence" is the operative word here. You won't actually see any beavers, unless perhaps you walk the trail at midnight and do your best lodgepole pine imitation. Beavers are nocturnal creatures and shy besides. But you will see what happens to a forest and meadow area when a bevy of beavers move in. The trail is a fascinating example of how one change in the order of things can drastically alter an ecosystem.

Sand Pond Interpretive Trail, Tahoe National Forest

The interpretive trail's story goes like this: Several beaver families discovered Salmon Creek in the mid-1980s. They decided the creek was a great place to live, dammed it, and flooded the surrounding forest. (Dammit, the beavers move in and there goes the neighbor-hood!) Entire stands of lodgepole pines drowned as their roots were submerged in water. This created a "ghost forest," an eery-looking marsh with tall, dead tree trunks poking upward. It makes a memorable sight, especially with the snow-covered Sierra Buttes in the background. The Forest Service has placed a wooden boardwalk over the flooded area, allowing hiker and wheelchair access.

Beyond the ghost forest, the trail leads into a thick conifer forest with signs identifying the different types of pines and firs. The most prevalent is the lodgepole pine, with scale-like bark and small, two-inch cones. Lodgepoles get their name from the Plains Indians, who made teepees with them. You'll see many tall, sturdy lodgepoles along this trail—some healthy and growing, others a "ghost forest" of dead trees, and still more just beaver-chewed stumps.

The end of the Sand Pond Trail brings you to Sand Pond, a small, shallow lake that attracts anglers. Sand Pond is a man-made body of water, formed by miners in the mid-1800s. The miners deposited tailings from the nearby Young America mine, then removed the tail-ings to sift through them for valuable ore. The removal of the tailings left the depression that is now filled with water and fish.

A great feature of the Sand Pond Trail is that it's rated as suitable for athletic wheelchair users, or wheelchair users with assistance. There are three different places where you can park and access the trail, and although some interpretive signs are posted, you don't need to start in any certain place to have it all make sense.

If you like, you can extend your walk from Sand Pond to the dam at Lower Sardine Lake, just 100 yards farther. You're likely to see plenty of campers and vacationers from Sardine Lake Lodge at both Sand Pond and Lower Sardine Lake. Both are popular spots for fishing; the lake is also popular with swimmers and boaters.

Make it more challenging: Add on a hike from Sand Pond to Lower Sardine Lake and then to Upper Sardine Lake (see the following story).

Trip notes: There is no fee. For more information, contact Tahoe National Forest, Downieville Ranger District, 15924 Highway 49, Camptonville, CA 95922; (530) 288-3231.

Directions: From Truckee, head north on Highway 89 for about 30 miles to Highway 49 heading west at Sattley. Turn west on Highway 49 and drive for about 10 miles to the town of Bassetts at the intersection of Highway 49 and Forest Service Road 24 (Gold Lake Highway). Drive 1.2 miles north on Road 24 to the turnoff for Sardine Lake and Packer Lake. Stay to the left and drive west on the Sardine Lake access road for a half mile to the parking area for the Sand Pond Trail (before the lake and the lodge). The trailhead for the Sand Pond Interpretive Trail is clearly marked. (The main trailhead has the largest parking area, but there are two other spots where you can park and access the trail.)

50. SARDINE LAKES TRAIL
Tahoe National Forest
Off Highway 49 near Bassetts
2.5 miles round-trip — 1.25 hours — rolling terrain

Upper and Lower Sardine Lakes are the *raison d'être* for Sardine Lake Lodge, a dream-like cabin resort where you can have your own boat on a lake for a week, stay in a cabin with mountain and lake views from your front porch, eat gourmet meals prepared by the lodge's chef, and hike and fish to your heart's content.

That's the good news. The even better news is that you don't have to be a guest at the lodge to enjoy the hiking (and shore-fishing and swimming) at Sardine Lakes, because all this land is national forest land—open and free to the public—even though the lodge has a lease to operate on it.

Of all the lakes in the Lakes Basin, the Sardine Lakes are perhaps the most scenic. They are framed by a spectacular backdrop of the jagged, snowy Sierra Buttes, at elevation 8,587 feet. The mountains tower imposingly behind the lakes. It's as perfect as any jigsaw-puzzle scene.

A great trail leads from Lower Sardine Lake, right by the lodge, to Upper Sardine Lake, about a mile away. The path, which is actually an old logging and mining road, heads straight for the upper lake, so you march head-

Looking out over Lower Sardine Lake

first toward the Sierra Buttes. You get a first-rate view the entire way, and it gets even better as you rise above the lower lake.

Start your walk at the lodge parking lot. Take the gravel road (it's paved for the first few yards) on the right side of the lower lake. The trail climbs gently the whole way and is completely exposed, so carry plenty of water with you. Keep looking to your left for increasingly spectacular views of the lower lake as you ascend beyond it. Watch for a huge boulder on your left, about two-thirds of the way up the trail, that marks an informal cutoff where you can scramble down some rocks and wind up on top of a small waterfall. Even if the waterfall is running low when you visit, this is a great place to sit by the stream.

At last you'll reach Upper Sardine Lake—a perfect alpine lake with a rocky shoreline and deep blue water. Its shoreline is too jagged to allow a trail to be built around it. However, you can climb on rocks and boulders and find a place to swim, fish, or lay out in the sun.

The water in Upper Sardine Lake becomes almost warm in summer, so bring a float tube or a swim suit. Fishing for trout is fair. Of course, like most people, you can also forget about fishing and swimming and instead find a big rock to lay on. Then simply gaze in admiration at the pretty lake and the massive, dramatic Sierra Buttes.

Make it easier: Just climb until you get good views of the lower lake, then turn around and head home.

Trip notes: There is no fee. For more information, contact Tahoe National Forest, Downieville Ranger District, 15924 Highway 49, Camptonville, CA 95922; (530) 288-3231.

Directions: From Truckee, head north on Highway 89 for about 30 miles to Highway 49 heading west at Sattley. Turn west on Highway 49 and drive for about 10 miles to the town of Bassetts at the intersection of Highway 49 and Forest Service Road 24 (Gold Lake Highway). Drive 1.2 miles north on Road 24 to the turnoff for Sardine Lake and Packer Lake. Stay to the left and drive west on the Sardine Lake access road for a half mile to the parking area for the Sand Pond Trail (before the lake and the lodge). Walk past the lodge and begin hiking on the fire road that leads from the far side of the lodge parking lot.

---

51. WILD PLUM LOOP
Tahoe National Forest
Off Highway 49 near Sierra City
3 miles round-trip — 1.5 hours — some steep terrain

We came to the Wild Plum Loop Trail in search of waterfalls, but we left empty-handed. We walked three miles, half of it climbing pretty hard, and never found what we wanted. Were we disappointed? Frustrated? Ready to throw our map out the window? Not at all. In fact, the Wild Plum Loop turned out to be our favorite hike of the week, in a week filled with several spectacular trails.

That's because plenty of rewards are found along this trail, which is a three-mile loop trip that begins and ends at Wild Plum Campground, just south of the Gold Lakes Basin. For starters, the trail provides an unusual look at the back side of the steep and craggy Sierra Buttes. Plus the trail runs alongside Haypress Creek and its deep canyon—a steep-walled rock gorge containing a stream that flows like a raging torrent after snowmelt. In addition, there's the peace and quiet of the forest you walk in, where solitude is almost guaranteed.

If you aren't camping at Wild Plum Campground, start your trip from the trailhead parking area a quarter mile before the camp. Hike the connector trail to the access road and bridge for the camp, where you'll see a sign that reads "Haypress Trail, Pacific Crest Trail, and Wild Plum Loop." This is your ticket. Off you go through a mixed forest of cedars, firs, and various hardwoods.

The trail stays level as it parallels Haypress Creek for a quarter-mile. Near a small hydroelectric building, it starts switchbacking up a ridge. Be prepared to work a little; this is a long series of switchbacks that will get your heart rate up. (Console yourself with the thought of what this hill would be like *without* switchbacks.)

After about 15 minutes of climbing, you'll top the ridge. Any grumbling is sure to end when you see the excellent view of the back of the Sierra Buttes. There is a small clearing where you can gaze in wonder at the canyon below you and the mountains above, while you pat yourself on the back for toughing out the climb.

After admiring the view, continue hiking along the ridge top. You'll meet up with the Pacific Crest Trail (PCT) and turn right. (If you turn left on the Pacific Crest Trail by mistake, you'll have to climb up the back of the Sierra Buttes. If you think the ascent you just made was serious, the Buttes are a nightmare.)

Your work is now over and you'll start to descend. The remaining part of the loop is either level or slightly downhill, so you can just relax and glide it out. Although the Wild Plum Loop is made up of sections of the Haypress Trail and the Pacific Crest Trail, with connecting portions that bring it all together, the trail is well-signed and easy to follow. Watch for the signs and you can't go wrong.

When you cross the footbridge over Haypress Creek, you've completed your stint on the PCT. Turn right and head back on the last leg of your loop, hiking along Haypress Creek in a dense conifer forest. Follow this pretty, shaded stretch until you reach a logging road. Follow the road downhill to Wild Plum Campground. You'll return to the opposite side of the bridge from your starting point. Finish out your walk on the connector trail to the day-use parking area and your car.

Make it easier: Hike out-and-back along the creek from the campground.

Trip notes: There is no fee. For more information, contact Tahoe National Forest, Downieville Ranger District, 15924 Highway 49, Camptonville, CA 95922; (530) 288-3231.

Directions: From Truckee, head north on Highway 89 for about 30 miles to Highway 49 heading west at Sattley. Turn west on Highway 49 and drive for about 15 miles west toward Sierra City. Turn left on Wild Plum Road one mile before Sierra City. Drive 1.2 miles to the end of Wild Plum Road and the trailhead parking area. The last half-mile is not paved. Begin hiking at the trail marker on the left side of the parking lot.

52. FULLER LAKE TRAIL
Tahoe National Forest
Off Highway 20 near Interstate 80
1.5 miles round-trip — 45 minutes — mostly level terrain

Dozens of lakes are located on Bowman Lake Road off Highway 20 in the Grouse Lakes area. But many of them require a four-wheel-drive vehicle to reach their shorelines, plus a long drive on rutted dirt and gravel roads. Even if you can gain access, the lakes' hiking trails are often buried under snow until late in the year, as I discovered one Fourth of July. On an attempted trip to Carr and Feely lakes, we had to park and walk over snow fields for the last half-mile to the trailhead, where we were greeted by a frozen lake and totally snowbound trails.

Fuller Lake is the exception to the rule in the Grouse Lakes area, and it's the perfect destination for an easy hiking trip. You don't have to drive for miles on Bowman Lake Road; it's the first lake you come to as you head north, just four miles in. There's no dirt-and-gravel access road; you just pull right off the pavement into the parking lot by the lake. Fuller Lake is set at 5,600 feet in elevation, so it's open and ice-free long before neighboring higher-elevation lakes. Best of all, the trail by the lake is an easy, pretty stroll just a few feet from the water's edge.

On my trip, I met a woman walking her two dogs, a pair of lovers picnicking in the shade, and an older couple on a search for the perfect shore-fishing hole. That was all the company I had, even though there were several dozen other folks at the lake and the parking lot was full. Most people were in boats on the water; the rest were fishing for brown and rainbow trout right by the dam. Because Fuller Lake has a good boat ramp and is generously stocked by the Department of Fish and Game, most people get so involved with fishing that they miss out on this terrific little trail.

Begin your hike by crossing the dam to the right of the parking area, then pick up the trail on the far side. The trail and the scenery improve as you hike farther from the dam; you leave the crowds and enter a dense mixed conifer forest. The trail is littered with soft pine needles, and hundreds of pine cones lay at your feet. This is the perfect place to bring a child for a lesson about the different kinds of conifers and their cones—the Douglas fir with its brownish-red bark and three-inch cones with winged seeds; the ponderosa pine with its yellowish, jigsaw-puzzle bark and four-inch round cones; the white fir with its grey, furrowed bark and barrel-shaped cones; and the red fir with its reddish-brown bark, downward-sweeping branches, and oblong, smooth cones.

Some of the lakeshore is private property, with signs posted telling you to keep away, but much of it is yours to explore at will. You can hike almost a mile from the boat ramp and dam before reaching any "keep out" signs. Be sure to watch for wildlife as you walk along the shoreline. (I followed a mother duck and eight ducklings for about 20 minutes as they floated around the water's edge.) A picnic or a fishing rod can make your trip even more enjoyable.

Make it easier: Just cut your walk short and turn around when you wish.

Trip notes: There is no fee. For more information, contact Tahoe National Forest, Nevada City Ranger District, P.O. Box 6003, Nevada City, CA 95959; (530) 265-4531.

Directions: From Auburn, drive east on Interstate 80 for about 45 miles, past Emigrant Gap. Take the Highway 20 exit and drive west for 3.5 miles, then turn right on Bowman Lake Road (Forest Service Road 18). Drive north for four miles to Fuller Lake, located on the right side of the road. The trail begins across the dam, to the right of the parking area.

53. WARD CREEK TRAIL
Tahoe National Forest
Off Highway 89 near Tahoe City
3 miles round-trip — 1.5 hours — mostly level terrain

If you've been vacationing at Lake Tahoe for a while, there may come a time when you start to crave a little solitude. Perhaps you've already hiked the well-traveled Rubicon Trail, walked to popular Eagle Falls, and visited crowded Vikingsholm Castle. Now you'd just like a pretty forest and some peace and quiet.

The Ward Creek Trail is the answer to your wish. It begins at an unmarked trailhead a few blocks off Highway 89. Because it's not on the lake side of the highway, few people make the trip. Only locals seem to use the trail regularly, particularly in the winter for cross-country skiing.

Of course, compared to the more famous hikes at Lake Tahoe, the Ward Creek Trail is rather tame: No stellar waterfall, no drop-dead gorgeous lake view, no architectural wonders. But then again, there are no crowds either. For many, the trade-off is a good one.

The trail is a logging road, so it's wide, level, and easy to walk. The forest it traverses is open enough so that you have views of nearby mountain peaks, but you're still surrounded by the beauty of the trees. Sugar pines and bright yellow mule's ears border the trail. Ward Creek courses along on your left. Hikers share the trail with bikers and equestrians, and even dogs are allowed. But even with all those potential trail users, there's a good chance you'll have the trail to yourself.

The best time to hike the Ward Creek Trail is in spring, when the weather is warming but patches of snow still cling to the ground and the surrounding mountain peaks are crowned in white. Hiking boots are a good idea, because the trail can be wet and muddy after snowmelt.

The trail leads for miles through Forest Service land, but after about a half mile of walking, you'll move away from Ward Creek (near a fenced-in meadow where the trail makes a sharp right turn). You might choose to walk only this far and turn around. If you continue for another mile, you'll come to a "Road Closed" sign. This makes a good turnaround spot for a three-mile round-trip hike.

After years of abuse by off-road-vehicles, this canyon is now being protected and improved by the Forest Service. Meadows are fenced off for restoration, and a fish habitat improvement program is in place along Ward Creek. Boulders and logs have been placed throughout the creek to provide habitat for resident fish, including trout, suckers, and minnows. That means good news for anglers: Fishing may soon be excellent along Ward Creek.

To sum it up, the Ward Creek Trail is ideal for people who just want to take a stroll and kick a few pine cones. If you're ready for some solitude, pack up a picnic, leash up your dog, and set off for this tranquil spot in Tahoe National Forest.

Make it easier: For a one-mile hike, turn around at the fenced-in meadow where the trail makes a sharp right turn.

Trip notes: There is no fee. For more information, contact Lake Tahoe Basin Management Unit, 870 Emerald Bay Road, South Lake Tahoe, CA 96150; (530) 573-2600.

Directions: From Tahoe City, drive approximately two miles south on Highway 89 to Pineland Drive, just north of Kilner Park. Turn right on Pineland Drive and continue for a half mile to Twin Peaks Drive. Turn left and drive 1.7 miles. (Twin Peaks Drive becomes Ward Creek Boulevard.) At 1.7 miles, you'll see a gravel pullout on the left at a gated dirt road, which is Forest Service Road 15N62 and the trailhead for Ward Creek Trail. Park in the pullout and begin hiking on the dirt road.

54. RUBICON TRAIL
D. L. Bliss State Park

Off Highway 89 on Lake Tahoe's west shore
2 miles round-trip — 1 hour — rolling terrain

Two big problems plague hikers in Tahoe: Too many other hikers and too much private property surrounding the lake. Put the two together and you've got lots of visitors trying to share a very small space in the outdoors. Combine this with the fact that the hiking season in Tahoe is only a few months of the year, and we're talking overload.

But if you want to hike and get an eyeful of azure-blue Lake Tahoe, the Rubicon Trail is the only way to go—crowds and all. Accept no substitutes: Drive yourself to D. L. Bliss State Park, pay the entrance fee, and head for the trailhead at Calawee Cove Beach parking lot, where the trail sign points you to the old lighthouse and Rubicon Point. To increase your chance of peace and quiet, go as early in the morning as possible.

The hike begins on a mostly level grade, but be prepared if you're afraid of heights. The path contours along a steep hillside, which drops off more than 100 feet straight down to the water's edge. Park rangers have put up safety cables in a few spots to keep hikers from falling off the trail.

Fannette Island on Lake Tahoe, as seen from the Rubicon Trail

You'll have plenty of company on the Rubicon Trail, and for good reason. Plain and simple, it offers some of the best views of Lake Tahoe you'll find from public land. You can see the casinos across the water in Nevada, get a bird's-eye view of boaters speeding around the lake, or just stare at all that blue H_2O and ponder this: At 22 miles long and 12 miles wide, Lake Tahoe holds more than 37 trillion gallons of water and is the largest alpine lake in North America. It's the tenth deepest lake in the world, with a greatest depth of 1,645 feet. From Rubicon Point, just a quarter mile in on the Rubicon Trail, you can see several hundred feet down into the lake's depths.

If all that vastness is too overwhelming, you can stick to your close-up view, which includes plenty of chipmunks running along the path, and one spectacular curve in the trail where you get a sudden, breath-taking view of the seasonally snow-capped mountains ahead of you.

You might want to ignore the signed right turnoff to the old light-house. The lighthouse no longer exists, and the trip uphill to its former site is very steep and has a disappointing conclusion, since there's nothing there. The Coast Guard built a gas-powered lighthouse on Rubicon Point in 1916, but keeping the light supplied with fuel proved too difficult. Even when lit, the lighthouse was so high above the shoreline that it just confused everybody. It was shut down in 1919 and replaced by a newer lighthouse which still stands at Sugar Pine Point.

Beyond the lighthouse cutoff, continue along the trail for a half mile

Rubicon Trail, D.L. Bliss State Park

until you come to the next right turn, where you have two options: Turn around and go back the way you came for more gorgeous lake views, or turn right and loop back for a change in scenery.

If you choose to loop back, you'll find two right turns, one after another; take either one. You'll exit the forest at a parking lot. Turn right and walk about 30 yards until you see a sign for the Lighthouse Trail; turn right again, heading away from the parking lot and back into forest. This alternate trail is higher on the hillside than the Rubicon Trail. It heads through a thick stand of ponderosa and Jeffrey pines, firs, and cedars. The sandy, rocky trail is easy enough to walk on, but it requires more climbing than the Rubicon Trail.

One section of the Lighthouse Trail leads through a recently burned area. Take note of the wildflowers, manzanita, and other brushy shrubs growing in the fire-scarred forest. These are the first plants to come back after a fire, and they will prepare the ground for larger shrubs and trees to grow.

A steep descent brings you back behind the old lighthouse site. Continue to the left, coasting downhill toward the start of the trail.

Make it easier: Return on the same trail rather than making the loop back.

Trip notes: A $5 day-use fee is charged by D.L. Bliss State Park. A trail map is available at the entrance station for 50 cents. For more information, contact D. L. Bliss State Park, P.O. Box 266, Tahoma, CA 96142; (530) 525-7277 or (530) 525-7232.

Directions: From Tahoe City, drive south on Highway 89 for 15 miles and turn left at the sign for D.L. Bliss State Park. Drive a half mile to the park entrance station. Continue straight for seven-tenths of a mile to a sign for "Camps 141-168 and Beach Area." Turn right and drive seven-tenths of a mile to the Calawee Cove Beach parking lot. The Rubicon Trail begins on the far side of the lot.

55. CASCADE FALLS TRAIL
Tahoe National Forest
Off Highway 89 on Lake Tahoe's west shore
1.5 miles round-trip — 45 minutes — rolling terrain

We'd been issued all sorts of warnings about Cascade Falls: "Parking lots fill up early." "This walk is so easy that it's always packed with people." And "Get ready for a parade."

To make matters worse, it was the Friday before the Fourth of

July weekend, and Tahoe was jammed with revelers. I cringed at the prospect of a carnival show at the falls.

My fretting was needless. We reached the trailhead at 9 A.M. and our car was the only one in the lot. We didn't see a soul on our hike to the stunning 200-foot falls, and only a few people passed us on our way out. There may be times when the Cascade Falls Trail gets a lot of traffic, but as with most places, if you visit early in the morning or late in the afternoon, chances are good you'll be free of the crowds.

The trail is pretty every step of the way, meandering in and out of pine forest and open sunshine, alternately providing shade and views. Cascade Falls is just plain spectacular, surging and gushing as it flows more than 200 feet over granite all the way to the southwest end of Cascade Lake.

Start the walk from the trailhead at the edge of Bayview Campground, where you'll find a self-serve permit station for backpackers heading into the Desolation Wilderness. (Day-hikers to Cascade Falls don't need a permit.) Take the clearly marked trail to the left.

In a mere five minutes of walking, you're rewarded with a tremendous view of Cascade Lake at 6,464 feet in elevation. It looks so big you may think it's part of Lake Tahoe. Simultaneously, you'll hear the rumbling of the falls, and in a few more minutes, you'll break out of the forest and get a clear view of the tumbling water.

The remainder of the trail is out in the open. Watch your footing; although the path is mostly sand, rocks are everywhere on the exposed hillside, and steep dropoffs abound. A lack of attention could send you tumbling.

As you near the falls, the trail disappears on granite slabs, but small rock-pile trail cairns show the way. Most people are satisfied to stop a few hundred feet before the falls to picnic on a rock or just enjoy the view. (The waterfall view is actually best from a distance.) If you have children with you, it's recommended not to hike too close to Cascade Falls, especially if the trail is slippery.

When you're ready to return, pick your way across the granite again until you regain the trail, then backtrack to the parking area.

Make it easier: Don't get too close to the falls—just walk until you're satisfied with the view, then turn around.

Trip notes: There is no fee. For more information, contact Lake Tahoe Basin Management Unit, 870 Emerald Bay Road, South Lake Tahoe, CA 96150; (530) 573-2600.

Directions: From South Lake Tahoe, drive northwest on Highway 89 to the Bayview Campground and Trailhead, located across from Emerald Bay's

Inspiration Point. Drive through the campground to get to the trailhead parking area, where there is space for about eight cars. If this parking lot is full, park across Highway 89 at Inspiration Point and walk across the road to the trailhead.

---

56. ANGORA LAKES TRAIL
Tahoe National Forest
Off Highway 89 south of Fallen Leaf Lake
1 mile round-trip — 30 minutes — rolling terrain

Warning: Do not hike on the Angora Lakes Trail unless you are accompanied by a person under the age of seven. Well, okay, you can go without a child's supervision, but you'll feel like an outsider. That's because Angora Lakes is especially popular with children's day camps and groups, and the whole place is the perfect setup for families.

The adventure begins before you get to the trailhead, with a scenic five-mile drive off Highway 89 near Fallen Leaf Lake. Much of the road is dirt, but it's easily navigated by passenger cars. Along the way, check out the far-and-away view from the Angora Fire Lookout: To your right and far below is Fallen Leaf Lake, to your left is a wide-open valley, and straight ahead is Angora Peak, elevation 8,588 feet.

There you are, winding down this narrow dirt road for miles, feeling like you're all alone in the middle of nowhere, and then—surprise!—you reach the Angora Lakes trailhead with its two huge parking lots, each filled with what seems like a million cars. It's clear that a few other folks know about this place.

Don't be scared off; Angora Lakes is well worth the trip. Start hiking on the dirt road that climbs upward from the upper parking lot's left side. In less than a half mile, the wide road climbs all the way to the first lake, Lower Angora Lake. I would have thought young children would find the 250-foot elevation gain difficult, but I saw plenty of five-year-olds doing laps around their parents all the way up the hill. My lesson: Never underestimate the energy of anyone under 10.

The trail levels out as it tracks the perimeter of the first lake. A few private houses can be seen on the far side, so most hikers just cruise by, walking for another few minutes to reach Upper Angora Lake, where Angora Lakes Resort is located. The resort has been around since 1917 and has picturesque little cabins for rent. Day-visitors can take advantage of the lake's small beach, fish from shore for trout, or rent rowboats for $7 an hour. Upper Angora Lake at 7,280 feet in elevation is a per-

Playing in the snow patches on the trail to Angora Lake

fectly bowl-shaped, glacial cirque lake. The granite wall on its far side is snow-covered most of the year, and in early summer a waterfall of snowmelt flows down its face. Some people paddle around the lake in rubber rafts. By late summer, swimmers will find the water warm enough to take a dip.

Even those who are only interested in hiking may choose to stop by the resort's refreshment stand, where you can buy a big pitcher of lemonade. With the uphill walk to the lake, that lemonade stand is a gold mine. Almost no one can pass it by. Another oddity at the lake's edge is the pay phone located by the picnic tables. I checked my voice mail at my office in San Francisco, just for the sheer novelty of it. Upper Angora Lake is a funny concoction—an odd mix of a place that is developed and set up for tourism, but still remains rustic and unspoiled at the same time.

Because this is national forest land, dogs are allowed on the Angora Lakes Trail, but you must leash your dog at the resort. The resort folks have posted signs about leash rules and are very serious about it, probably because of all the little kids running around.

Make it easier: The work is on the uphill approach to the lakes; then it's downhill all the way home. Let kids explore around on rocks and snow patches to keep their enthusiasm up for the hike.

Trip notes: There is no fee. For more information, contact Lake Tahoe Basin Management Unit, 870 Emerald Bay Road, South Lake Tahoe, CA 96150; (530) 573-2600.

Directions: From Lake Tahoe's Emerald Bay, drive south on Highway 89 for five miles to Fallen Leaf Lake Road and turn right. In eight-tenths of a mile the road splits; stay to the left (do not head toward Fallen Leaf Lake) and continue for four-tenths of a mile. At the junction, turn right on Forest Service Road 12N14, which alternates as paved and unpaved. Drive for 2.3 miles, past the Angora Fire Lookout, to the parking lot at the road's end. The trailhead is on the left side of the upper parking lot.

57. HORSETAIL FALLS TRAIL
Eldorado National Forest
Off U.S. 50 west of Echo Lake
2 miles round-trip — 1 hour — some steep terrain

You'll know why they call it Horsetail Falls the minute you see it from the highway. Straight and narrow at the top and fanning out to a wide inverted "V" at the bottom, Horsetail Falls swishes its way down Pyramid Creek's glacier-carved canyon, its powerful stream reinforced by four different lakes: Toem, Ropi, Pitt, and Avalanche.

We were still a couple miles away on U.S. 50 when we first spotted Horsetail Falls. Even from the highway, it took my breath away. Somehow I hadn't expected it to be so *big*. Even more surprising was the parking area at Twin Bridges, which was packed with dozens of cars.

It turned out the crammed parking lot was a false alarm. Many of the cars belonged to backpackers who were far off in the Desolation Wilderness on multi-day trips, and many more belonged to people just milling around the trailhead, picnicking and admiring the falls, with no intention of walking more than a few hundred feet.

The trail is very well marked at its start, and you'll have plenty of company for the first quarter-mile. No problem, though; it seems like everybody on this trail is in a good mood—they've brought their dogs, kids, picnic baskets, and swimming trunks. Everyone's smiling because they're off the freeway and in a dense, gorgeous cedar forest that smells just like grandma's cedar chest in the attic, only fresher and better.

As you climb, you'll notice more and more people dropping off the trail, most of them choosing a spot along Pyramid Creek where they can relax for a while and maybe take a dip in a rock-lined pool. If you continue hiking, you'll walk out of the forest and into an exposed granite area, moving away from the creek. You'll cross wide slabs of granite and then pick up the trail again on the far side. Sometimes the granite slabs are marked with trail cairns, sometimes not. If you're unsure of which way to go, just continue straight until you spot the trail again. There are enough other hikers around so that you are unlikely to get too lost.

Your hike ends at the Desolation Wilderness boundary, where the creek rages by. A sign is posted warning you that to go any farther requires a wilderness permit. Even more critical is that to go any farther requires some serious backcountry knowledge; many inexperienced hikers have gotten lost or injured trying to make their way to the base of the falls. Turn around at the boundary, and don't worry about what you're missing. Seeing Horsetail Falls from a distance is as good as seeing it from close up, with the added bonus that you can be sure you'll return from the trip. And here's more incentive: The return route to your car is as spectacular as the trip in, with views of Lover's Leap and surrounding peaks to the south, far across the highway.

Make it easier: Go only part way on this trail and you'll still have a lovely alpine walk and good view of the falls. Pick a spot along the creek and watch the water roll by.

Trip notes: There is no fee. A permit is necessary only if you're going to travel farther than the trip described above. For more information, contact Eldorado National Forest, 3070 Camino Heights Drive, Camino, CA 95709; (530) 644-6048. Or contact Lake Tahoe Basin Management Unit, 870 Emerald Bay Road, South Lake Tahoe, CA 96150; (530) 573-2600.

Directions: From South Lake Tahoe, drive south on Highway 89 to U.S. 50. Take U.S. 50 west for approximately 15 miles to Twin Bridges, where there is a huge pullout on the right side of the highway just before the bridge. (The pullout is a half mile after the turnoff for Camp Sacramento.) Park here, then walk across the highway bridge about 500 feet to the signed trailhead.

North San Francisco Bay Area

(For locations of trails, see map on page 9.)

58. TOMALES POINT TRAIL
Point Reyes National Seashore
Off Highway 1 near Olema
5 miles round-trip — 2.5 hours — rolling terrain

👣

If seeing wildlife is one of the reasons you enjoy hiking, the Tomales Point Trail is sure to satisfy. You'll have a good chance at spotting big, furry animals before you even get out of your car (and not just the usual Point Reyes bovines).

The wildlife is plentiful because the Tomales Point Trail is located in Point Reyes National Seashore's tule elk preserve. Before 1860, thousands of native tule elk roamed Tomales Point, but in the late nineteenth century, the animals were hunted out of existence. The tule elk reserve is part of the park service's effort to re-establish the elk in their native habitat. Today the herd is numbered at more than 200 and going strong.

Seeing the magnificent tule elk is almost a given. Frequently they're hanging out in large numbers near the trailhead parking lot, and often you can see them as you drive in on Pierce Point Road. Once you're out on the trail, you may see more elk, as well as other wildlife. If you hike early in the morning before a lot of other people have traipsed down the trail, check the dirt path for footprints. I've seen mountain lion tracks as well as the more common raccoon and elk prints. While hiking, I've encountered large jackrabbits, various harmless snakes, big fuzzy caterpillars, and more birds than I could possibly remember. Once my hiking partner and I had to make a wide circle off the path to avoid a big skunk who insisted on walking down the trail ahead of us. He was just moseying along, indifferent to our presence.

It's 4.7 miles to the trail's end at the tip of Tomales Point, but you don't have to walk that far to have a great trip. Only a mile or two of hiking will provide you with splendid coastal and Tomales Bay views, plus a probable wildlife encounter. Set your own trail distance; turn around when you please. Just make sure you pick a clear day to take this trip. Although you may still see tule elk in the fog, you'll miss out on the trail's world-class views. And be sure to carry a few extra layers; if the weather is clear, the trail is likely to be windy.

The Tomales Point Trail begins at Pierce Point Ranch, one of the oldest dairies in Point Reyes. The ranch manufactured milk and butter for San Francisco dinner tables in the 1850s. Begin by hiking around the western perimeter of the ranch, or take a few minutes to inspect its

Female elk along the Tomales Point Trail

buildings. Interpretive signs describe the history of the ranch and its dairy business. The trail curves uphill around the ranch, then heads northwest along the blufftops toward Tomales Point, the northernmost tip of Point Reyes. Wildflowers bloom profusely in the spring, particularly poppies, gold fields, tidy tips, and bush lupine.

The trail is wide, smooth, and easy to hike. At a half mile out, you reach your first climb, in which you gain about 100 feet. Turn around and look behind you as you ascend—you've got the ocean on one side, and Tomales Bay on the other. Views are spectacular in all directions. Look for forested Hog Island in Tomales Bay, a popular pull-up spot for kayakers.

At 1.8 miles, the trail starts to descend, and you get a good view of Bird Rock out at sea, and the town and campground at Lawson's Landing across Tomales Bay. At 2.5 miles, you've climbed to the trail's highest point. Views of Bodega Bay and the Sonoma Coast to the north are excellent. This high point makes an excellent turnaround point for a five-mile round-trip. Although it may appear that the tip of Tomales Point is close at hand, don't be fooled—it is in fact another two miles further. Enjoy the vistas and then retrace your steps back to the trailhead.

Make it easier: Just cut the trip short. Chances are you'll be able to see the elk within your first 20 minutes on the trail, so just turn around whenever your wish.

Trip notes: There is no fee. A free map of Point Reyes National Seashore is available at the Bear Valley Visitor Center on Bear Valley Road. For more information, contact Point Reyes National Seashore, Point Reyes, CA 94956; (415) 663-1092.

Directions: From San Francisco, cross the Golden Gate Bridge and drive north on U.S. 101 for 7.5 miles. Take the Sir Francis Drake Boulevard exit west toward San Anselmo and drive 20 miles to the town of Olema. At Olema, turn right (north) on Highway 1 for about 150 yards, then turn left on Bear Valley Road. Drive 2.2 miles on Bear Valley Road until it joins with Sir Francis Drake Highway. Bear left on Sir Francis Drake and drive 5.6 miles, then take the right fork onto Pierce Point Road. Drive nine miles to the Pierce Point Ranch parking area.

59. KEHOE BEACH TRAIL
Point Reyes National Seashore
Off Highway 1 near Olema
1 mile round-trip — 30 minutes — mostly level terrain

At most beaches in California, you just drive up, park your car in the paved parking lot, and then walk a few feet and plop down in the sand. Kehoe Beach beats that by a mile. Exactly a mile, in fact, because that's how far it is to hike there and back. The distance is long enough for a pleasant, level walk, and it can be combined with another mile or so of sauntering along the wide strip of beach.

The trail proves that the journey can be as good as the destination. The fun starts right where you park your car. In late spring and summer you'll find a huge patch of blackberries growing just across the road from the trailhead. If you're wearing long sleeves and long pants, you can pick enough berries to sustain you as you hike.

The trail is gravel, almost completely level, and wide enough for hand-holding. You walk alongside Kehoe Marsh, which provides excellent habitat for birds and birdwatchers. Songbirds are nearly as abundant as the non-native iceplant that weaves thick cushions of matted foliage alongside the trail. Grasses and vines also grow in profusion, encouraged by the proximity of the marshy creek and its underground spring. As you get closer to the ocean, the marsh land transforms to sandy dunes, where you may see big jackrabbits hopping among the grasses.

Before you sprint down to Kehoe's brayed tan sands, take the spur trail that cuts off to the right and up the bluffs above the beach. In springtime, the bluffs are completely blue and gold with lupine and poppies—a glorious sight to behold. Once you've admired them, head to the beach for more walking or a picnic lunch. You'll return on the same trail.

Dogs are allowed on leash at Kehoe Beach, which is a great bonus for dog-lovers and their canine companions. There is little that makes a dog happier than going to a huge, wide open beach, and there are only a few beaches in Point Reyes where dogs are permitted. Keep your canine friend leashed, though. The strict leash rules protect harbor seals that occasionally haul out on Kehoe Beach. Take care not to disturb them—they need to rest for an average of seven hours per day, and they nurse pups on land from late March through June.

Make it easier: The only way to make this hike easier would be to ride your bike (which you may do on this trail).

Trip notes: There is no fee. A free map of Point Reyes National Seashore is available at the Bear Valley Visitor Center on Bear Valley Road. For more information, contact Point Reyes National Seashore, Point Reyes, CA 94956; (415) 663-1092.

Directions: Follow the directions on page 134 to the town of Olema in western Marin County. At Olema, turn right (north) on Highway 1 for about 150 yards, then turn left on Bear Valley Road. Drive 2.2 miles on Bear Valley Road until it joins with Sir Francis Drake Highway. Bear left on Sir Francis Drake and drive 5.6 miles, then take the right fork onto Pierce Point Road. Drive 5.5 miles to the Kehoe Beach Trailhead on your left. Park along either side of the road in the pullouts.

---

60. TOMALES BAY TRAIL
Point Reyes National Seashore
Off Highway 1 near Point Reyes Station
2 miles round-trip — 1 hour — rolling terrain

🏃🏃

Now don't get the Tomales Bay Trail confused with the Tomales Point Trail, just because both are in Point Reyes. The Tomales Point Trail is the hike with the tule elk on the northern tip of Point Reyes (see page 132). The Tomales Bay Trail is one of the few paths on the east side of Tomales Bay—not actually on the Point Reyes peninsula— that's administered by the park service. It gives you a unique view of the far southern end of Tomales Bay, just before the bay transitions into marshland.

Tomales Bay Trail, Point Reyes National Seashore

A side attraction is that the hike leads right across the San Andreas Fault line, where the North American Plate and the Pacific Plate divide and conquer. The waters of Tomales Bay cover the northern end of the fault.

From the trailhead at Highway 1, you hike along rolling hills to the edge of the bay. This is an easy hike, and a good path for a contemplative walk on a foggy day—the norm in summer in Point Reyes. In the fog, the green hillsides and meandering waterways of the bay have a brooding, moody look to them, making you feel like you're hiking in Scotland's moors or the diked farmlands of the Netherlands.

Head straight west from the parking area on the only possible trail. At a few points, narrower spur trails branch off the Tomales Bay Trail, but stay on the main path and keep heading for the water. You'll walk downhill first, then uphill again to the top of a ridge with a wide view of Tomales Bay and the town of Inverness across the water.

Just after topping the ridge, you'll descend again and skirt a couple of small ponds. They're surrounded by tall reeds and cattails. Red-winged blackbirds can be seen here, as well as coots and mallards.

Make a final drop down to the bay's edge, where you'll find an old lock system on a levee that's no longer in use. In the early 1900s, the North Pacific Coast Railroad cut through this marsh. Its tracks were built around levees that channeled the flooded wetlands. The remains of the large trestles that once supported the tracks are still in place.

Walk to the north along the water's edge for a few hundred yards until you come to the trail's end at a fence. From this point, you can see how Tomales Bay divides into tiny shallow inlets here at its southern terminus, before draining into marshlands of willow, coyote brush, and grasslands.

Make it easier: Hike in about three-quarters of a mile, past the ponds, until you get a nice view of the bay. Skip the last downhill that takes you right to the water's edge.

Trip notes: There is no fee. A free map of Point Reyes National Seashore is available at the Bear Valley Visitor Center on Bear Valley Road. For more information, contact Point Reyes National Seashore, Point Reyes, CA 94956; (415) 663-1092.

Directions: Follow the directions on page 134 to the town of Olema in western Marin County. At Olema, turn right and drive north on Highway 1 for four miles, passing through the town of Point Reyes Station, to the Tomales Bay Trail parking area on the left. (It is 1.8 miles beyond Point Reyes Station.)

---

61. MARSHALL BEACH TRAIL
Point Reyes National Seashore
Off Highway 1 near Point Reyes Station
2.4 miles round-trip — 1.5 hours — rolling terrain

The Marshall Beach Trail is one of the best kept secrets in Point Reyes. Few visitors know about Marshall Beach because the trailhead is situated on a dirt road to nowhere, at the northeastern tip of the Point Reyes peninsula. While thousands of visitors pour into neighboring Tomales Bay State Park for its protected bay waters and stunning white beaches, few realize that right next door is Marshall Beach, with all the same advantages but none of the crowds, and no entrance fee.

On your first trip to the trailhead, you may wonder if you are going the right way, because the road leads through cow country, with no beach in sight. The paved road turns to dirt, and you keep driving along flat coastal bluffs until you reach a nondescript trailhead sign. Then you hike through cow pastures. This is one trail where you must keep a vigilant lookout for meadow muffins—the stuff can stay on your boot soles for days.

Cattle and dairy ranches have been operating in Point Reyes since the 1850s. The 1962 law that authorized Point Reyes National

Hiking to Marshall Beach

Seashore made allowances so that the original ranch owners could continue operating within the seashore boundaries. Ranching is considered to be part of the "cultural history" of the park. Currently, seven dairies operate within Point Reyes, milking about 3,200 cows and producing over five million gallons of milk each year. Just wave and smile at Bessie as you walk to the beach.

The hike is a simple out-and-back, with no trail junctions. Just amble down the wide ranch road, which curves around the hillside and descends to the water's edge. There is no shade along the way, except for at the edge of Marshall Beach's cove, where you'll find a grove of windswept cypress trees with thick lichen hanging from their branches.

Marshall Beach is a nearly perfect beach, with coarse white sand and azure blue Tomales Bay water. It's a small slice of paradise overlooking the hamlet of Marshall on the other side of the bay. You can swim in the calm bay waters, which are protected from the wind by Inverness Ridge. Typical visitors to the beach are kayakers who have paddled over from the town of Marshall across the bay, or from Tomales Bay State Park to the south.

Essentials for this trip include a picnic, a bathing suit, a good book, and some binoculars for birdwatching. Settle in for a perfect afternoon, then drag yourself away—and back up the hill—when it's time to leave.

Make it easier: A mountain bike would make the trip up and down the fire road a breeze.

Trip notes: There is no fee. A free map of Point Reyes National Seashore is available at the Bear Valley Visitor Center on Bear Valley Road. For more information, contact Point Reyes National Seashore, Point Reyes, CA 94956; (415) 663-1092.

Directions: Follow the directions on page 134 to the town of Olema in western Marin County. At Olema, turn right (north) on Highway 1 for about 150 yards, then turn left on Bear Valley Road. Drive 2.2 miles on Bear Valley Road until it joins with Sir Francis Drake Highway. Bear left on Sir Francis Drake and drive 5.6 miles, then take the right fork onto Pierce Point Road. In 1.2 miles you'll see the entrance road for Tomales Bay State Park. Drive just past it to Duck Cove/Marshall Beach Road; turn right and drive 2.6 miles. The road turns to gravel and dirt; stay to the left where it forks. Park in the gravel parking area, taking care not to block any of the dirt roads that connect here.

---

62. INDIAN NATURE TRAIL & JOHNSTONE TRAIL
Tomales Bay State Park
Off Highway 1 near Inverness
2 miles round-trip — 1.5 hours — rolling terrain

👫

We might as well get clear on this right away: The whole point of making this trip is not really the hiking. It's that Tomales Bay's beaches are so gorgeous, you simply have to come and explore them. You can swim, picnic, or just wander around for a while and then lay on the beach and take a nap. Now this is easy hiking.

Although it's quite large, Tomales Bay is shallow enough that its water warms up somewhat. The bay is surf-free for swimming—an activity that is nearly impossible at the turbulent beaches of neighboring Point Reyes. The water is nearly calm much of the time, and the bay is blessed with good weather. Protected by Inverness Ridge, Tomales Bay is often sunny and warm, even when the nearby ocean coastline is fogged in or windy. Another bonus is that the water of Tomales Bay is a lovely light blue, making the white sand beaches look like a tropical paradise.

My preferred route at Tomales Bay State Park is a start-in-the-middle and head-in-both-directions path on the Indian Nature Trail and Johnstone Trail. This provides a glimpse at the best features of this 1,000-acre park.

Begin on the north side of Heart's Desire Beach and take the Indian Nature Trail for a half mile to Indian Beach. The Indian Nature Trail is an interpretive trail with signs explaining the park's various plants and their uses by the coastal Miwok Indians. The trail climbs a bit to start. When it divides, stay to the right (the left trail is the return loop). In about 15 minutes of walking, you'll descend to Indian Beach, a lovely sandy strip that extends from an inland marsh into Tomales Bay. Birds and wildlife are plentiful both in the marsh and along the shoreline. On one trip, we stood on the footbridge by the marsh and watched a group of bat rays feeding in the oceanbound stream. The rays hovered in the water, moving their fins just enough to hold their position in the current as they munched on tiny organisms being filtered out of the marsh and into the ocean.

You can take the bridge at the north end of the beach to loop back on a dirt service road, but the road isn't terribly scenic. You're better off retracing your steps on the Indian Nature Trail, while quizzing your hiking partner about toyon, coffee berries, and bracken fern, which you learned about on the way in.

Pebble Beach, Tomales Bay State Park

When you return to Heart's Desire Beach, walk to the south side of the beach and take the Johnstone Trail. You'll travel for a half mile through a forest of oaks, bay, and madrone, getting frequent views of Tomales Bay as you peek through the trees. You will pass through a large picnic area, which could mar the solitude of your hike, but the area is mostly empty except at midday on weekends.

At a half mile out, a short side trail descends to Pebble Beach, a gorgeous and secluded little beach composed of tiny—guess what?—pebbles. If you visit this park on a busy weekend and Heart's Desire and Indian beaches have too many people for you, Pebble Beach could be your chance to leave the crowds.

So there you have it: You hike around for two easy miles and you gain access to three beautiful beaches. If that isn't entertainment enough, you can even go clamming if you have a valid California fishing license. (For me, the greatest thing about clamming is that I never suffer a guilty conscience for murdering little bivalves. In about a dozen attempts at clamming, I've never even dug up one.)

Of course, with all these pretty beaches to explore, you'll probably find that you're happy as a clam yourself. A clam at high tide, that is.

Make it easier: Just hike to one of the beaches. Indian Beach is most likely to be crowded; it's especially popular with school groups. Pebble Beach is smaller than Indian Beach and more secluded.

Trip notes: A $5 state park day-use fee is charged by Tomales Bay State Park. A trail map/brochure is available at the park for 50 cents. For more information, contact Tomales Bay State Park, Star Route, Inverness, CA 94937; (415) 669-1140 or (415) 893-1580.

Directions: Follow the directions on page 134 to the town of Olema in western Marin County. At Olema, turn right (north) on Highway 1 for about 150 yards, then turn left on Bear Valley Road. Drive 2.2 miles on Bear Valley Road until it joins with Sir Francis Drake Highway. Bear left on Sir Francis Drake and drive 5.6 miles, then take the right fork onto Pierce Point Road. Drive 1.2 miles to the access road for Tomales Bay State Park. Turn right and drive one mile down the park road. Turn left and park at the Heart's Desire Beach parking lot.

63. FERN CANYON NATURE TRAIL
Point Reyes Bird Observatory
Off Highway 1 near Bolinas
0.75 mile round-trip — 30 minutes — some steep terrain

Many hikers make the journey to the Palomarin Trailhead near Bolinas to walk to Bass Lake or Pelican Lake, two classic Point Reyes destinations, or maybe to backpack to Wildcat Camp and see Alamere Falls, a spectacular waterfall dropping 50 feet from the blufftop to the sea. In the process, they drive right by the nondescript little building that is the Point Reyes Bird Observatory.

I had passed it by dozens of times myself until one day I stopped in to find out about the observatory's bird banding program. I parked my car in their lot right in front of a sign that said "Nature Trail." A trail, here? How come I'd never heard of it? It turns out the trail is used as a research area for this field station, where biologists and volunteers study breeding, territoriality, and habitat preferences of several resident bird species.

The trail leads through a canyon that is a prime research area because it's located at the intersection of two distinct biological environments: coastal scrub on the open oceanside bluffs and riparian forest in the deep shaded canyon. Where two types of habitat meet, animals and birds thrive. These are the best places to look for wildlife, and for that reason alone, you should make the trip. The list of birds studied in the canyon includes red-tailed hawks, song sparrows, wrentits, bushtits, towhees, scrub jays, winter wrens, black-headed grosbeaks, Swainson's thrushes, and purple finches.

Another reason to walk the Fern Canyon Nature Trail is that you leave the wide, open grasslands and coastal bluff territory you've been driving in and enter an unexpectedly lush, rain-forest-like canyon, filled with ferns, big trees, and deep green foliage.

The walk begins on the bluffs above the sea, where the primary plant you see is coyote brush, the tough, leathery shrub with tiny leaves that thrives in harsh coastal scrub environments. In only about 100 yards, you'll reach the edge of the canyon, where you can look down between the trees and get a glimpse of the habitat change you'll soon experience. (It's easy to walk right past the canyon and miss it, because trails on the bluff head in several directions. Keep watching on your left for the first place where the trail turns and heads downhill.)

Follow the trail as it descends quickly and steeply into the green, plant-filled ravine. If it has rained recently, hiking boots are a must, or you may find yourself sliding all the way down. Go slowly, watch your footing, and notice all the ferns lining the canyon walls and the "old man's beard" draped over the bay trees. These lichens look like Spanish moss but are actually two different plants, an algae and a fungus, growing together.

At the bottom of the canyon, a small ladder takes you the last few steps to the streambed. (If the ladder isn't in place on your visit—it wasn't when I was here—you just have to jump a few feet.) Before crossing the stream and rejoining the trail on the other side, take a few minutes to look around at all the different types of ferns growing on the canyon walls, nourished by underground seepage in the rock.

The stream you're crossing is Arroyo Hondo Creek. It runs year-round and is the main drainage for the Bolinas watershed, emptying into the Pacific Ocean. Although the creek is fullest in winter and spring, the ravine stays wet enough year-round to supply water for numerous bird and plant species. Moist, thick air envelops you in the quiet of the canyon.

Continue up the trail on the far side of the creek. A dozen wooden steps lead you up and out of the canyon, then the trail switchbacks uphill to a large meadow, once the site of a Miwok Indian village. I recommend a turnaround here; then retrace your steps through the fern-filled canyon. If you choose to follow the loop instead, you'll have to walk back on the road for a half mile.

Make it more challenging: If you follow the loop trail out to the road, you can add on an out-and-back hike on the Arroyo Trail, which begins just across Mesa Road. Return to your car by retracing your steps through the fern canyon or walking a half mile west on the road.

Trip notes: There is no fee. For more information, contact Point Reyes Bird Observatory, 4990 Shoreline Highway, Stinson Beach, CA 94970; (415) 868-1221.

Directions: From San Francisco, cross the Golden Gate Bridge and drive north on U.S. 101 for four miles. Take the Mill Valley/Stinson Beach/ Highway 1 exit and continue straight for one mile to a stoplight at Shoreline Highway (Highway 1). Turn left on Shoreline Highway and drive to Stinson Beach, then continue north on Highway 1 for another five miles to an unsigned road on the left, which is Olema-Bolinas Road. It's just beyond the Bolinas Lagoon. Follow Olema-Bolinas Road west for two miles to Mesa Road. Turn right and follow Mesa Road for 3.8 miles (it's marked "Not a Through Road") to the Point Reyes Bird Observatory, just past the Coast Guard Station. (The road turns to gravel.) Park at the observatory lot, then take the trail marked "Nature Trail" that begins on the ocean side of the parking lot.

---

64. KENT, GRIFFIN, & NORTH LOOP TRAILS
Audubon Canyon Ranch/Bolinas Lagoon
Off Highway 1 near Stinson Beach
3 miles round-trip — 1.75 hours — some steep terrain

When I pulled into the parking lot at Audubon Canyon Ranch at Bolinas Lagoon, I thought I was in the midst of some major event. A row of cars lined the driveway, more cars kept coming in, and somebody was in charge of directing all the traffic. What was it, John Muir's birthday or something? Fearing a crowd scene, I considered not even stopping, but for some unknown reason I persevered.

The traffic director informed me that this was no special event, just a busy day at Audubon Canyon Ranch, and she had counted 380 visitors. I cringed at the possibility of meeting 380 people on my hiking trip, but set out anyway, just to see what all the fuss was about.

Now that I've seen it, I understand. The Bolinas Lagoon Preserve is one of three preserves in Marin and Sonoma counties run by Audubon Canyon Ranch. It's open only from mid-March to mid-July, on Saturdays, Sundays, and holidays, from 10 A.M. to 4 P.M. The preserve's chief attraction is the Henderson Overlook, a hike-in birdwatching platform from which you can witness the miracle of great egrets and herons nesting in the tops of redwood trees.

With visitation periods so limited, there's no way to avoid the crowds in the parking lot, except maybe to show up on a rainy day. But most all of the visitors are either right by the parking lot or on their way to and from the Henderson Overlook. That means that if you're willing to hike a little further, you can explore a beautiful protected wildlife preserve and find some solitude, too.

North Loop Trail, Audubon Canyon Ranch

But first you should make a trip to the overlook. The Alice Kent Trail begins behind the preserve's buildings, and it climbs moderately but pleasantly enough for a half mile. You might not find solitude on this trail, but about halfway up you'll see what you've come for—snow-white great egrets nesting in their treetop colony on the neighboring hillside. At the overlook platform, you'll probably find quite a few people sitting on the viewing benches, which are

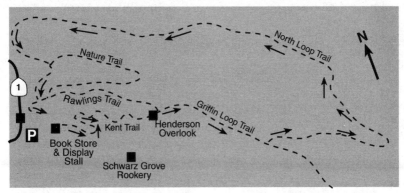

Kent, Griffin, & North Loop Trails

stacked like bleacher seats at a football game. The Audubon people set up sighting scopes and everyone takes turns looking at the birds.

On my trip, I was amazed at how polite all these perfect strangers were to each other. Everyone was very quiet and excited, as if they were in on some big secret. And they were. It was mid-May, so the egret eggs had hatched. By looking through the sighting scopes, you could see right into the nests to the baby egrets—two or three per nest—who were clamoring for food.

We also got a wonderful magnified view of the adult egrets in all their white feathered finery. The adults are so large that they appear almost clumsy in the tree branches—the branches sway and drop dramatically as the birds land and take off. Lucky visitors may also get to see a great blue heron in its nest. There are presently only nine pairs of herons in the preserve, compared to about 100 egret pairs.

After you've marveled at the birds, continue beyond the overlook on Griffin Trail, the only trail that keeps heading uphill through the oak and bay forest. When I say uphill, I'm not exaggerating. The trail heads straight up, with nary a switchback. This section of trail is only another half-mile, but it's what gives this hike a resounding "steep" rating. Take it at your own pace, and conserve your energy by not grumbling under your breath.

When you reach the marked intersection of Griffin Trail and North Loop Trail, the choice will be easy because North Loop Trail heads downhill, and you won't want to climb any more. Take North Loop and immediately descend into a fern-filled redwood forest. Congratulate yourself on your stamina and enjoy the mostly downhill trip along a small, gurgling stream. After about 10 minutes, you'll swing away from the stream, lateraling the ridge on a narrow path and then climbing ever-so-slightly to top out at an open bluff with a view of Bolinas Lagoon and the ocean. The best way to enjoy the view is to have a seat on the preserve's strategically placed wooden swing, which is wide enough for about four people. Sway back and forth to your heart's content as you review the day's wonders. Then follow the trail back down the sloping hillside. It curves gently all the way back to Audubon Ranch headquarters, providing fine views all the way.

On my hike, I shared the trail to Henderson Overlook with 20 or 30 people, plus there were about that many at the viewing area, watching the egrets. But once I left the overlook and started climbing, I saw no one for the rest of the afternoon until I returned to the parking area. I had the whole forest, and all the stunning lagoon and coastal views, to myself.

Make it easier: Just take the Kent Trail to the overlook and enjoy the birds. You can return the way you came, or, for variation, return on the Rawlings Trail, which begins just above the overlook. Either route will give you a one-mile round-trip.

Trip notes: There is no fee. Bolinas Lagoon Preserve is open mid-March to mid-July, weekends and holidays only from 10 A.M. to 4 P.M. For more information, contact Audubon Canyon Ranch Headquarters, 4900 Highway 1, Stinson Beach, CA 94970; (415) 868-9244.

Directions: From San Francisco, cross the Golden Gate Bridge and drive north on U.S. 101 for four miles. Take the Mill Valley/Stinson Beach/Highway 1 exit and continue straight for one mile to a stoplight at Shoreline Highway (Highway 1). Turn left on Shoreline Highway and drive to Stinson Beach, then continue north on Highway 1 for another 3.7 miles. Look for the entrance to Audubon Canyon Ranch on the right. First you'll pass an entrance marked "Volunteer Canyon"—don't turn there; take the next entrance.

---

65. STAIRSTEP FALLS TRAIL
Samuel P. Taylor State Park
Off Sir Francis Drake Boulevard near Lagunitas
2.5 miles round-trip — 1.25 hours — rolling terrain

Samuel P. Taylor State Park gets somewhat overshadowed by its large and famous neighbor, Point Reyes National Seashore, but that's okay with the people who know and love the place. Even when the state park campground is filled with campers on summer weekends, it's rare to find many people on Samuel P. Taylor's hiking trails. This means

that Stairstep Falls
has managed to
remain something of
a secret in Marin
County. Tucked into
the back of a shady
redwood canyon, it's
a tranquil spot where
you can find some
solitude at the base
of a waterfall.

The trailhead
isn't at the main
Samuel P. Taylor
park entrance; rather
it's a mile west on Sir
Francis Drake Bou-
levard at Devil's
Gulch Horse Camp.
Park in the dirt
pullout across the

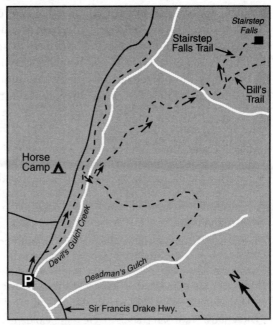

Stairstep Falls Trail

road from the camp, then walk up the paved camp road for about 150
yards until you see a trail leading off to the right along Devil's Gulch
Creek, paralleling the road. Take it, and immediately you descend into
a stream-fed canyon filled with Douglas firs, redwoods, oaks, bay laurel,
and about a million ferns. By April, the ground near the stream is
covered with forget-me-nots, buttercups, and milkmaids.

A few minutes of upstream walking brings you to a bridge over
Devil's Gulch. Just ahead is a huge, hollowed-out Sequoia. It's the only
Sequoia around, situated among many other kinds of hardwoods. Go
ahead, climb inside—the tree's charm is irresistible.

By the Sequoia, turn right and cross a footbridge, then turn left on
the far side of the bridge, following the sign marked "Trail to Barnaby
Peak." You'll climb very gently above the creek, marveling at the walls of
ferns and the long limbs of mossy oaks, gaining 350 feet over three-
quarters of a mile. Soon you get a nice view of the bald, grassy ridge on
the far side of the creek (on your left).

After crossing a bridge over a feeder stream, look for the Stairstep
Falls Trail cutting off to the left from the main trail. Sometimes it is
signed, sometimes not. Bear left and in 10 minutes of walking, you'll
reach the trail's end near the base of Stairstep Falls.

True to its name, 40-foot-tall Stairstep Falls drops in three main cascades, with a rocky "staircase" at its base producing dozens of rivulets of water. Trail maintenance crews try to keep the area around the falls cleared of fallen trees and branches, so you can stand close to the cascading flow. Some waterfall-lover has fashioned a makeshift bench and carved the fall's name into a downed tree limb. It makes a lovely spot, perfect for quiet contemplation in the good company of ferns, forest, and water.

Make it easier: There isn't any easier way to get to the waterfall, but you can just skip it and enjoy the lovely forested trail along Devil's Gulch Creek. Instead of crossing the bridge at the hollowed-out redwood tree, remain on the level trail that runs along the north side of the creek. You can walk all the way to the trail's end and return the same way for a 1.5-mile round-trip.

Trip notes: If you park along the highway at legal turnouts, there is no fee. A $5 state park day-use fee is charged if you park in the main paved parking areas. A trail map/brochure is available at the ranger kiosk for 75 cents. For more information, contact Samuel P. Taylor State Park, P.O. Box 251, Lagunitas, CA 94938; (415) 488-9897 or (415) 893-1580.

Directions: From San Francisco, cross the Golden Gate Bridge on U.S. 101 and drive north for seven miles. Take the Sir Francis Drake Boulevard exit west toward San Anselmo, then drive about 15 miles (through the towns of Ross, Fairfax, and Lagunitas) to the entrance to Samuel P. Taylor State Park. Don't turn here; continue on Sir Francis Drake (past the main park entrance) for one mile. Park across the road from Devil's Gulch Horse Camp, where there is a dirt parking area. Walk across the road and hike on the paved road to the campground.

66. BON TEMPE LAKE LOOP
Marin Municipal Water District
Off Bolinas-Fairfax Road near Fairfax
3 miles round-trip — 1.5 hours — rolling terrain

When most people think of public parkland around Mount Tamalpais, they think of the towering redwoods of Muir Woods National Monument or the dense forests and stunning coastal views of Mount Tamalpais State Park. But fewer people know that five sparkling lakes are also a part of the Mount Tam landscape. They're located in the Mount Tamalpais Watershed on the northwest side of the mountain. The five lakes are Alpine, Bon Tempe, Kent, Lagunitas, and Phoenix,

Bon Tempe Lake

and together they provide five more reasons why the Mount Tam area is so spectacular for outdoor recreation.

For easy hiking, my favorite of the lakes is Bon Tempe. It's uncrowded, it's closed to mountain bikers but open to dogs on leash, and by linking together a couple of trails, you can walk all the way around the lake in about an hour and a half.

Start by parking near the dam at Bon Tempe. Walk uphill to the dam and cross it, and you'll get pretty views right away of bright blue Bon Tempe Lake on your left and the marshes and lowlands of Alpine Lake on your right. The unmistakable profile of Mount Tamalpais looms to the south. On the far side of the dam, pick up the single-track trail that leads to your left around the lake. It climbs only slightly as it travels into a thick mixed forest of oaks, madrones, firs, and redwoods.

If you like the trail so far, you're going to enjoy the whole trip, which offers plenty more of the same. About a mile down the trail, you leave the forest and enter a grassy area where you can look westward over the entire lake, all the way back to the dam where you started. This vista is particularly stunning if the sun is sinking low in the sky. Then the trail heads back into the woods for a short distance until you come out at the parking and picnic area for neighboring Lake Lagunitas. Cross a small footbridge just before the pavement, then walk to your left for a few feet across the parking lot and pick up the trail again on a dirt and gravel fire road.

Here and in several other places around Bon Tempe you'll find many trails crisscrossing and heading away from the lake. However, your mission is always to stay as close to the lakeshore as possible. When the fire road splits off with a single-track leading to the left along the lake, follow the single-track. Just ignore all trails that don't stay close to the water. There's only one short section on the lake's north side (about three-quarters of the way around the loop) where a feeder stream and marsh force the trail to move away from the lake and up along the edge of paved Sky Oaks Road. Walk along the road for an eighth of a mile until you see a gravel pullout for cars on the right side. Look to your left to pick up the single-track trail again, which returns you to the water's edge.

If you enjoy seeing wildlife, rest assured that you're almost guaranteed to see deer on this trail, usually black-tails. They've gotten used to human visitors in the watershed and are not flighty. Often they'll stare you down for a while or move only a few feet away when you approach. On my last visit to Bon Tempe, I saw a doe and two yearlings on one side of the lake, then a young antlered buck on the other side.

You're almost guaranteed to see anglers at the lake as well, because Bon Tempe is stocked with trout by the Department of Fish and Game from November to April. Even in summer, when the lake level drops and catch rates are much lower, some fishermen persevere in their work along the shoreline. However, because Bon Tempe is a reservoir, no boating, swimming, or wading is allowed on the lake. Even your dog must be kept leashed and out of the water.

Late winter and spring are the best seasons to visit Bon Tempe, when the lake is brimming full and the hillsides are covered with wild-flowers, particularly Douglas irises. The best times of day for hiking are early in the morning or just before sunset, when the crowds are down and the animals show themselves. For many local people in western Marin County, this is a favorite after-work walk, a way of regaining perspective after a hectic day.

Make it easier: Just walk across the dam and along the south side of the lake as far as you like, then retrace your steps rather than completing the loop.

Trip notes: The entrance fee is $3 on weekdays, $4 on weekends from April to October, and $3 on weekends from November to March. The park is open from sunrise to sunset. For more information and a $2 map, contact Marin Municipal Water District at 220 Nellen Avenue, Corte Madera, CA 94925; (415) 924-4600. Or phone Sky Oaks Ranger Station at (415) 945-1181.

Directions: From San Francisco, cross the Golden Gate Bridge on U.S. 101 and drive north for seven miles. Take the Sir Francis Drake Boulevard exit west toward San Anselmo, then drive six miles to the town of Fairfax. Turn left at the first gas station in Fairfax (by the "Fairfax" sign on unsigned Pacheco Road), then turn right immediately on Broadway. In one block, turn left on Bolinas Road. Drive 1.5 miles on Bolinas Road to Sky Oaks Road, where you bear left. Drive straight for four-tenths of a mile to the ranger station and entrance kiosk, then continue for three-tenths of a mile to a fork in the road. Bear right on the gravel road. (The left fork takes you to Lake Lagunitas.) Drive four-tenths of a mile until you reach another fork, then bear left and park in the gravel parking area next to a gated fire road. Start hiking at the gate, heading uphill to Bon Tempe Dam.

67. CASCADE FALLS TRAIL
Elliott Nature Preserve/
Cascade Canyon Open Space
Off Bolinas-Fairfax Road, near Fairfax
2 miles round-trip – 1 hour — rolling terrain

Here's proof that the true measure of a waterfall is not how big it is or how much water flows over it, but the overall impression it creates. Little Cascade Falls in Fairfax is no Niagara, but it's perfectly set in a hidden rock grotto in a deep canyon. It features a single cascade that drops about 15 feet from the edge of a boulder to a small pool below. The pool is surrounded by many large and small mossy rocks, perfectly placed for waterfall-watching. It's the kind of place where once you arrive, you never want to leave.

At its start, the Cascade Falls Trail doesn't seem like it could possibly lead to a waterfall. To get to the trailhead, you drive through a suburban neighborhood. Then when you start hiking, you head out on a dry and dusty fire road. The only water you'll see at the beginning of the trail looks stagnant, except during the heaviest rains. Things don't look promising.

But they get better. Stay close to San Anselmo Creek as you hike, avoiding the wide fire roads wherever you can and taking the single-track hiking paths. (Leave the fire roads for bicyclists.) Cross a wooden footbridge about a quarter-mile in and head to your right into a lovely oak and laurel forest, walking right beside the creek. The stream has many quiet pools and pretty rocky sections.

In less than a mile from the trailhead you'll round a bend and hear the sound of falling water, then get your first glimpse of the waterfall. In winter or early spring, Cascade Falls flows with enthusiasm, but it dwindles to a trickle in summer.

On my first visit, I was pleasantly surprised by the beauty of the little waterfall, but I was even more surprised to find two musicians at its base, sitting cross-legged on a big boulder, playing a duet on the violin and guitar. I stayed and listened to their music, combined with the music of the falls, for more than an hour.

While I can't promise you'll be serenaded when you hike to Cascade Falls, I can tell you that this is a perfect short walk for after work or a midday stroll. You can even bring your four-legged friend, because leashed dogs are allowed in Cascade Canyon. I saw one particularly happy Labrador dunk himself again and again in the small pool below the fall. His tail never stopped wagging.

If you don't mind a short climb, follow the trail up and over the waterfall. You'll find rocks to sit on above and alongside the falls, as well as others down below, surrounding the waterfall pool. Any of these spots would be perfect for picnicking. The trail continues further uphill, out of the shaded canyon and into Marin Open Space District lands, eventually connecting to other trails. But the best may be right here, so I recommend going only as far as the waterfall, then turning around and heading back to your car.

Make it more challenging: Beyond the waterfall, the trail continues for miles, connecting with Repack fire road and eventually San Geronimo Ridge fire road. You can hike out and back as far as you like.

Trip notes: There is no fee. Please take special care to respect the private property that borders this Marin Open Space preserve. Be courteous and park carefully so as not to block driveways. For more information, contact the Marin County Open Space District, 3501 Civic Center Drive, San Rafael, CA 94903; (415) 499-6387.

Directions: From San Francisco, cross the Golden Gate Bridge on U.S. 101 and drive north for seven miles. Take the Sir Francis Drake Boulevard exit west toward San Anselmo, then drive six miles to the town of Fairfax. Turn left at the first gas station in Fairfax (by the "Fairfax" sign on unsigned Pacheco Road), then turn right immediately on Broadway. In one block, turn left on Bolinas Road. Follow Bolinas Road for three-tenths of a mile to a three-road intersection. Bear right on Cascade Drive (the middle road) and continue for 1.5 miles. The road becomes very narrow and ends at Elliott Nature Preserve. Park alongside the road (be careful to avoid blocking driveways and obey the "no parking" signs in the last 100 feet before the trailhead). Begin hiking at the gate.

68. PINE MOUNTAIN & CARSON FALLS TRAILS
Marin Municipal Water District
Off Bolinas-Fairfax Road near Fairfax
3 miles round-trip — 1.5 hours — some steep terrain

Quiz question: Name three waterfalls located on or nearby Mount Tamalpais, all within six miles of each other, that start with the letter C.

Answer: Cascade Falls in Marin County Open Space off Bolinas-Fairfax Road (see page 151), Cataract Falls near Laurel Dell, just over the border from Mount Tamalpais State Park (see page 160), and Carson Falls in Marin Municipal Water District land.

It's a good idea to learn them all and know which is which, because it saves a lot of confusion when you start telling other people about the great waterfall hike you had. Carson Falls? Isn't that the one with the trail that starts at Alpine Dam and climbs the whole way? Nope, that's Cataract. Cataract Falls? Isn't that the one that falls in a long, skinny stream through several steps into a canyon? Nope, that's Carson. Cascade Falls? Isn't that the one that's just outside the Fairfax suburbs? Well, you got one right.

Carson Falls

Let's set the record straight. Carson Falls is an unusual waterfall set in the middle of a dry grassland canyon in Marin Municipal Water District land, high above Alpine and Kent lakes on the back slope of Mount Tamalpais. It's a long chain of pool-and-drop cataracts pouring into granite pools. The trail to reach the waterfall is not well-marked, so it gets minimal traffic. To get there, you have to hike up to a ridge, then down into a canyon, and you have to have some idea where you're going, because there are few signs.

Carson Falls' main trailhead is along Bolinas-Fairfax Road at 1,078 feet in elevation. From the parking area, you cross Bolinas Road and pick up Pine Mountain fire road, climbing uphill for one mile, gaining more than 300 feet in elevation. Keep your eyes and ears out for mountain bicyclists on this trail, who sometimes come flying downhill, usually after experiencing the agony and the ecstasy of climbing Pine Mountain. Be sure to look over your right shoulder occasionally to check out the wide views of Mount Diablo, San Pablo Bay, much of Marin County and the East Bay, and even the San Rafael-Richmond Bridge. The climb will get your heart pumping, but the views more than compensate you for your efforts.

After a mile of climbing, turn left on clearly marked Oat Hill Road, also a fire road. As you descend on Oat Hill, start paying attention to the telephone lines strung up above your head, because they'll be your only indicator of when to make a right turn to the watershed for Carson Falls. When you see the telephone lines make a right turn, you should, too. (There's a "no bikes" sign on the telephone pole at the turnoff.) You'll leave the fire roads and begin walking on a downhill single-track trail into the Carson Creek drainage. It's pretty steep going down, so watch your footing.

After descending a couple hundred feet in elevation, you'll notice a change in the landscape. Although you're still in dry, grassy country, with no hint of a waterfall nearby, you'll notice some trees growing in a little slot in the hillside—evidence of an underground spring. Get closer and you'll see they are buckeye trees, flowering exuberantly in the spring and dormant in the summer. Buckeyes are a dead giveaway that water is close at hand. Now you're in the watershed, and within moments you're right on top of the falls.

Don't expect that usual thunderous moment of wow!—a waterfall!—because Carson Falls is more subtle, more mysterious than that. This waterfall reveals its pleasures slowly, one pool at a time. To see it all, keep descending along the rough trail that parallels its cascades,

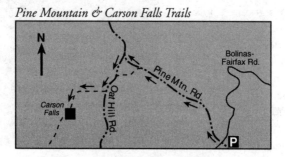

Pine Mountain & Carson Falls Trails

North San Francisco Bay Area

dropping in elevation along with the waterfall. I recommend going as far as the third pool, just before the trail gets *really* steep on its way to the fourth pool.

Choose a rock near one of the waterfall pools, have a seat, and listen to the water for a while. Even in summer, when Carson Falls is reduced to a mere trickle, sitting nearby is a great experience, like resting in a zen garden with the sound of the wind and the tinkling of water as your only companions.

When it's time to return, head back to your car by reversing the hike, climbing uphill out of the canyon and then downhill along Pine Mountain fire road.

Make it more challenging: The trail continues beyond the waterfall's pools, and if you descend on it you can connect with two possible loop trails—one to the north and one to the south—for a longer hike. Get a good map of the area before you make the trip.

Trip notes: There is no fee. For more information and a $2 map, contact Marin Municipal Water District at 220 Nellen Avenue, Corte Madera, CA 94925; (415) 924-4600. Or phone Sky Oaks Ranger Station at (415) 945-1181.

Directions: From San Francisco, cross the Golden Gate Bridge on U.S. 101 and drive north for seven miles. Take the Sir Francis Drake Boulevard exit west toward San Anselmo, then drive six miles to the town of Fairfax. Turn left at the first gas station in Fairfax (by the "Fairfax" sign on unsigned Pacheco Road), then turn right immediately on Broadway. In one block, turn left on Bolinas Road. Drive 3.8 miles on Bolinas Road, past the golf course, to the trailhead parking on the left side of the road. Park and walk across the road to the trailhead.

69. SHORELINE TRAIL
China Camp State Park
Off U.S. 101 near San Rafael
3 miles round-trip — 1.5 hours — mostly level terrain

China Camp State Park covers 1,500 shoreline acres on San Pablo Bay and the Shoreline Trail traverses much of it. But you don't have to march all five-plus miles of the trail to experience the park's best features. Instead, you can start at two different trailheads and, with two short and very special walks, see many of the highlights of China Camp.

Begin on the Shoreline Trail from the Back Ranch Meadows Campground parking area. One early May, I had only walked a few hundred yards from my car when I was surprised by a mother deer, two yearlings, and two tiny fawns, still wearing their spots, happily munching the grasses about 20 feet from me. The fawns must have been only a few weeks old.

Cross the road and take the Jake's Island Trail. When bay waters were higher, Jake's Island was an actual island, but now it's a shoreline hill surrounded by saltwater marsh. All along the trail, views of San Pablo Bay are excellent. Jake's Island may be closed to the public in the next few years—some environmentalists fear that visitors may harm the fragile marsh—but right now you can walk around the island (except in rare high tides) and then return on the Pickleweed Marsh Trail. This interpretive nature trail takes you around Turtle Back, another big hill that was once an island.

On a rainy day on this trail, I saw an adorable group of three-year-olds in raincoats walking this trail on a preschool field trip, as well as a group of older women—clearly experienced hikers—who were quite seriously identifying birds and plant life along the way. Birdwatching is excellent at China Camp State Park.

For your second short walk, drive back to North San Pedro Road, and follow the road east (to your right) for slightly over a mile to the Bullhead Flat parking area on the left. Cross the road and walk up the service road to the China Camp State Park office (a trailer). Take the Shoreline Trail to your left and hike seven-tenths of a mile to China Camp Village.

Shoreline Trail to Turtle Back and Jake's Island

China Camp Village is the well-preserved remains of a 19th-century Chinese fishing village, one of more than 30 such villages that sprung up on the shores of San Francisco and San Pablo bays. The people who lived in the village would fish for plentiful grass shrimp in spring, summer, and fall, and in winter, they would mend their nets and work on their boats. Some of the shrimp were sold at local markets, but most were exported to China, because Chinese people would eat dried shrimp while Americans only liked it fresh-cooked. Eventually laws were passed that forbid the

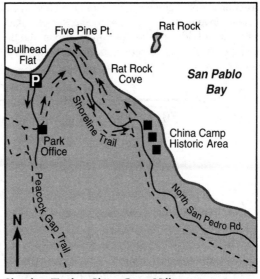

Shoreline Trail to China Camp Village

Chinese method of fishing for shrimp with bag nets. In 1905, the export of dried shrimp was banned, and this village along with others like it were slowly deserted.

A pier and four buildings, some partly furnished, are all that remain of the village. You can tour around the old camp, then follow the Rat Rock Cove Trail from the China Camp Point parking lot for 200 feet to a quiet little beach that is popular with great egrets. You'll probably see more of these graceful white birds out on Rat Rock, a few hundred yards offshore. The water in this shallow part of the bay is relatively warm, and children will enjoy playing on the beach.

Depending on the tide, you can sometimes walk around a small marshy pond and down the beach to Five Pine Point. Your return from the beach to Bullhead Flat and your car is less than a half mile, either following the Shoreline Trail or walking along the road.

Make it easier: Park at either Back Ranch Meadows Campground or Bullhead Flat and walk one of the trails or the other. Try China Camp if you're in the mood for a little cultural history, and Turtle Back and Jake's Island if you're in the mood for a little natural history.

Trip notes: A $5 state park day-use fee is charged by China Camp State Park. A free trail map is available at park headquarters across from the Bullhead Flat parking area. For more information, contact China Camp State Park, 1455A East Francisco Boulevard, San Rafael, CA 94901; (415) 456-0766 or (415) 893-1580.

Directions: From San Francisco, cross the Golden Gate Bridge on U.S. 101 and drive north for 11 miles to San Rafael. Take the North San Pedro Road exit and drive east for four miles. Park at the Back Ranch Meadows Campground parking area on your right. The trailhead for the Shoreline Trail is on the bay side of the parking lot.

70. PHYLLIS ELLMAN TRAIL
Ring Mountain Preserve
Off U.S. 101 near Corte Madera
3 miles round-trip — 1.5 hours — rolling terrain

Now here's a trail that comes as a real surprise—the good kind of surprise. The Nature Conservancy's Ring Mountain Preserve is located smack in the middle of the Corte Madera suburbs, not far from Paradise Drive's paradise of shopping malls. But while all the pavement around here may bring your spirits down, the Phyllis Ellman Trail will lift them right back up again, with a lovely grasslands walk and outstanding North Bay views.

The Nature Conservancy acquired this hillside land tucked between neighborhood houses primarily to protect the Tiburon mariposa lily, which grows nowhere else in the world. Six other species of Ring Mountain wildflowers grow in few other areas, which lands them a spot on the rare plant list. They share these hills with many more common wildflowers and grasses, as well as bay trees, live oaks, deer, grey fox, quail, and songbirds. We saw almost all of the above in one spring visit.

The Phyllis Ellman Trail is a loop, and you should take the left side of it first, leaving the right (steeper) side for your return. From the trailhead, things don't look all that promising, but just be patient. Start climbing and take your time—there's nowhere to go but up.

As you ascend, be sure to turn around every few minutes to check out the view behind you. You'll gain elevation quickly on this trail, and with every few footsteps your view will expand to include more and more of the North and East bays. You're situated directly across San Francisco Bay from the Larkspur Ferry Terminal and San Quentin Prison. As you scan the horizon, you'll see the East and West Brothers Islands near Richmond, the East and West Marin Islands near San Rafael, Point San Pedro, the Richmond Bridge, and even parts of the East Bay. The islands are perhaps the most intriguing sight, and this is the only spot I know of where you can see both the Marin Islands, which are state-owned and unoccupied, and the East and West Broth-

California's state flower at Ring Mountain Preserve

ers Islands, the larger of which (East Brother Island) has a lighthouse and bed and breakfast inn.

As you hike uphill, you'll probably want to take a few side trips to climb on some of the large serpentine outcrops that jut out from the hillside. You'll be in open sunshine for most of this walk, but every now and then the trail passes through small groves of live oaks. Each grove has only a few trees, but they are large enough to create a huge canopy of branches and leaves, giving you the feeling of being in a miniature forest. It's very shady and dark underneath.

Near the top of the ridge (at interpretive post number 11), the trail meets up with a wide fire road. Turn right. When you reach the highest point on the ridge, at what seems like the top of the world (or at least Corte Madera), you get a complete picture to the north and south: San Francisco, Angel Island, Alcatraz, Tiburon, and Sausalito are visible on your left (to the south), and the whole of the East and North bays are on your right. You can also see both San Francisco Bay and San Pablo Bay at the same time. For some close-up entertainment, there are more rock outcrops to examine along the ridgetop.

Note that many spur trails cut off from the main loop trail. If you're concerned about losing your way, keep watching for the numbered posts along the main loop. From the ridgeline fire road, you turn right at the clearly signed Phyllis Ellman Trail and begin your descent. The views will continue to inspire you all the way back downhill.

Make it easier: Don't climb all the way to the top, but do go as far as you can, because the view just keeps getting better. Return the way you came instead of making the loop.

Trip notes: There is no fee. For more information, contact Marin County Open Space District, 3501 Civic Center Drive, San Rafael, CA 94903; (415) 499-6387. Or contact The Nature Conservancy at (415) 435-6465 or (415) 777-0487.

Directions: From San Francisco, cross the Golden Gate Bridge and drive north on U.S. 101 for seven miles. Take the Paradise Drive exit in Corte Madera. Follow Paradise Drive east for 1.6 miles through a residential neighborhood to the preserve entrance on the right. Park in the gravel pullout on the side of the road.

---

71. LAUREL DELL & CATARACT TRAILS
Marin Municipal Water District
Off Panoramic Highway near Mill Valley
2.25 miles round-trip — 1.25 hours — rolling terrain

Every time I hike the Cataract Trail uphill from Alpine Lake, I come across people who are panting and gasping for breath, clearly unhappy about the climb. "How far is it to the waterfall?" they ask. Since they've already gone this far, I spare them the ugly details and tell them they're almost there. In truth, they could be taking a much easier trail to Cataract Falls. It's a downhill hike, not a thousand-foot elevation-gaining march. Hey, why do it the hard way if you don't have to?

The trick is to start your trip from the right trailhead, which for easy hiking is the small parking area northwest of Rock Springs on West Ridgecrest Boulevard. You start at 1,800 feet in elevation. The falls are at 1,400 feet. Mr. and Mrs. Gasp-for-Breath are starting down by Alpine Dam, where the elevation is 680 feet. Guess who's going to have more fun?

Start walking at the trail marker for Laurel Dell. You'll head downhill along a fire road, heading into a thick mixed forest of bay laurel and Douglas fir. Continue for seven-tenths of a mile until you come to a clearing and see Laurel Dell on your left. During late winter and spring you may have to cross Cataract Creek; the fire road can be completely submerged by the flooded stream. In summer, it's an easy walk and the route is completely dry.

Laurel Dell isn't signed or marked; it's just a grassy meadow area and an intersection of trails. Be careful that you don't pass it by, because the fire road you're walking on continues far beyond it. You must turn left at Laurel Dell and walk through it to connect with Cataract Trail.

From this point the scenery starts to get really pretty, as you parallel Cataract Creek heading downhill into the canyon. Watch for a junction in four-tenths of a mile with High Marsh Trail on the right. Just past this trail intersection is your destination, one of the prettiest cascades of Cataract Falls. The Cataract Trail curves in tightly, bringing you close to the stream, and you'll see the water tumbling over huge boulders as it rushes downhill.

Unlike many waterfalls, Cataract Falls isn't one single rushing torrent, but rather a series of small waterfalls that reveal themselves, one after the other, as you walk down the canyon of Cataract Creek. If you're feeling energetic, you can continue downhill along Cataract Trail and visit more of cascades. But keep in mind that the trail loses another 700 feet in elevation as it descends all the way to Alpine Lake; the return trip is all uphill.

Cataract Trail

If you are satisfied with this destination, pick a rock and settle in for a while, enjoying the wide, toppling shower of water over boulders, and admiring the many pools the fall creates. In late summer Cataract Falls can dry up completely, so make sure you time your visit for winter or spring, preferably after a rain. The only thing sadder than watching people hike this trail the hard way (uphill from Alpine Dam) is watching people hike it the hard way during August and September, when there is no waterfall at all, or only the tiniest trickle.

When you're ready, head back uphill to Laurel Dell and then return to your starting point. If you like, you can take a short side-trip into Mount Tamalpais State Park starting from your parked car on West Ridgecrest Boulevard. If you cross the road, you'll see a single-track hiking trail leading up and over a grassy knoll. Follow it for 100 yards to reach a stunning vista of the ocean, 2,000 feet below you, in stark contrast to the grassland hills all around you.

Make it easier: Walk to Laurel Dell and back, losing only 300 feet in elevation instead of 500 feet to the cascade. Or walk the little side trail into Mount Tam State Park and have a picnic on the grassy bluffs.

Trip notes: There is no fee. For more information and a $2 map, contact Marin Municipal Water District at 220 Nellen Avenue, Corte Madera, CA 94925; (415) 924-4600. Or phone Sky Oaks Ranger Station at (415) 945-1181. Because this trip borders Mount Tamalpais State Park, rangers there can also help you. Contact Mount Tamalpais State Park, 801 Panoramic Highway, Mill Valley, CA 94941; (415) 388-2070.

Directions: From San Francisco, cross the Golden Gate Bridge and drive north on U.S. 101 for four miles. Take the Mill Valley/Stinson Beach/Highway 1 exit and continue straight for one mile to a stoplight at Shoreline Highway (Highway 1). Turn left on Shoreline Highway and drive 2.5 miles, then turn right on Panoramic Highway. Drive nine-tenths of a mile until you reach an intersection where you can go left, straight, or right. Take the middle road (straight), continuing on Panoramic Highway for 4.3 more miles to Pantoll Road. Turn right on Pantoll Road and drive 1.4 miles to its intersection with Ridgecrest Boulevard. Turn left on West Ridgecrest Boulevard and drive 1.6 miles to a small parking area on the right. Park there and take the trail from the parking lot that is marked "Laurel Dell."

72. BENSTEIN, MICKEY O'BRIEN, & CATARACT TRAILS
Marin Municipal Water District
Off Panoramic Highway near Mill Valley
4 miles round-trip — 2 hours — rolling terrain

If you just want an easy walk in the woods, maybe with a little picnicking or a nature lesson along the way, here's a trail loop that's just right. Lots of people come to Mount Tamalpais to see the majestic coastal redwoods or take in the sweeping coastal views, but there's plenty to be said for a simple hike in a mixed hardwood forest, combining a little exercise, some solitude, and the sound of the birds and your own breathing.

The plethora of cars parked at Rock Springs parking area on the weekends might make you worry that this trail will be packed with people, but I've often seen only one or two others on it. Many people come to Rock Springs, but they head out to see the scenic lookout at O'Rourke's Bench or Mountain Theater. On one weekend hike, the only folks I saw on this trail were a group of senior hikers, many who looked to be in their 70s or 80s, who were speeding up Benstein Trail like they were on their way to a fire, arguing all the way about what species of oriole they had just seen. They passed me near Potrero Camp and I never caught up with them.

It's a good idea to carry a park map with you. Although the trail is well-signed, you have to make quite a few turns to complete the loop. Start by walking straight from the parking area, heading out on Cataract until it splits—Cataract to your left and Benstein to your right. Take Benstein north, heading immediately into the forest, where you'll likely be greeted by the sound of woodpeckers.

Benstein, Mickey O'Brien, & Cataract Trails

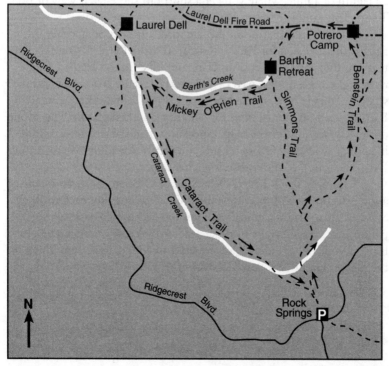

Trail markers lead you toward Potrero Meadows, and you climb all the way until you come to a joining of Benstein Trail with the Rock Springs/Lagunitas fire road. Take the fire road to the left for only a few dozen yards before Benstein veers off again to the left, back on single-track.

Prepare for a sudden change as you come out of the hardwoods and on to the rocky back side of this ridge, where you enter a contrasting world of manzanita, chamise, small Sargent cypress trees, and rocks and gravel made of serpentine. Spend some time examining the foliage; it consists of plants that need little in the way of nutrients and are often dwarfed in size. This is a classic example of flora in a serpentine environment. Serpentine, which is California's state rock, is formed by water mixing with peridotite. It's a pretty grayish-green on Mount Tamalpais, although in other places it can be almost all gray.

Descending from this gravelly, exposed ridge, follow Benstein for another quarter mile until you reach Laurel Dell fire road, which leads to Barth's Retreat and eventually Laurel Dell. (A picnic area can be found across the road at Potrero Camp if anyone in your group is getting hungry or tired.) Turn left on the fire road and hike for about an eighth of a mile, where you get a short but spectacular view of Bon Tempe Lake and the Marin Watershed valley to the north.

After your short stint on the fire road, turn left on another fire road at the trail sign for Barth's Retreat. (Barth's Retreat is an old camp that was built by the poet, musician, and hiker in the 1920s.) Turn right and cross a bridge, pass by yet another picnic area, and continue straight. You are now on the Mickey O'Brien Trail heading west along Barth's Creek, in a thick forest of oak, bay, and Douglas fir. This is one of the best sections of the loop, especially when the stream is running in spring, as Mickey O'Brien leads you gently downhill toward Laurel Dell. The sound of the stream is enchanting.

Before you reach Laurel Dell, Mickey O'Brien comes to an end at an intersection with Cataract Trail, which is your ticket back to Rock Springs. Turn left on Cataract and it's just over a mile back to the parking area. If you want to make a sidetrip to picnic at Laurel Dell, head to your right for less than a quarter of a mile, have your lunch in the picnic area, then follow Cataract home.

Make it easier: At Barth's Retreat, you can head back to the parking area on Simmons Trail and cut one mile off your trip.

Trip notes: There is no fee. For more information and a $2 map, contact Marin Municipal Water District at 220 Nellen Avenue, Corte Madera, CA 94925; (415) 924-4600. Or phone Sky Oaks Ranger Station at (415)

945-1181. Because this trip borders Mount Tamalpais State Park, rangers there can also help you. Contact Mount Tamalpais State Park, 801 Panoramic Highway, Mill Valley, CA 94941; (415) 388-2070.

Directions: From San Francisco, cross the Golden Gate Bridge and drive north on U.S. 101 for four miles. Take the Mill Valley/Stinson Beach/Highway 1 exit and continue straight for one mile to a stoplight at Shoreline Highway (Highway 1). Turn left on Shoreline Highway and drive 2.5 miles, then turn right on Panoramic Highway. Drive nine-tenths of a mile until you reach an intersection where you can go left, straight, or right. Take the middle road (straight), continuing on Panoramic Highway for 4.3 more miles to the Pantoll parking lot. Turn right on Pantoll Road and drive 1.4 miles to its intersection with Ridgecrest Boulevard, where there is a large parking area called Rock Springs. Park here and take the trail from the parking lot that is marked "Cataract Trail."

73. COASTAL & MATT DAVIS TRAILS
Mount Tamalpais State Park
Off Panoramic Highway near Mill Valley
3.2 miles round-trip — 1.5 hours — rolling terrain

Is it a clear spring day in the San Francisco Bay Area? If so, then there's really only one thing to do: Lace up your hiking boots and head for the Coastal Trail in Mount Tamalpais State Park.

The clear-day views from the Coastal and Matt Davis trails on Mount Tamalpais are truly jaw-droppers, even for those whose jaws are not dropped by your average stunning view. The trick is to pick a day when the fog is either nonexistent or hovering far out to sea, when visibility is at its best. Then just follow the trail, which meanders in and out of the trees, providing the best of both worlds—secluded forest groves laced with small, coursing streams, and wide open grasslands covered with lupine and poppies in the spring.

There is some confusion about this trail's name. Both Coastal and Matt Davis are two lengthy trails which traverse Mount Tam. For the duration of the route described here, they are the same trail. Matt Davis Trail splits off from this route and descends to the ocean, while Coastal Trail continues straight and eventually ends at the intersection of Ridgecrest Boulevard and Bolinas-Fairfax Road.

After an initial glimpse at the ocean near the start of the trail, you'll head into a dense mixed hardwood forest and remain there for just shy of a mile. The beauty is close at hand—thick moss growing like fur on the bay laurel trees, dense ferns clustered around seasonal

Coastal Trail, Mount Tamalpais State Park

streams, and dappled sunlight filtering through the canopy of leaves.

Just as your eyes grow accustomed to the low light of the forest, the trail suddenly opens out to wide, sloping grasslands and bright sunshine. In spring, the mountain's wildflowers burst into colorful display, spurred on by cooling fog and plentiful sunlight. Because you can see so far and wide along the grassy slopes of Mount Tamalpais, you may spot deer as much as a mile away, or a couple of miniature hikers having lunch on a rock, looking like pieces out of a model train set. This trail is an incredible place for getting an idea of how small we are in the big scheme of things.

From the trail's vantage point, the mountain slopes drop more than 1,000 feet to the ocean. The further you walk, the wider your view becomes, until it finally extends from the San Francisco skyline to Stinson Beach and Bolinas, then north to Point Reyes. If you ever wanted to explain to somebody how large the ocean is in relation to the size of the land, this would be the place to do it.

The best turnaround spot is 1.6 miles in, at a small unmarked spur trail to the left that makes a short climb to a knoll. (If you reach the junction where the Coastal Trail and Matt Davis Trail split off, you've gone past it.) Take this spur trail, which in about 50 feet will lead you to the most awesome view of the day, taking in the entire Marin County coast. It's a good place to picnic or just sit and admire the world before heading back.

Make it more challenging: You can continue on Coastal Trail past its junction with Matt Davis Trail for nearly three miles, until it intersects with West Ridgecrest Boulevard, adding up to six more miles to your out-and-back trip.

Trip notes: A $5 state park day-use fee is charged if you park at the paved parking lot at the Pantoll Ranger Station. If you park legally in any pullout along the road, there is no fee. A trail map is available at Pantoll Ranger Station for $1. For more information, contact Mount Tamalpais State Park, 801 Panoramic Highway, Mill Valley, CA 94941; (415) 388-2070.

Directions: From San Francisco, cross the Golden Gate Bridge and drive north on U.S. 101 for four miles. Take the Mill Valley/Stinson Beach/Highway 1 exit and continue straight for one mile to a stoplight at Shoreline Highway (Highway 1). Turn left on Shoreline Highway and drive 2.5 miles, then turn right on Panoramic Highway. Drive nine-tenths of a mile until you reach an intersection where you can go left, straight, or right. Take the middle road (straight), continuing on Panoramic Highway for 4.3 more miles to the Pantoll Ranger Station and parking area. Turn left to park in the parking area, then walk across Panoramic Highway to the start of Pantoll Road. There is a small dirt parking area there, and across from it, on the southwest side of Pantoll Road, is the signed trailhead for the Coastal/Matt Davis Trail.

---

74. PANORAMIC, LOST TRAIL, & FERN CREEK LOOP
Muir Woods National Monument
Off Panoramic Highway near Mill Valley
3.4 miles round-trip — 1.5 hours — rolling terrain

The redwoods at Muir Woods National Monument are beauties. The foliage in the understory of the big redwoods—bays, tanoak, thimbleberry, sword ferns, and sorrel—is lush, green, and pretty year-round. Redwood Creek, which cuts through the center of the park, is a pristine, coursing stream.

Muir Woods is good—no doubt about it. The only problem with Muir Woods is its location: it's situated a bit too close to a major urban area. That means this little tiny national monument, not much larger than a few city blocks, gets visited by more than one million people each year.

How do you hike in the park and see its lovely redwoods without getting run over by the crowds? It's not easy. Summer is the busiest time, of course, so it's best to avoid May to September all together.

Weekends tend to be more crowded than weekdays, but weekdays bring school groups. (Thirty sixth-graders on a field trip can be pretty boisterous.) The best choice? Try to show up early in the morning, as in 8 A.M. when the park gates open. During the week, the first school buses and tour buses don't usually arrive till 9 or 10 A.M. On the weekends, most visitors don't show up till mid-morning. An 8 A.M. start any day of the week should give you at least a two-hour window of peace among the redwoods. Winter and early spring are the least crowded and also the loveliest seasons, when Redwood Creek runs full and high.

And don't worry about visiting on a rainy day; just pack along your rain gear. A redwood forest is the best place to hike in the rain. You'll be partially protected by the big trees, and the drops of water on every fern, branch, and leaf only accentuate the beauty.

Start your trip from the entrance gate to Muir Woods, near the small visitor center. The only trail choice is the wide, paved path that runs along the bottom of the canyon, passing the most impressive redwoods. You'll walk the entire length of this trail on your return; for now, bear right and in about 100 yards you'll reach a fork with Panoramic Trail. Panoramic Trail (once named the Ocean View Trail, although it has no ocean views) ascends up the hillside to the right. Take it and leave the pavement behind.

The path is completely forested, but the redwood trees are younger and smaller here, and interspersed with many Douglas firs. The climb is very moderately graded, and curves around the canyon until it reaches a junction with Lost Trail at 1.5 miles. Note this junction; then continue straight past it for another 200 yards until Panoramic Trail exits the forest just below Panoramic Highway, a busy road. A large boulder rests on the hillside between the trail and the road; this is the only spot along the trail where you can get a long-distance view. On a sunny day, it's a good resting place, looking down over the forests of Muir Woods below.

When you've had your fill of sunshine, return to the shady woods and the previously noted junction. Turn right on Lost Trail, now heading downhill. Lost Trail is very similar to Panoramic Trail in that it cuts through a young redwood, Douglas fir, and bay forest. Soon it descends more steeply on railroad-tie stairsteps, and in seven-tenths of a mile it connects with Fern Creek Trail. Fern Creek is a narrower offshoot of Redwood Creek, the main stream that flows through Muir Woods' canyon. The path follows Fern Creek's delightful course for nearly a half mile, crossing it on two footbridges.

Near the end of the Fern Creek Trail you pass a sign marking

Blooming sorrel in Muir Woods

the border of Muir Woods National Monument. In a few more steps, you're standing at the base of the Kent Memorial, a very large Douglas fir tree dedicated to the man who was responsible for the creation of Muir Woods National Monument. Congressman William Kent and his wife donated this land to the federal government; President Theodore Roosevelt declared it a national monument.

The loop trail ends with a three-quarter-mile walk from the Kent Memorial back up the main trail to your starting point. Although this stretch of trail has the largest and most impressive redwoods, it also has the most people. Fortunately some of the pavement has been removed in recent years; it has been replaced by a wooden boardwalk that allows the redwoods' roots to grow better. Admire the big trees and the clear stream of Redwood Creek, then head back to your car.

Make it easier: Hike the paved main trail only, heading out and back for a 1.5-mile round-trip. If you choose this path, try to arrive early in the morning so you have a chance of seeing the redwoods without the crowds.

Trip notes: A $2 day-use fee is charged per adult; children 16 and under enter free. A free park map/brochure is available at the entrance station. For more information, contact Muir Woods National Monument, Mill Valley, CA 94941; (415) 388-2595.

Directions: From San Francisco, cross the Golden Gate Bridge and drive north on U.S. 101 for four miles. Take the Mill Valley/Stinson Beach/

Highway 1 exit and continue straight for one mile to a stoplight at Shoreline Highway (Highway 1). Turn left on Shoreline Highway and drive 2.5 miles, then turn right on Panoramic Highway. Drive nine-tenths of a mile and turn left on Muir Woods Road. Drive 1.5 miles to the Muir Woods parking area.

75. LAGOON TRAIL
Golden Gate National Recreation Area
Off U.S. 101 near Sausalito
1.75 miles round-trip — 1 hour — mostly level terrain

You have to look long and hard to find a hiking trail in the Marin Headlands that is nearly level. Or you can head directly for the Lagoon Trail and spare yourself a lot of searching. The trail begins conveniently at the Marin Headlands Visitor Center, where you can get a few natural and cultural history lessons before heading out on the scenic, remarkably easy path.

Start walking directly toward the ocean and Rodeo Beach. A trail veers off to the right, but continue straight ahead, marching toward the sea. You're on a wide gravel path, listening to the rhythm of the ocean breakers and watching the birds in Rodeo Lagoon. The natural lagoon is separated from the ocean by a narrow strip of beach. Winter storm

Lagoon Trail near Rodeo Beach, Golden Gate National Recreation Area

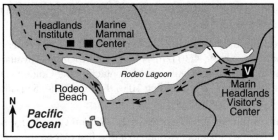

Lagoon Trail, Marin Headlands

waves occasionally wash over the beach and into the lagoon, mixing fresh and salt water. This combined freshwater and saltwater environment makes the lagoon a happy home for brown pelicans, snowy egrets, and other water birds. Red-winged blackbirds and other songbirds like it too.

For a brief stretch, the foliage beside the trail is very dense and high, and you can't see much in any direction. You pass a feeder stream, with horsetail ferns growing thickly alongside it. Then the trail starts to climb a bit, taking you 100 feet above the lagoon and expanding your view. Across the water, you can see the Headlands Institute and the Marine Mammal Center, a nonprofit organization that rescues and rehabilitates injured marine animals.

When the trail drops back down again, nearly at the ocean beach, you are surrounded by poppies, ice plant, and purple lupine. You can follow the sandy trail straight out to the breakers and explore Rodeo Beach. The beach is usually peopled by a mixed collection of fishermen, surfers, birdwatchers, and beach-lovers. When it's sunny on Rodeo Beach, it's often fiercely windy; when it's foggy, it's quieter and more peaceful. Look closely at the tiny, colorful pebbles on the beach. Some are semiprecious stones, such as carnelians and agates, but collecting them is prohibited. Swimming at this beach is not recommended because of rip tides; the lagoon is also off-limits to swimming.

If you have the energy, climb up on the bluffs to the left of the beach for a fine view of rocky sea stacks and the coast to the south. To finish out your trip, you can loop back around the far side of the lagoon by exiting the beach on a wooden bridge, then walking alongside the parking lot and road. I'd recommend a turnaround instead; just reverse your steps and enjoy this trail all over again.

Make it more challenging: Trails lead up the bluffs from both the north and south sides of Rodeo Beach, adding extensive out-and-back possibilities. Be sure to check posted signs for seasonal trail closures on these bluffs due to erosion problems.

Trip notes: There is no fee. The Marin Headlands Visitor Center is open daily from 9:30 a.m. to 4:30 p.m. A free map/brochure is available at the Marin Headlands Visitor Center, or by contacting the Golden Gate National Recreation Area, Building 1056, Fort Cronkite, Sausalito, CA 94965; (415) 331-1540 or (415) 556-0560.

Directions: From San Francisco, cross the Golden Gate Bridge on U.S. 101 and take the Alexander Avenue exit (the first exit on the Marin County side of the bridge). Turn left and loop back under the freeway; then turn right on Conzelman Road. In about one mile, turn right on McCullough Road and continue less than a mile. Turn left on Bunker Road and continue two miles. (Follow the signs for the Marin Headlands Visitor Center.) Park at the visitor center and locate the Lagoon Trail marker near the rest rooms on the west side of the parking lot.

East San Francisco Bay Area

(For locations of trails, see map on page 9.)

76. CLARK BOAS & BELGUM TRAIL LOOP
Wildcat Canyon Regional Park
Off Interstate 80 near Richmond
3 miles round-trip — 1.75 hours — some steep terrain

Never judge a trail by its trailhead, sage hikers always say. When you park your car at Wildcat Canyon Regional Park and see the trailhead, you'll think, "Aha, a forested hike through eucalyptus and oaks." But then, when you start walking on the Wildcat Creek Trail, you'll think, "Aha, a paved, flat trail along the bottom of a canyon."

Wrong on both counts, because looks are deceiving at Wildcat Canyon. What begins as a flat, paved, tree-shaded road at a low elevation becomes a hilly, dirt path that takes you up nearly 1,000 feet for wide views of the East Bay and North Bay. That means you have to be prepared to climb on this trail—those great views come with a price.

But the cost is not out of reach for most people, and I'll tell you how you can get a discount. Begin your hike by walking two-tenths of a mile on the Wildcat Creek Trail, a paved path that starts on the east side of the parking lot. It turns to dirt after about 150 yards, but then it becomes pavement again in another 50 yards. Watch for the wide dirt path (unmarked) that veers off to the left while you're on the short dirt section of the trail. If you reach pavement again, you've gone too far and missed the turnoff. (You'll also know you've gone too far if you come to a trail marker for the Belgum Trail.)

Take this wide dirt path and begin climbing up the grassy hillside. This ascent is the most challenging part of the trip, but you'll be well rewarded for your efforts. As you climb, notice the variety of grassland plant life around you. On the surrounding hills, you'll see purple Canada thistles, which in autumn bear dried-out, rust-colored pom-poms that look like metal modern art sculptures. They grow as tall as four feet high. In spring, you'll see big yellow sunflowers and plenty of blue-eyed grass.

Head toward the houses on the ridge ahead of you, and then follow the trail as it veers off to the right. This puts you on the Clark Boas Trail, although it may not be signed. The dirt trail becomes gravel, and now you've gained enough elevation to be rewarded with wide-angle views of the San Francisco Bay Area, from Vallejo to San Francisco and the southern East Bay. Pick out the famous landmarks: the Bay Bridge, the Transamerica Tower, Twin Peaks, the Golden Gate Bridge, Angel Island, and so on. (When it comes to views, I've always preferred a sea of conifers to a sea of civilization. Still, I have to say that this vista—truly an urban view—makes a lasting and memorable impression.

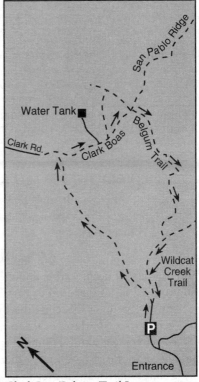

Clark Boas/Belgum Trail Loop

No matter how calm and warm it was when you started your hike, it's likely to be windy on top of the ridge. Numerous raptors and songbirds (including red-wing blackbirds) take advantage of the lofty breezes up here.

A paved road heads left to a water storage area; follow the dirt road that veers to the right. The dirt road splits into a gravel road and a single-track trail; follow the single-track trail to the right, heading slightly downhill and then mostly level. You'll walk along the edge of a pine grove; the trees are fenced in and marked as private property. Walk through a cattle gate, now heading due east and away from the bay. Climb steeply for about 40 yards to a high knoll—this is your last push—and take in the views of San Pablo Ridge.

At last you reach the intersection with the Belgum Trail (it may not be signed). Turn right and you're on a downhill cruise. As you descend from the ridge, the environment around you changes. First you see one palm tree all by itself, and then a little oasis and more trees—palms, willows, and eucalyptus—planted by a long-gone landowner. When you drop all the way to the pavement again, turn right on paved Wildcat Creek Trail and head a half mile back to your car.

Make it easier: In order to obtain the best views on this hike, you just have to climb. But you can shorten your trip by climbing only the first leg (the unmarked dirt trail leading to Clark Boas Trail) and then returning the way you came. A slightly longer option would be to follow Wildcat Creek Trail and then turn left on Belgum Trail, ascending as high as you like.

Trip notes: There is no fee. Free trail maps are available at the parking area. For more information, contact the East Bay Regional Parks District, 2950 Peralta Oaks Court, P.O. Box 5381, Oakland, CA 94605-0381; (510) 635-0135.

Directions: From Interstate 80 northbound in Richmond, take the Amador/Solano exit and drive three blocks on Amador. Turn right on McBryde Avenue and head east. After passing Arlington Boulevard, continue straight (the road becomes Park Avenue) and bear left into the Wildcat Canyon parking area. The Wildcat Creek Trail begins on the far side of the parking lot and is paved at the start.

77. OLD BRIONES ROAD & LAGOON TRAIL LOOP
Briones Regional Park
Off Interstate 680 near Pleasant Hill
5 miles round-trip — 2.5 hours — some steep terrain

For years I'd been hearing about how great the views were at Briones, but I never managed to make the trip. I had an attitude problem: Every time I looked at the Briones map, I envisioned a dry, hot desert, with giant dusty peaks to surmount, and maybe a few tumbleweeds blowing around. Hiking this far inland in the East Bay? Gee, I'm pretty sure I have some other real important things to do.

Well, I finally made it over to Briones, and I've got a new vision of how things can be. The secret is to go on a clear day in late fall, winter or spring (to get the best views and the coolest weather) and to start from the higher-elevation trailhead at Briones Road rather than the main trailhead at Alhambra Creek. This way your car does some of the climbing instead of your feet, and you get within easy hiking distance of some excellent vistas.

There are two prerequisites for enjoying this hike: 1) Don't go in the midday heat of summer; and 2) You must like bovines, or at least be amenable to them. Cows are grazing all over Briones.

The trail does have some fair ascents. Plus it's a long walk in wide open sunshine, so you need to come prepared, which means to carry plenty of water and maybe a snack. When you're ready, start at the main trailhead at Briones Road, just to the right of the ranger's residence driveway, and begin climbing on Old Briones Road, a fire road. (Don't forget to pick up your free trail map at the trailhead kiosk.)

Old Briones Road climbs gently for three-quarters of a mile and then levels out near—surprise—a small lagoon. On my first trip here, I had noticed "Maricich Lagoon" on the map, but with my attitude problem, I had imagined a crusty dust bowl with hawks circling overhead and maybe a desiccated skull or two. Instead, I found a pretty little pond, fenced in to keep the cows out. Two ducks were peacefully floating on its surface.

At the lagoon, check the trail marker and make sure you continue right on Old Briones Road for another quarter mile. Then turn right on the Briones Crest Trail, heading for another set of ponds, Sindicich Lagoons. Now prepare to start getting those remarkable views.

Remarkable? How about Mount Diablo, San Pablo Bay, Point Pinole, Suisun Bay, and Honker Bay in the

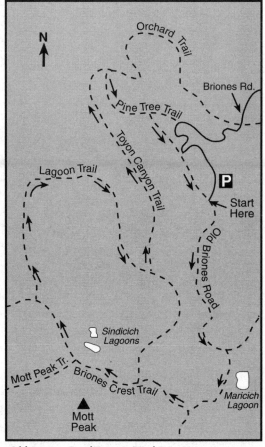

Old Briones Road/Lagoon Trail Loop

distance? Hey, what are all those ships lined up down there? That's the Mothball Fleet—old military ships that have been put out to pasture, and Jacques Cousteau's *Glomar Explorer* sitting all by itself between the last Navy ship and the bridge. You'll see the oil refineries along Contra Costa County's shoreline, often referred to as the Oil Coast. Not enough for you? Okay, let's toss in the Berkeley hills and the distinctive profile of Mount Tamalpais to the west. Kind of brings the whole Bay Area into reach, doesn't it? And you're not even seeing it from the highest point in this park, which is Mott Peak to the south, named after William Penn Mott, champion of parks.

If you're feeling a bit tired from all the climbing you've done, now is the time to consider the "make it easier" option (see page 179).

Old Briones Road & Lagoon Trail Loop, Briones Regional Park

You've just climbed up to 1,200 feet, and you may think it's all down-hill going back. Wrong. Shortly past the intersection with the Mott Peak Trail on the left, the Briones Crest Trail begins to descend. The only way to loop back to your car is to drop down below the trailhead and then circle around, which involves some climbing. A more direct route doesn't exist. The trail marker for the Mott Peak Trail, or some-where close to it, is an excellent turnaround point for a four-mile round-trip hike.

Energetic types should continue further on the Briones Crest Trail and bear right on the Lagoon Trail. Follow the Lagoon Trail for 1.25 miles and loop around to Toyon Canyon Trail. You'll head into a live oak forest, a nice change of pace from the sunshine and grasslands. Turn left on Toyon Canyon Trail and continue for one mile, then turn right for a quarter mile on the Pine Tree Trail, coming near some estate homes. When you see the paved road you drove in on, either follow the road back to your car or the unsigned single-track trail that parallels the access road.

The trails at Briones have a lot of different users, besides hikers and all the bovines—dogs, bicyclists, horses and their riders—so keep your ears and eyes open for them. Always remember to give horses plenty of room. The trails are plenty wide here, so there should be no problems. I saw every kind of trail user on my trip, and all of them were polite and friendly. Seems like at Briones, everyone, including me, gets their attitude adjusted.

Make it easier: Make this an out-and-back hike instead of a loop. When you reach the trail sign for Mott Peak Trail, turn around and head back the way you came. If you continue on the loop, you'll have more mileage and more climbing.

Trip notes: There is no fee. Free trail maps are available at the parking area. For more information, contact the East Bay Regional Parks District, 2950 Peralta Oaks Court, P.O. Box 5381, Oakland, CA 94605-0381; (510) 635-0135.

Directions: From Interstate 680 north of Pleasant Hill, take Highway 4 west for three miles to the Alhambra Avenue exit. Turn south on Alhambra Avenue, drive a half mile and bear right on Alhambra Valley Road. In about 50 yards, turn left on Briones Road and continue 1.5 miles to the trailhead.

78. MACDONALD TRAIL
Anthony Chabot Regional Park
Off Interstate 580 near Oakland
3.5 miles round-trip — 1.5 hours — rolling terrain

A little piece of paradise is available to hikers in the East Bay, and the big surprise is that it's only a 20-minute drive from the heart of downtown Oakland. Here's the scoop: Anthony Chabot Regional Park is nearly 5,000 acres of grasslands and forest surrounding Lake Chabot, a bright blue gem of a lake that provides quality fishing and boating as well as a reserve water supply for the city of Oakland. The East Bay Skyline National Recreation Trail, a 31-mile trail that traverses Contra Costa County between Berkeley and Walnut Creek, has an easement throughout the park. The Macdonald Trail is one portion of it.

Begin walking on the Macdonald Trail at the Bort Meadow Staging Area. The trail climbs gently right away, and keeps climbing for the first half hour of hiking. The hills give you plenty of reason to take your time and examine the grassy slopes and abundant wildflowers in spring, and to pause to check out the views in all directions.

You'll pass through two cattle gates, one right at the beginning of

Macdonald Trail, Anthony Chabot Regional Park

the trail and one further on. Close them behind you. In a few places, the main trail will branch off to narrower trails, but stay on the wide main path. At 1.5 miles, you'll reach an intersection with the Parkridge Trail to your left, which connects to a bordering neighborhood. Stay on the Macdonald Trail as it starts to slope downward. Before it goes too far downhill—"too far downhill" is that delicate point where you know you won't enjoy the return trip uphill—you should do an about-face and head back the way you came.

If you keep your eyes peeled, you will find my favorite destination point on this hike. A quarter-mile past the Parkridge Trail junction, look for a tiny spur trail on the right that heads into thick foliage. This short spur leads you to a hidden wooden bench, which provides a place to rest and take in the view of the hills and grasslands to the east. It's a peaceful little spot overlooking a stunning vista. If you retrace your steps from here, you won't have to climb at all on your way back.

The Macdonald Trail is great for testing your knowledge of plants and grasses, especially in spring. With the help of my trusty handbook, I've identified more than 20 varieties of wildflowers. Most prevalent is blue-eyed grass, which for years I knew only as "the little purple jobs."

But you don't have to know anything about botany to enjoy the walk. Pick a clear day in winter or spring, preferably one that combines blue skies with some big puffy clouds, or an early morning in summer before the temperatures heat up, and head to Chabot Park in the East Bay hills. You'll find that paradise is a lot closer than you thought.

Make it easier: Just shorten your route, and be sure to stop for a picnic somewhere along the trail or in Bort Meadow.

Trip notes: There is no fee. Free trail maps are available at the parking area, or from any ranger kiosk in the park. For more information, contact the East Bay Regional Parks District, 2950 Peralta Oaks Court, P.O. Box 5381, Oakland, CA 94605-0381; (510) 635-0135.

Directions: From Interstate 580 in Oakland, take the 35th Avenue exit and drive east (left). 35th Avenue becomes Redwood Road; follow it. You'll cross Skyline Boulevard and continue for just over four miles to the Bort Meadow Staging Area on the right. The trailhead is on the northwest end of the parking lot.

---

79. NORTH PEAK TRAIL to PROSPECTORS GAP
Mount Diablo State Park
Off Interstate 680 near Danville
2.25 miles round-trip — 1 hour — some steep terrain

Most everybody thinks about making a trip to 3,849-foot Mount Diablo from time to time. After all, you see it from just about everywhere in the Bay Area. It's not that it's the tallest mountain around San Francisco Bay (Mount Hamilton is taller); it just has a way of making its presence known, looming in the background of the lives of millions of East Bay residents.

When your time to visit Diablo arrives, the first thing you should do is drive up to the summit and see what it's like to look at the greater Bay Area from Mount Diablo, rather than vice versa. Park as close to the summit building as possible, walk around the summit parking lot, and check out the view in all directions (on the clearest days, you can see all the way to the Sierra!) Then go inside the visitor center and take 10 minutes to learn a bit about this big mountain.

Just make sure you don't tell anybody you're here on Mount Diablo to do some easy hiking. They'd probably laugh at you, because this mountain has a reputation for being hot, dry, steep, and mean. Most of the trails are fire roads, patrolled by hard-core bicyclists with a

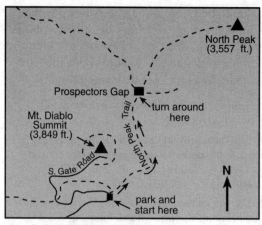

North Peak (3,557 ft.)

Prospectors Gap

turn around here

Mt. Diablo Summit (3,849 ft.)

North Peak Trail

S. Gate Road

N

park and start here

North Peak Trail to Prospectors Gap

penchant for heat and dust. Those who choose to hike usually begin in the canyons and take long, steep, multiple-hour climbs up the mountain. No wonder they named this place Diablo, Spanish for "devil."

Nonetheless, Diablo has a multitude of charms. Although its spectacular summit vista is the main attraction, easy hikers will be pleased to find a trail near the summit that makes a great trip in winter or spring. To reach the trailhead, drive back down the summit road for about one mile to a gravel parking area signed as "Summit Trail." You'll find two trails here; don't take the upper Summit Trail, but rather the unsigned lower trail, which is the North Peak Trail. Start walking the path across the shoulder of the mountain at 3,800 feet in elevation, less than 100 feet below the summit.

Mount Diablo has two summits, the main one with the paved road to the top and North Peak, which is 292 feet shorter at 3,557 feet. The North Peak Trail takes you around the east side of the higher summit, then down to a saddle between the peaks called Prospectors Gap. From there, North Peak Trail climbs on a fire road to the top of North Peak. Easy hikers should follow North Peak Trail only as far as Prospectors Gap, unless they're in the mood for a steep tromp up to North Peak (a 500-foot elevation gain in less than a mile). The trail to Prospectors Gap weaves in and out of chaparral and grasslands, occasionally catching breezes from the north and west. The route is shaded by the summit in the afternoon, and the gap offers unimpeded views to the east and west.

The trail is not entirely easy, however. It drops 400 feet in elevation on the way to Prospectors Gap, then climbs back up on the return. The "up" is a bit of a challenge for your thighs, heart, and lungs, while the down gives your feet and knees a workout. I'd definitely advise wearing hiking boots on this trail, as there are some steep pitches with loose gravel and an uneven surface.

The flora on Mount Diablo is quite unique. Even on this short walk on the North Peak Trail, you may see several spring wildflowers that are rarely seen in the rest of the Bay Area. Lucky hikers will spot Mount Diablo fairy lanterns, which grow nowhere else in the world. They have yellow, waxy-looking, nodding heads on stalks about five inches high. More prevalent are hooker's onions (foot-tall thin stalks with pink flower clusters at the top), purple fields of clarkia, red larkspur, dark blue lupine, orange California poppies, and tall mariposa lilies, with white tulip-shaped bowls and reddish-brown spots.

If you visit after the March-to-May wildflower season has passed, you'll still have California laurel, scrub oaks, and gray pines to keep you company along the trail. The scraggly-looking gray pines are similar to coulter pines, which also grow on Mount Diablo, but they have forked trunks and a grayish color to their needles. Coulter pines grow straighter and taller. The gray pine is most remarkable for its big cones, which weigh between one and four pounds and are six to ten inches long. (The coulter pine's cones are even bigger.) As I walked, I heard a gray pine cone hit the ground with a resounding "bonk." Watch your head if you decide to sit under one of these trees.

You'll probably run across some wildlife on your trip to Diablo, too. I saw two deer on the summit road, a plethora of sagebrush lizards on the trail (they're the speediest lizards around), a big jackrabbit, and several varieties of butterflies flitting about the brush. At the summit, I was virtually surrounded by a swarm of ladybugs. There must have a ladybug convention, or perhaps they all took a tour bus to see the view.

There is only one important thing to remember about visiting Mount Diablo: Never, ever go in the blazing heat of summer; it just ruins all your fun. The best seasons to visit are winter, when you may even find snow on the summit; or spring, when the grasses are green and the wildflowers put on their show. Sunsets and sunrises are particularly spectacular, as is any day when the valley is fogged in. Diablo's summit usually sits above the fog, so you get the heavenly perspective of gazing down over a feather-mattress layer of puffy white clouds.

Make it easier: After 10 minutes of hiking on the North Peak Trail, you'll reach a small cutoff trail, which leads to a rock outcrop with wide valley views. The cutoff reconnects to the main trail after 40 feet. This is an excellent resting place for those who don't want to hike all the way to Prospectors Gap.

Trip notes: A $5 state park day-use fee is charged by Mount Diablo State Park. A map is available for $1 at the ranger kiosk and at the interpretive center; the interpretive association also publishes a more extensive map, which is available for $5. For more information, contact Mount Diablo State Park, 96 Mitchell Canyon Road, Clayton, CA 94517; (925) 837-2525 or (650) 726-8800.

Directions: From Interstate 680 at Danville, take the Diablo Road exit. Follow Diablo Road for 1.5 miles to Mount Diablo Scenic Boulevard, then turn left. Mount Diablo Scenic Boulevard becomes Blackhawk Road. Continue to South Gate Road and turn left, then drive to the summit parking area. After seeing the view from the summit, drive back down South Gate Road for about one mile to a gravel parking area that is signed "Summit Trail." There are two trails here; take the lower, unsigned trail, not the upper Summit Trail.

South San Francisco Bay Area

(For locations of trails, see map on page 9.)

80. BROOKS CREEK & MONTARA MOUNTAIN TRAILS
San Pedro Valley County Park
Off Highway 1 near Pacifica
3.5 miles round-trip — 1.5 hours — some steep terrain

🚶🚶

The first time you drive to San Pedro Valley County Park, you'll think you have the wrong directions. You head down Highway 1 into Pacifica, a good-sized beach town, and then turn off at a shopping center, complete with three different fast-food chains. Plenty of wilderness out here, you'll say to yourself. But hold on, because you need only drive for five more minutes until you arrive at the park entrance. In a few minutes of hiking, you'll be heading up and away from the parking lots, noise, and traffic lights, and entering a vastly different world.

Still, the biggest surprise is yet to come. By hiking the Brooks Creek Trail in winter or spring, you have a chance to see one of the Bay Area's prettiest waterfalls: Brooks Falls, a tall, narrow cascade of water that drops 175 feet in three tiers. It is similar in appearance to the majestic tropical waterfalls of Hawaii.

Locate the trailhead for the Montara Mountain Trail alongside the restrooms in San Pedro Valley County Park. A few feet past the trailhead, the trail splits, with the Montara Mountain Trail heading right and the Brooks Creek Trail heading left. Follow the Brooks Creek Trail as it leads uphill through the eucalyptus, eventually breaking out to wide, open views of the canyon. At trail junctions, look for small signs that say "To Waterfall Viewing Area." Stay on the Brooks Creek Trail, bearing right at two forks, and keep heading uphill.

Twenty minutes of well-graded climbing delivers your first glances at the waterfall, far off in the canyon on your left. Look for a narrow plume of water cascading down the mountainside. Unfortunately, no trails lead to the base of the waterfall; you can only view it from a distance. The best viewpoint is at a conveniently placed bench right along the trail. After a hard rain, you can hear as well as see the water crashing down the slopes, a quarter-mile across the canyon.

By the time you reach this overlook point on the Brooks Creek Trail, you've climbed above the eucalyptus trees and are surrounded by manzanita and coastal brush. Your options are to turn around and head back, or continue on an excellent 3.5-mile loop trail. If you choose the latter, you get continual views of Brooks Falls as you continue upward, switchbacking to a trail junction and an overlook of the Pacific Ocean,

Pacifica Beach, the Marin Headlands, and even the Farallones on a clear day. This is also the junction with Montara Mountain Trail. Turn right on Montara Mountain Trail and start your descent back down the slope. (The left fork climbs even higher to the top of Montara Mountain.) Remain on Montara Mountain Trail, descending about 600 feet in elevation through stands of eucalyptus, until you return to the trailhead and parking area.

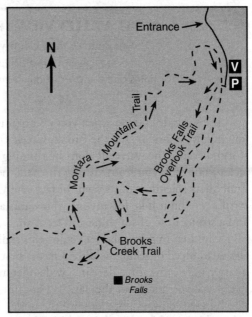

Brooks Creek & Montara Mountain Trails

When planning your trip, remember that Brooks Falls is a seasonal waterfall. It is best viewed in late winter or early spring, especially soon after a rain. This loop trip makes a pleasant hike year-round, but only in the rainy season will you see the waterfall.

Make it easier: You can shorten your hike considerably by just stopping at the viewing bench for Brooks Falls and then returning the way you came. This would make your walk about two miles round-trip, including a moderate 400-foot climb up to the falls' viewing spot.

Trip notes: There is a $3 entrance fee, usually only collected on weekends and holidays. Free trail maps and park brochures are available at the park trailheads. For more information, contact San Pedro Valley County Park, 600 Oddstad Boulevard, Pacifica, CA 94044; (650) 355-8289.

Directions: From San Francisco, take Highway 1 south into Pacifica. Turn east (left) on Linda Mar Boulevard and follow it until it dead-ends at Oddstad Boulevard. Turn right and drive to the park entrance, located about 50 yards ahead on the left. Park in the upper parking lot (to the right of the visitor center as you drive in). You'll find a trailhead marked "Montara Mountain Trail" directly behind the public rest rooms.

81. VALLEY VIEW TRAIL
San Pedro Valley County Park
Off Highway 1 near Pacifica
2 miles round-trip — 1 hour — rolling terrain

🚶‍♂️ ♿

If it's the dry season when you visit San Pedro Valley County Park, you might choose to skip the Brooks Creek Trail (see the previous story), because the waterfall won't be running anyway. But don't let a lack of rain stop you from visiting the park, because the Valley View Trail offers splendors of its own. In fact, the Valley View Trail is a terrific one-hour hike for anyone who wants a little bit of a workout and a strong dose of sunshine and fresh air.

Children in particular will enjoy this trail, because they are virtually guaranteed of seeing wildlife. On my first hike here, within the first quarter-mile I saw three deer in a wide open meadow, despite the fact that it was the middle of the day. As I continued, I spotted more than a dozen lizards (always popular with the under-12 crowd), several species of songbirds and hawks, and a rabbit. You may even see a bobcat or coyote on rare occasions.

An interesting feature of this trail is that it's rated for use by disabled persons with "mountain wheelchairs" and a buddy. The hard-packed dirt trail has a 400-foot elevation gain, and parts of it become quite narrow and uneven, so some wheelchair users may choose to travel only a portion of the trail. Weiler Ranch Road, which is the return leg of this loop hike, is even more wheelchair-friendly. It's also popular with people pushing baby strollers.

It takes about 30 minutes to gently ascend the Valley View Trail. You'll have to work just hard enough to say hello to your cardiovascular system. As you climb, you'll be rewarded with lovely meadow, canyon, hillside, and finally ocean views. When you reach the top of the ridge, you'll be surprised at how high you've climbed, because the trail has an easy grade that makes the ascent smooth. In springtime, you'll find several huge patches of purple Douglas irises on the ridgetop—as many as 100 showy flowers in each patch. From this high point, you have 20 minutes of easy walking down to Weiler Ranch Road, where you turn right and head back to your starting point.

Make it easier: If you don't want to climb, or if you are pushing a baby stroller, a great alternative is simply to head out and back on Weiler Ranch Road. It's two miles round-trip on this flat dirt trail.

Douglas iris on the Valley View Trail in San Pedro Valley County Park

Trip notes: There is a $3 entrance fee, which is usually only collected on weekends and holidays. Free trail maps and park brochures are available at park trailheads. For more information, contact San Pedro Valley County Park, 600 Oddstad Boulevard, Pacifica, CA 94044; (650) 355-8289.

Directions: From San Francisco, take Highway 1 south into Pacifica. Turn east (left) on Linda Mar Boulevard and follow it until it dead-ends at Oddstad Boulevard. Turn right and drive to the park entrance, located about 50 yards ahead on the left. Park in the lower parking lot (to the left of the visitor center as you drive in). Look for the sign at the northeast end of the parking lot pointing toward the group picnic area. Follow the paved path over a bridge, through the group picnic area, and then straight ahead for the trailheads for Weiler Ranch Road and the Valley View Trail.

82. WHITTEMORE GULCH TRAIL
Purisima Creek Redwoods Open Space Preserve
Off Highway 35 on the San Francisco Peninsula
2.2 miles round-trip — 1 hour — some steep terrain

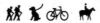

Everyone who has ever been to Purisima Creek Redwoods Open Space Preserve knows that it's a hiker's heaven. The preserve provides visitors with breathtaking ocean views, towering redwood and fir trees, a beautiful creek, and lots of wildlife and wildflowers. There isn't much more a nature-lover could ask for, except not to have to hike straight down to get there and then straight back up to return.

Purisima delivers on its Spanish name—it is pristine and secluded. It is also *steep*. But the Whittemore Gulch Trail can make your trip easy, provided you don't follow it for too many miles. The trail offers you the best of the park—pretty woodlands and coastal vistas—but it does so gently, without brutalizing your feet. And because this trail was specifically designed with hikers in mind, it is closed seasonally to bikers and equestrians, who can use the fire roads in the park instead.

From the trailhead, you switchback your way down the trail, enjoying the dense forest at the start and the views of Half Moon Bay and the coast as you progress. You have an excellent chance of seeing some local wildlife, most likely in the form of a deer or bunny, or any of the myriad bird species that soar here. From February to June, the sides of the trail are littered with light blue forget-me-nots, more dense than I've seen anywhere else. As you hike among the flowers and look down at your feet, you feel like you are walking on acres of light blue clouds.

For easy hikers, the key to enjoying the Whittemore Gulch Trail is not to get too ambitious. Since you are going downhill for the first part of your trip, the hiking is effortless. Because the trail and views are so pretty, you may be tempted to keep going. But be sure to rein yourself in, or be prepared for a long uphill return. After traveling a half mile on the hikers-only, single-track trail from the trailhead, you'll turn right on a fire road for a short distance and then turn left back on to single-track. (The trail is well-signed.) On this second single-track section, as you switchback downhill, look for a short spur trail to an informal overlook with a railing to lean against. It offers a fine view of the coast near Half Moon Bay, and it's a good place to hang out for a while before you gear up for the climb home. If you miss it, turn around at the trail marker shortly beyond that reads "Skyline Parking—1.1 mile."

If you don't pay attention to the trail markers, you may continue switchbacking down the slope all the way to the bottom of the canyon and Purisima Creek. While this is a splendid trip for those who are prepared for it, the hike is 3.5 short miles down and then 3.5 seemingly endless miles back up.

Purisima Creek Preserve is one of the most beautiful regions of open space in the Bay Area. The Whittemore Gulch Trail makes the park's wildlands accessible, even for those of us who prefer our hiking to be easy.

Make it easier: If this trail involves too much huffing and puffing for your taste, you can access Purisima Creek Redwoods two miles further south on Highway 35 and walk on the quarter-mile, wheelchair-accessible Redwood Trail.

Trip notes: There is no fee. The preserve is open from dawn until sunset. Free trail maps are available at the trailhead. For more information, contact the Midpeninsula Regional Open Space District, 330 Distel Circle, Los Altos, CA 94022; (650) 691-1200.

Directions: From San Francisco, drive south on Interstate 280 for 19 miles to the Highway 92 cutoff. Head west on Highway 92 toward Half Moon Bay for 2.7 miles, then turn south (left) on Highway 35 (Skyline Boulevard) and drive 4.2 miles to the Purisima Creek Redwoods Open Space Preserve parking area on the right, just past a small store. The Whittemore Gulch Trailhead is at the southwest end of the parking lot.

---

83. TAFONI TRAIL
El Corte de Madera Open Space Preserve
Off Highway 35 on the San Francisco Peninsula
2.6 miles round-trip — 1.5 hours — rolling terrain

The main attractions of the 600-acre El Corte de Madera Open Space Preserve are the monolithic sandstone formations at the end of the Tafoni Trail. The formations stand completely alone in the forest; they're unlike anything else you see along the trail. For the majority of your walk, it's just trees and more trees, including some magnificent old spruce and younger redwoods. Then suddenly they appear: huge sandstone beasts looming 50-feet high. Then just as suddenly, there are no more of them, just forest again. It's as if Mother Nature told the delivery company to drop the sandstone off at the wrong location.

Many trails run through the preserve, but for the majority of this trip you stay on the wide main fire road, signed as Tafoni Trail. You'll hike on a mostly level grade for the first mile, then reach a major junction where signs direct you a short distance to a vista point or a shorter distance to the sandstone formations. Turn sharply right to head for the sandstone first. (This part of the trail is open only to hikers, but the rest of the trail and all other trails in the preserve are open to bikes and horses.) In just a few hundred feet, you'll reach a sign announcing the sandstone formations ahead, called "tafoni." No, it's not some kind of Italian dessert; tafoni is a type of sandstone that is formed by years of weathering. The "glue" that holds the individual sand grains together

Tafoni Trail, El Corte de Madera Open Space Preserve

eventually erodes away, leaving fascinating crevices and holes in the sandstone.

Be sure to follow the use trails that circle around the formations. The informal paths are quite steep, so use caution as you scramble around. Take your time, watch your footing, and enjoy the unique geologic slabs. They're off-white, smooth, and pocked with caves and hollows. It's important not to touch the sandstone; the pressure of human hands will speed erosion.

When you've finished exploring, retrace your steps back up the hill to the previous junction and head right on the spur trail to the vista point. This spot offers a nice view of the coast and a level, open area for picnicking, in strong contrast to the dense woods you've been hiking in.

Make it easier: Skip the vista point and shave a quarter-mile off the trip.

Trip notes: There is no fee. The preserve is open from dawn until sunset. Free trail maps are available at the trailhead. For more information, contact the Midpeninsula Regional Open Space District, 330 Distel Circle, Los Altos, CA 94022; (650) 691-1200.

Directions: From San Francisco, drive south on Interstate 280 for 19 miles to the Highway 92 cutoff. Head west on Highway 92 toward Half Moon Bay for 2.7 miles, then turn south (left) on Highway 35/Skyline Boulevard and drive 8.5 miles to the Skeggs Vista Point parking area on your left. (It is 1.6 miles south of the intersection with Kings Mountain Road, and 3.8 miles north of Skylonda.) You can't enter the parking area from this direction; you must drive up the road and find a safe place to make a U-turn. After parking, cross Skyline Boulevard and walk north about 50 feet to the trailhead.

84. PALO ALTO BAYLANDS NATURE TRAIL
Palo Alto Baylands Preserve
Off U.S. 101 in Palo Alto
1.25 miles round-trip — 30 minutes — mostly level terrain

I was a bit skeptical about a hike that parallels the Palo Alto Municipal Airport runway. As I drove in, I even thought that perhaps the whole thing was a joke. A nature center in the midst of suburban sprawl? It didn't seem likely. But there it was, the Baylands Interpretive Center, a wooden structure resting on stilts above pickleweed in the mudflats of the South Bay. And the hike, which follows the airport runway for some distance, has many pleasant and surprising features.

For one thing, the place is teeming with birdlife. One particular species caught my eye because of its unique markings—black stripes on its wings and a pale orange head. It was an American avocet, well-known for the side-to-side motion it makes with its head as it feeds in shallow water. Orioles zoomed back and forth across the trail, doing the ambitious work of building their nests underneath the pilings of the interpretive center. Also present were the usual cabal of wetlands birds: herons, egrets, ducks, coots, and pelicans, not to mention western sandpipers (more than 100,000 of them, I was told). The sandpipers fly in precise patterns right along the water's edge, as if the entire flock was radio-controlled.

All these birds can't be wrong. The Palo Alto Baylands is a great place with more than 2,000 acres of preserved marshland. It's a sanctuary amid the chaos of the Silicon Valley. The birds don't seem to mind the neighboring airport, nor the power lines and electrical towers that line the bay, and to my surprise, neither did I.

The walk is as flat as can be, but never dull. You start walking on the trail in front of the interpretive center, head out for a half mile until you reach a bench at the end of the trail, then head back. When you're not watching the wildlife, it's quite interesting to watch the small planes taking off at the airport. You're far enough away so that their noise is not bothersome, but close enough to make out the details of the planes. You may even find yourself embroidering some elaborate metaphor comparing human flight to bird flight. The Baylands Trail invites the comparison.

Don't miss this side trip: the interpretive center has a wooden boardwalk extending from its back side for 800 yards across the tidal marshlands. The 15 minutes it takes to walk it are well worth the trip. At the boardwalk's end is an observation deck, situated at the exact boundary where marshland meets open water. It's the kind of place you can sit for a long time, just gazing at the always-in-motion bay flow.

The Palo Alto Baylands Preserve was created in the 1960s by some smart folks in Palo Alto. More acreage was added later to include a huge salt marsh, a duck pond, and a seasonal freshwater marsh that is fed by millions of gallons of treated wastewater from the nearby Palo Alto sewage treatment plant. The preserve is a fine example of the right way to protect precious wetlands.

One more surprise is in store for birdwatchers: The Palo Alto Baylands are home to a healthy population of colorful ring-necked pheasants, exotic birds imported from Asia that were introduced in the United States in the 1800s as a game bird. For many years, a pheasant farm was located just north of what is now the interpretive center. After the farm's demise in the 1960s, the birds continued to thrive in the wild. If you're lucky, you may hear a pheasant making its clamorous call, or catch sight of its bright gold and forest-green colors as you hike.

Make it easier: Walk out and back on the boardwalk to the observation deck instead of walking the entire trail.

Trip notes: There is no fee. For more information, contact Palo Alto Baylands Interpretive Center, 1451 Middlefield Road, Palo Alto, CA 94301; (650) 329-2261 or (650) 329-2506.

Directions: From U.S. 101 in Palo Alto, take the Embarcadero exit east. Drive about a half mile, passing the golf course, airport and yacht harbor, until you reach a sharp right turn. Park in the lot on the right. The interpretive center is across the road; the trailhead is directly in front of it.

85. HAWK RIDGE TRAIL LOOP
Russian Ridge Open Space Preserve
Off Highway 35 on the San Francisco Peninsula
1.5 miles round-trip — 1 hour — rolling terrain

The first time I hiked at Russian Ridge Open Space Preserve, I knew I had a major problem on my hands. My task was to chronicle

Northern California's most beautiful, easy hikes, and I'd just come upon a park that was almost too good to be true. Russian Ridge is free to the public, has great trails and easy access, and is so spectacularly beautiful that it defies description. Mere words don't do it justice. How many ways can I say "This place is just plain incredible"?

I'm not exaggerating when I say that Russian Ridge Open Space Preserve is more than 1,500 acres of paradise. First, we're talking location, location, location, as in directly off Skyline Boulevard (Highway 35), near the well-to-do town of Woodside. That's right, folks; there's a reason that one-bedroom cottages here cost half a million dollars—just look out the window. The first time I visited the weather was foggy along the coast, but the sun was shining brightly on Skyline. From the preserve's 2,300-foot elevation, I could look out and over the blanket of fog that covered the ocean. From this perspective, the fog looks absolutely gorgeous—like layers of white cotton candy. You get to appreciate the beauty of it without being stuck in the middle of it.

As you admire the vistas, you walk on an easy path through rolling hills that will make you want to sing songs from *Brigadoon*. But unlike that legendary place, Russian Ridge doesn't just appear once every 100 years. Thanks to some smart buying on the part of the Midpeninsula Regional Open Space District, this preserve is a permanent fixture.

The Hawk Ridge Trail Loop provides you with some of the highlights of the preserve. After parking at the Cal Trans Vista Point, walk across Highway 35 and head straight (toward the ocean) on the main trail, which is a connector trail for Mindego Ridge Trail. Follow it downhill for three-tenths of a mile until you reach a trail sign for Alder Spring Trail and Hawk Ridge Trail. Turn right here and walk three-tenths of a mile until the trail splits—Alder Spring to your left and Hawk Ridge to your right. You may want to venture a short way on Alder Spring

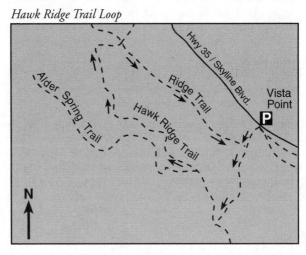

Hawk Ridge Trail Loop

Trail before you continue your loop on Hawk Ridge. The spring creates a lovely oasis of live oaks in the midst of wet grasses and profuse and pretty yellow wildflowers.

Follow the Hawk Ridge Trail for a mostly level half-mile. At the junction with Ridge Trail, turn right and hike through another half mile of bliss. On a clear day, your mind will be blown by expansive views all the way to the Pacific. If it's spring, you'll be charmed by colorful wildflowers and verdant grasslands. If it's summer or fall, you'll see the hillsides turned to gold, and watch the grasses sway in unison to the ridgetop winds.

Although many people visit this preserve for the views, Russian Ridge offers plenty more. Its acreage combines several plant environments, including lush grasslands, creeks, springs, and oak-shaded canyons. The area is ideal for wildlife, including a variety of raptors, coyotes, and mountain lions. What impressed me most here one April day were the wildflowers—I had never seen such an explosion of natural color, particularly poppies, goldfields, and blue-eyed grass. Later on I found out that this preserve is considered to be one of the five best places to see wildflowers in the entire Bay Area. Well, you won't get any argument from me.

There are only eight miles of trails at Russian Ridge, but all of them are delightful. You may share the trails with mountain bikers, but fear not; most of the paths are wide, and this place has a way of slowing everybody down.

Make it easier: Go out and back on Ridge Trail, the final leg of this loop, instead of descending to Hawk Ridge Trail. You'll still get the views but without any climb. Start at the main trailhead and walk only a few hundred yards until you come to a wide trail on your right, which is Ridge Trail. You can head out and back for a half mile each way.

Trip notes: There is no fee. The preserve is open from dawn until sunset. Free trail maps are available at the trailhead. For more information, contact the Midpeninsula Regional Open Space District, 330 Distel Circle, Los Altos, CA 94022; (650) 691-1200.

Directions: From Interstate 280 or U.S. 101 on the San Francisco Peninsula, take Highway 84 west through the mountains to Skyline Boulevard (Highway 35). Turn left on Highway 35 and drive 5.7 miles south to the CalTrans Vista Point parking area on your left. Park there, then cross the road to reach the trailhead. (The vista point is one mile north of the junction of Alpine Road, Page Mill Road, and Highway 35. The main entrance to Russian Ridge is located at this junction of roads.)

86. HORSESHOE LAKE LOOP
Skyline Ridge Open Space Preserve
Off Highway 35 in the Los Altos hills
1.5 miles round-trip — 45 minutes — rolling terrain

👫 ♿

Skyline Ridge Open Space Preserve is probably the most developed of all the Midpeninsula Regional Open Space preserves. It has a big entrance sign on Skyline Boulevard and three decent-sized parking lots, rather than meager dirt pullouts along the road. If your reason for hiking is to get away from it all, you might want to head somewhere else. But Skyline Ridge's Horseshoe Lake Trail is such a special little walk, I say come here anyway and check it out.

The preserve is easy to spot—it's located right next to a huge Christmas tree farm. (This explains why all those conifers are exactly the same size, and growing in such neat rows like good soldiers.) From the parking lot, you head out on the trail by the map and signboard, walking through fields of wildflowers to little Horseshoe Lake. Along the way, you'll cross a parking lot reserved for wheelchair-users so they can take a wheelchair-accessible trail to the lake.

The walk to the lake's western edge is only three-tenths of a mile. Once there, you can stay for a while and then head back for a half-mile walk, or make a loop around the lake for a 1.5-mile walk. Lots of people do the former—you'll see plenty of picnickers, families, and older folks who just show up for a short stroll to the lake. Benches are provided so you can sit and enjoy the scene. True to its name, the lake is horseshoe-shaped. It is nicely protected from the wind by ridges on the north and south side.

If you hike the loop, you'll connect to a trail that's open to bikers and equestrians for a quarter mile, then climb above the lake and wind up at yet another parking lot—this one for cars with horse trailers. From there, you have a hillside meadow walk (open to hikers only), which brings you back to the north side of the lake and then to the wheelchair-user parking lot. Simply retrace your steps back to your car.

Horseshoe Lake is particularly popular with families and children, because parents with baby strollers can maneuver the route and older children enjoy exploring the lake's shoreline and watching for wildlife. Numerous picnic tables are situated near the water. Because the trail is so short, you can leave the Power Bars at home and pack a real picnic.

The trail is also a good place to teach children about wildflowers.

Horseshoe Lake Loop, Skyline Ridge Open Space Preserve

Skyline Ridge has basically the same variety of plant life as nearby Russian Ridge and Long Ridge, but you can see more flowers in a shorter walk. Purple, vine-like spring vetch, orange California poppies, and dark blue lupine are most prevalent.

A hiking trip to Horseshoe Lake is not the solitary experience you get at other Midpeninsula Open Space preserves, but for many people, it's the perfect way to spend an afternoon. Almost no one wears hiking boots here; tennis shoes are the norm. If you just want a pretty walk and maybe a picnic or a conversation in a peaceful spot, the Horseshoe Lake Trail provides the perfect setting for it.

Make it easier: Take the Horseshoe Lake Trail out and back rather than looping around the lake.

Trip notes: There is no fee. The preserve is open from dawn until sunset. Free trail maps are available at the trailhead. For more information, contact Midpeninsula Regional Open Space District, 330 Distel Circle, Los Altos, CA 94022; (650) 691-1200.

Directions: From Interstate 280 or U.S. 101 on the San Francisco Peninsula, take Highway 84 west to Skyline Boulevard (Highway 35). Turn left on Highway 35 and drive 7.8 miles south to the Skyline Ridge parking area on the right. (From the South Bay, take Highway 9 west to the junction with Highway 35. Turn north on Highway 35 and drive 5.4 miles to the Skyline Ridge parking area on the left.) Park in the lot farthest to the right. Wheelchair users can follow the signs and park in the lot closer to the lake and the wheelchair-accessible trail.

87. PETER'S CREEK TRAIL & LONG RIDGE ROAD
Long Ridge Open Space Preserve
Off Highway 35 in the Los Altos hills
4 miles round-trip — 2 hours — rolling terrain

👭 🚶 🚲 🐎

Long Ridge is one of those special places in the outdoors that you might want to keep all to yourself. It's a peaceful 600-acre preserve along Skyline Boulevard on the San Francisco Peninsula, an area that is perfect in all seasons: Warm and windy in summer, covered with golden waves of grasses in fall, clear and crisp in winter, and almost overwhelmed by wildflowers in spring.

At the start, there's only one trail to follow at Long Ridge. It's a half-mile connector trail that leads downhill from the parking area into the preserve, where it joins with Peter's Creek Trail. Once you begin hiking, the sight and sound of Skyline Boulevard quickly disappears as the trail drops below the road and into a pristine canyon of grasslands and forest. All you see are fields of wildflowers and grasses close by and a forest of Douglas firs and oaks ahead. Many visitors just walk this short connector trail to the meadow, spread out a picnic, and head back home. In addition to being a pastoral spot, the meadow is the only place in Long Ridge Preserve where you can bring your dog; once you follow the trail into the forest, canines are *verboten.*

But you should keep on walking. Turn left on Peter's Creek Trail and start to climb gently uphill. Peter's Creek meanders along at your side. As you ascend, take a break to try an experiment: Stop for a few minutes, sit by the stream with your back against a big tree, close your eyes, and listen. See how many different sounds you can identify, and the wide range of tones you can hear. I tried this exercise, remembering it from elementary school days, and was amazed at what I was missing as I trudged along.

Bring your wildflower field guide with you if you are visiting between February and June. The variety of flower color and shape is amazing, from tiny two-eyed violets (heart-shaped leaves with white and purple flowers) to two-foot-tall dandelions. Look for pink hooker's onions with their long leafless stems, red-and-yellow columbine, pink wild roses, blue-eyed grass, white irises, poppies, lupine, and huge ceanothus bushes with sprays of blue flowers.

The trail wanders in and out of meadows and forest, passing a pretty little pond with huge reeds and a sea of horsetails growing near it. Finally you climb all the way to the top of the ridge and meet up

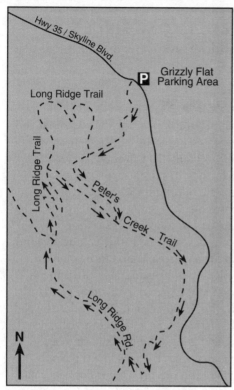

Peter's Creek Trail & Long Ridge Road

with Long Ridge Road, a wildflower-lined dirt road. You're now at 2,500 feet in elevation and have walked two miles. The expansive views from the ridge are your reward. Make a right turn on Long Ridge Road and wander along it, oohing and aahing at the views of neighboring Butano Ridge and the forests of Big Basin State Park.

At the signed border of the preserve, turn right again on to Long Ridge Trail, heading back into the trees. (Before you re-enter the forest, you might want to find a spot on the ridge for a picnic or a nap in the sun. The trip back is another two-plus miles.)

The only drawback to this preserve is that on some days, when the wind blows just right, you can hear the pow-pow-pow from the shooting range at the Los Altos Rod and Gun Club, and also the occasional whine of motorcycles speeding down Skyline Boulevard. Sound travels along the ridge.

You may share portions of your trip with mountain bikers or equestrians, but if that bothers you, wait until the rainy season to hike here, when the Open Space District closes the trails to everyone but hikers. Mountain bikers are usually only on the connector trail and Long Ridge Trail, anyway.

At the final trail junction, you can continue straight on Long Ridge Trail or go right to Peter's Creek Trail to return. Long Ridge Trail drops a little too abruptly and invites speeding mountain bikers, so I'd recommend heading back on Peter's Creek. With one last left turn on Peter's Creek Trail, you're back on the connector trail to the parking area.

Hiking down Long Ridge Road in Long Ridge Open Space Preserve

Make it easier: If you turn around and retrace your steps from Long Ridge Road instead of looping back, you can cut a half mile off your trip.

Trip notes: There is no fee. The preserve is open from dawn until sunset. Free trail maps are available at the trailhead. For more information, contact Midpeninsula Regional Open Space District, 330 Distel Circle, Los Altos, CA 94022; (650) 691-1200.

Directions: From Interstate 280 or U.S. 101 on the San Francisco Peninsula, take Highway 84 west to Skyline Boulevard (Highway 35). Turn left on Highway 35 and drive 10 miles south to the Long Ridge/Upper Stevens Creek County Park/Grizzly Flat parking area. (From the South Bay, take Highway 9 west to the junction with Highway 35. Turn north on Highway 35 and drive 3.2 miles to the Long Ridge/Upper Stevens Creek County Park/Grizzly Flat parking area.) The trail is on the west side of the road.

---

88. SKYLINE TRAIL to SUMMIT ROCK
Sanborn-Skyline County Park
Off Highway 35 near Saratoga Gap
0.8 mile round-trip — 30 minutes — mostly level terrain

Although there is another, more prominent entrance to Sanborn-Skyline County Park, the Summit Rock trailhead offers the shortest, prettiest walk possible to Summit Rock, which is the best lookout

---

around for viewing the South Bay. Why the best? Because Summit Rock is perched at 3,000 feet in elevation, high enough to get an occasional dusting of snow in winter, in a dramatic contrast to the flat—oh so flat—peninsula baylands below. From Summit Rock, you can see the Santa Clara Valley spread out below you in all its urban splendor.

In addition to the far-and-away views, you'll have a chance to see lots of action close up at Summit Rock. Local rock climbers use the steep east side of the rocky outcrop to practice their stuff. Anyone can hike up the western, back side of the rock—that's where this trail takes you—but the steep front side is reserved for those with ropes and harnesses. It's fascinating to sit on top of the rock and watch the climbers below inch their way up.

The Skyline Trail to Summit Rock leads through a pretty hardwood forest, filled with Douglas firs, oaks, California laurels, and madrones. As you walk on a dirt path lined with fir needles, you may find yourself having thoughts (or at least olfactory memories) of Christmas. To reach your destination, simply head out on the Skyline Trail, which is clearly signed to Summit Rock. When you come to a four-way intersection, turn left, toward the valley of the South Bay, and walk out of the forest and into an open area. A short climb up a steep dirt hill will put you right at the base of Summit Rock. From there you can climb up and around to find the best view.

There's one more bonus to hiking to Summit Rock from this

Enjoying the view from Summit Rock

trailhead. The alternate entrance to Sanborn-Skyline County Park is directly across the street from popular Castle Rock State Park, and it gets a ton of overflow traffic from Castle Rock. This trailhead gets less use, which guarantees you a peaceful walk.

Make it easier: This is the easiest trail to Summit Rock, but if you want views that are just as good with an even shorter walk, start at the Sanborn-Skyline County Park entrance across from Castle Rock State Park (one mile south of here) and take the quarter-mile walk to Indian Rock instead.

Trip notes: There is no fee. Park hours are 8 a.m. to dusk. For more information and a free map, contact Sanborn-Skyline County Park, 16055 Sanborn Road, Saratoga, CA 95070; (408) 867-9959.

Directions: From Interstate 280 or U.S. 101 on the San Francisco Peninsula, take Highway 84 west to Skyline Boulevard (Highway 35). Turn left on Highway 35 and drive 14.6 miles south, past Highway 9, to the Summit Rock parking area on the left. (From the South Bay, take Highway 9 west to the junction with Highway 35. Turn south on Highway 35 and drive 1.4 miles to the Summit Rock parking area on the left.) The trailhead starts on the south side of the parking lot.

---

89. SARATOGA GAP & RIDGE TRAIL LOOP
Castle Rock State Park
Off Highway 35 near Saratoga Gap
5 miles round-trip — 2.5 hours — some steep terrain

Hello, hikers, and welcome to Swiss Cheese State Park. Oops, that's Castle Rock State Park, of course, but all those holey rocks look more like *fromage* than *châteaus*. Call it what you like; Castle Rock is one of the most surprising and spectacular parks in the entire San Francisco Bay Area.

Why surprising? In less than five miles of easy hiking, you get to see a 50-foot waterfall in winter and spring, gaze at miles of Santa Cruz Mountains wildlands, and explore several large sandstone formations, including the local rock climbers' favorite, Goat Rock.

From the parking lot, head right on the Saratoga Gap Trail. The pleasure begins immediately as you travel gently downhill, walking alongside a gurgling creek through a mixed forest of Douglas firs, black oaks, and madrones. It's a mere eight-tenths of a mile to Castle Rock Falls. In about 15 minutes of walking, you find yourself standing on a wooden viewing deck almost directly on top of the gushing cataract (in the wet season), with a delightful view of the forested canyon below.

Seems pretty good, right? Keep going; there's more. Continue on Saratoga Gap Trail beyond the falls for another 1.8 miles. When you intersect with Ridge Trail, turn right. You'll notice that the scenery transitions from a shady forest canopy to an exposed chaparral ridge with views all the way out to Monterey Bay and the Pacific Ocean. Spring and summer showcase bright yellow Scotch broom, orange bush monkeyflower, and other sun-loving flowers along this trail section, plus purple Douglas iris in shadier areas. In any season, as you travel you'll notice an ever increasing number of sandstone slabs, hollowed and sculpted by wind erosion. In some places, the sandstone becomes the trail surface. You'll have to scramble over a few small boulders to continue on your way.

When you reach the spur trail for Goat Rock, take it. You will only stray a quarter mile off your loop route, and Goat Rock is worth the effort. You may see rock climbers strutting their stuff on the steep front side of the rock, but the back side is easily accessible by plain old ordinary hikers. Park officials encourage hikers to take the vista point spur next to Goat Rock instead of climbing on the rock itself, and with good reason—Goat Rock is quite steep. But if you're sure-footed and cautious, the smooth back side of Goat Rock is a great place to have a picnic lunch, examine some of the sandstone's Swiss-cheese-style crevices, enjoy the view of the San Lorenzo Valley and the Pacific Ocean, and maybe take a little siesta. I took a cue from the many lizards I saw and did a little sunbathing.

Your loop finishes out on Ridge Trail, which roughly parallels Saratoga Gap Trail but at a higher elevation, and offers even broader

Saratoga Gap Trail/Ridge Trail Loop, Castle Rock State Park

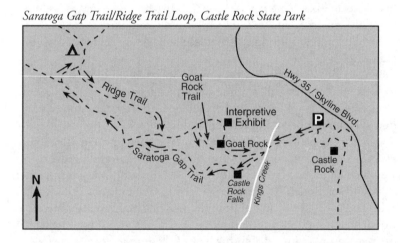

views. Ridge Trail eventually connects back with Saratoga Gap Trail. Turn left and make a short, four-tenths-of-a-mile climb back up the creek canyon to the trailhead and your car.

Make it easier: Just walk the 1.6-mile round-trip on Saratoga Gap Trail to Castle Rock Falls. Then hike out and back from the parking area to Castle Rock, the park's namesake 40-foot sandstone formation. This will add another one mile round-trip.

Trip notes: A $3 state park day-use fee is charged by Castle Rock State Park. A trail map/brochure is available at the trailhead for 50 cents. For more information, contact Castle Rock State Park, 15000 Skyline Boulevard, Los Gatos, CA 95020; (408) 867-2952 or (831) 429-2851.

Directions: From Interstate 280 or U.S. 101 on the San Francisco Peninsula, take Highway 84 west to Skyline Boulevard (Highway 35). Turn left on Highway 35 and drive 15.7 miles south, past Highway 9, to the Castle Rock State Park parking area on your right. (From the South Bay, take Highway 9 west to the junction with Highway 35. Turn south on Highway 35 and drive 2.5 miles to the Castle Rock State Park parking area.) The trailhead is on the west side of the parking lot, opposite the entrance.

---

90. SEQUOIA AUDUBON TRAIL
Pescadero Marsh Natural Preserve
Off Highway 1 near Pescadero State Beach
2 miles round-trip — 1 hour — mostly level terrain

There's only one prerequisite to enjoying a spring hike in Pescadero Marsh Natural Preserve: Make sure you wear long pants and long sleeves. Pescadero happens to be the tick capital of the world, and it may also be one of California's greatest natural greenhouses for poison oak.

Sounds like you want to stay home instead? Don't make that mistake. The preserve at Pescadero is one of the best places for level, easy hiking on the Northern California coast. It's a 600-acre natural marsh, the largest one between San Francisco and Monterey Bay. A veritable jungle of wetlands and coastal foliage, the marsh attracts more than 200 species of birds, as well as numerous mammals and amphibians.

Almost everyone who comes to Pescadero Marsh gets rewarded with wildlife sightings. On one trip, we saw two deer on the trail, half a dozen bullfrogs under a little bridge by the creek, one large turtle, scads of minnows and water bugs, plus birds galore: ducks, great egrets, redwing blackbirds, swallows, and four great blue herons doing a little fishing.

If that's not enough wildlife for you, you might see steelhead trout swimming up Pescadero Creek in late winter to spawn, or the rare endangered San Francisco garter snake slithering along the path. Animals just plain like it here.

The preserve's Sequoia Audubon Trail is soft sand at the start, which is a bit hard to walk on, but shortly turns to hard earth as it moves away from the ocean and heads inland. You'll notice that the ground heats up as you get away from the coastal winds and move into thick vegetation. Spring and summer wildflowers bloom along the trail, including coastal paintbrush, nonnative purple and yellow ice plant, and yellow bush lupine. A couple of gnarled, low-lying eucalyptus trees also grow along the path.

The far end of Sequoia Audubon Trail climbs above the marsh to a viewing area, where a bench affords you a vista of the entire wetlands and the ocean beyond, one mile away. An interpretive sign identifies different types of hawks, kites, and owls—birds of prey you may see soaring above you, if you're lucky.

At one time a short loop trail led from this viewing bench back to the main trail, but it is terribly overgrown with poison oak. Don't try to take it—just head back the way you came.

Of the three trails at Pescadero Marsh, I like Sequoia Audubon Trail the best because it travels right up Pescadero Creek, one mile up and one mile back, giving you the best chance at seeing wildlife. If you wish to extend your hike, the trail connects to North Pond Trail, which will add another two miles to your trip, but North Pond is open only during the fall and winter months because of the breeding season of resident birds.

A side trip that's a "must" is a little coastal walk along Pescadero's rocky beaches, starting from anywhere near where you parked your car. The coastline has long sandy stretches, interesting rock formations, tidepools, and plenty of harbor seals lounging around on the rocks.

Make it more challenging: Add on a hike on one of the two other trails in the preserve. They are detailed on posted trail map signs.

Trip notes: There is no fee. The marsh is open from 8 A.M. to sunset. For more information, contact California State Parks, Bay Area District, 250 Executive Park Boulevard, Suite 4900, San Francisco, CA 94134; (415) 330-6300.

Directions: From San Francisco, drive approximately 40 miles south on Highway 1 to its intersection with Pescadero Road, near Pescadero

State Beach. Park in the first parking lot south of the Highway 1 bridge over Pescadero Creek, on the ocean side of the highway. Walk to the north side of the bridge (there is a pedestrian walkway on the west side), then take the trail underneath the bridge and continue up the canyon.

91. DAVENPORT BEACH WALK
City of Davenport
Off Highway 1 in Davenport
2 miles round-trip — 1 hour — mostly level terrain

Many beaches in Northern California are spectacular, but some beaches are a cut above. Davenport Beach is one of them. The beach is usually sunny, not foggy, it is typically uncrowded, and it graciously provides its admirers with a fine hike along coastal bluffs and then down a rocky staircase to the sand. From the water's edge, you can walk to the north to visit sea caves at low tide, or south to an ocean-bound stream that carves a sculpted canyon through the bluffs.

Start the hike from the parking area across from the Davenport Post Office, right by the flashing yellow light that warns drivers on Highway 1 to slow down as they cruise through town. Cross the railroad tracks, then look to your left to pick up the trail again (about 15 feet away). Then simply walk along the oceanside bluff, paralleling the beach.

The bluff is a classic example of a wave-cut terrace. It's the result of this part of the coast rising and jolting upward from geological activity. Have no fear, though—the process happens slowly, over the course of several hundred thousand years. The story of a wave-cut terrace goes something like this: Eons ago, as a warming climate melted glaciers, the sea rose and cut into the land mass. This created beaches and bluffs that grew larger as sand and gravel were washed down them. Subsequent geologic activity moved the earth's plates, lifting the beaches to form seaside terraces. The nonstop action of waves and wind sculpts and erodes the terraces. Even now, new terraces are being formed under water. As the coastline continues to rise, the bluffs will continue to change.

Besides being ancient geological wonders, the grass-topped bluffs provide exposed, windblown habitat for coastal wildflowers, including Indian paintbrush, wild strawberry, coast lupine, and monkeyflower. Even if the flowers aren't blooming, there is plenty to admire from this perch above the sea. The carved-out rocks along the shore and the

Davenport Beach

continual crashing of the waves will compete for your attention.

Head south along the bluffs for a little more than a quarter mile until you reach the chalky sandstone cliffs that have eroded into a wide natural staircase to the beach. Descend to the sand and walk to the south side of the cove, where you can hike up and around a high-walled streambed that carries runoff from the hills to the sea, or examine the eroding cliffs that drop right to the water's edge.

If the tide is low, walk to the north end of the beach, where you'll find sea caves carved deep into the wave-cut terraces. Some extend back into the land mass farther than your eyes can see in the darkness. The sandstone and mudstone of the terraces erodes in little carved pockets, which create a rippled effect on the rock. It's like a miniaturized surface of the moon.

The wind is almost always blowing on the Davenport coast, so come prepared for it. In summer, this is often a great beach for sun-bathing and swimming, but you're likely to need warmer clothes for hiking on the windswept bluffs.

Make it easier: Just hike along the bluffs and back, without descending to the beach, for a mile-long hike.

Trip notes: There is no fee or managing agency for this beach. For food and lodging in Davenport, contact the Davenport Cash Store/Bed and Breakfast Inn, (831) 426-4122.

Directions: From Santa Cruz, drive north on Highway 1 for 11 miles to the yellow flashing light in Davenport. Turn left at the light into the dirt parking area (across from the post office and Ocean Street). The trail starts at the north end of the parking lot.

92. OLD LANDING COVE TRAIL
Wilder Ranch State Park
Off Highway 1 near Santa Cruz
2.5 miles round-trip — 1.5 hours — mostly level terrain

🚶 🚴

Wilder Ranch State Park is a favorite park of mountain bikers, and often what bikers find appealing, hikers don't. Bikers like long fire roads that go forever so they can pedal to their heart's content; hikers like narrow paths that lead to a stellar destination in not too many miles. Bikers like the wide-open road; hikers like the meandering trail.

The good news is that Wilder Ranch has trails that are good for both parties. The park is large enough to have a variety of paths, plus plenty of room for everybody. Most riders stick to the inland side of the park, across Highway 1, where the fire roads crisscross the grassy hillsides. If hikers stay on the ocean side of the park, they don't have to fear being mowed down by speeding mountain bicyclists. And luckily, on the ocean side of the park lies the Old Landing Cove Trail, a gem of a coastal walk that offers several great surprises, including a seal rookery, some spectacular beaches, and a hidden fern cave.

Old Landing Cove Trail

The Old Landing Cove Trail starts from the parking lot, at a sign that simply reads "Nature Trail." Begin walking on a level dirt road through the park's agricultural preserve of brussels sprouts fields. Yes, it's true, Wilder Ranch's biggest claim to fame is not its historic ranch buildings, nor its excellent trail system, nor its spectacular beaches and coastal vistas. It's the fact that 12 percent of our national brussels sprouts production happens right here within the park's boundaries. One question: Who's eating all of them, anyway?

Follow the trail toward the coast, then turn right and head out along the sandstone and mudstone bluffs. The first beach you'll reach, Wilder Beach, is a critical habitat area for the endangered snowy plover and is fenced off and protected as a natural preserve.

No matter; there are plenty of other beaches to explore. In another eighth of a mile you'll come to the trail's namesake, the old landing cove. The cove is a remarkably narrow inlet where small schooners pulled in to anchor and load lumber in the late 1800s. Sizing up the limited cove, you gotta think: Those guys sure must have known how to steer.

Just off Old Landing Cove is a huge flat rock where harbor seals hang out, laying around in the sun all day to keep their flippers warm.

Inside the fern cave in Wilder Ranch State Park

You can't get a good look at the seals on the rock until you walk past the Old Landing Cove and turn around, which means your best view of the seals comes on your return trip.

For now, keep walking along the blufftops. The highlight of this hike is the descent to the beach to see Wilder Ranch's fern cave, the oceanside home of a collection of bracken and sword ferns. They hang from the small cave's ceiling just low enough to tickle the top of your head. The fern cave is hidden in the back of a U-shaped cove, but the trick is that it's almost impossible to know which cove is the right one. (The spur trail to the beach can be difficult to spot.) Here's the key to finding the fern cave: The Old Landing Cove Trail is a numbered interpretive trail, so keep your eyes peeled for post number 8. A few yards beyond it is the cove with the fern cave; a narrow spur trail leads down to it. (Another way to know you're in the right spot is to look back toward the park entrance; you should be directly across from the California and United States flags that fly over the entrance kiosk.)

Because it's located in the back of the cove, the fern cave is partially protected from the salty ocean air. An underground spring gives the ferns life and keeps them moist and cool. The floor of the cave is covered in driftwood that has been collected from the sea by the constant motion of the tide.

After exploring and admiring the sea cave, return to the top of the bluffs and the Old Landing Cove Trail. Walk a quarter mile farther north, heading to the next beach cove. This one has a wider and more visible trail leading down to it, and it features a perfect crescent-shaped strip of sand—the ideal place to have a picnic lunch or sit and watch the waves come in.

Make it easier: You can just cut this hike short and skip the descent to the beach coves.

Trip notes: A $6 day-use fee is charged by Wilder Ranch State Park. A map is available for free from the entrance kiosk. For more information, contact Wilder Ranch State Park, 1401 Old Coast Road, Santa Cruz, CA 95060; (831) 423-9703.

Directions: From Santa Cruz, drive north on Highway 1 for four miles. Turn left into the entrance to Wilder Ranch State Park, then follow the park road to its end and park in the main parking area. Take the trail marked "Nature Trail" from the southwest side of the parking lot.

93. SEQUOIA TRAIL
Big Basin Redwoods State Park
Off Highway 9 near Felton
3.6 miles round-trip — 1.5 hours — rolling terrain

Sure, everybody knows that Berry Creek Falls is the prime destination of hikers in Big Basin Redwoods State Park. The catch is that it takes four to six hours to make the round-trip hike, covering about nine miles with a lot of up-and-down in between. But what everybody doesn't know is that there's another pretty waterfall in Big Basin, and you can get to it in less than two miles of nearly level hiking from park headquarters.

Sempervirens Falls is a waterfall that anyone can hike to, even small children with their parents. The Sequoia Trail takes you there in 1.8 miles. After you see it, you can just turn around and hike back (for a round-trip of 3.6 miles) or you can make a longer loop trip out of it by returning on the Shadowbrook Trail (for a round-trip of five miles).

The best time to visit is after winter or early spring rains. The wet season turns Sempervirens Falls into a gushing 25-foot-tall cascade of water, about four feet wide at the top, with two miniature cascades flowing into it from above. The waterfall is perfectly framed by fallen redwood trees on either side and a large clear pool at its base.

Even if the waterfall is not flowing hard when you visit, the trail that leads to it is still a delightful journey into a redwood world. The big trees, which reach more than 300 feet tall in Big Basin, never fail to take your breath away, no matter how many times you've seen them.

Sequoia Trail, Big Basin Redwoods State Park

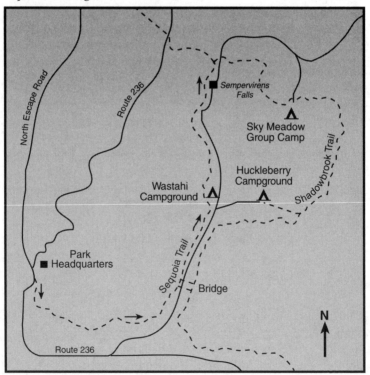

South San Francisco Bay Area

Mixed in with the redwoods are Douglas fir, tan oak, and California laurel, as well as thousands upon thousands of ferns lining the forest floor. Springtime brings wild ginger, trillium, and azalea blooms.

To get started, follow the Sequoia Trail from park headquarters. You don't even need to remember the trail's name, because all the trail markers read "Sempervirens Falls" on your way out and "Park Headquarters" on your way back. What could be easier than that?

Portions of the Sequoia Trail are routed near a park road, but it gets little traffic and shouldn't disturb your hike. Most of the time, you won't even notice it's there, and no wonder—the forest surrounding you is certain to keep your attention.

A nice feature of this hike is its convenient location to park campgrounds. If you are staying at Sky Meadow Group Camp, Wastahi Campground, or Huckleberry Campground, you can access the falls directly from your campground by either the Sequoia or Shadowbrook trails, rather than driving and parking at park headquarters.

Make it easier: If you head to the falls from Sky Meadow Group Camp, Wastahi Campground, or Huckleberry Campground, Sempervirens Falls is only a half mile to one mile away, making for an even shorter trip.

Trip notes: A $6 state park day-use fee is charged at Big Basin Redwoods State Park. A trail map is available at park headquarters for $1. For more information, contact Big Basin Redwoods State Park, 21600 Big Basin Way, Boulder Creek, CA 95006; (831) 338-8860 or (831) 429-2851.

Directions: From Santa Cruz, take Highway 9 north and drive approximately 12 miles to Boulder Creek. At Boulder Creek, turn left on Highway 236. Follow it for about 10 miles to Big Basin Redwoods State Park Headquarters. Park in the lot across from park headquarters, then walk back toward the headquarters building. The trailhead is located to the right of the building near the 15-minute parking spots.

94. LOCH TRAIL
Loch Lomond Recreation Area
Off Highway 9 near Felton
2 to 5 miles round-trip — 1 to 2 hours — rolling terrain

Every summer when I was a kid, my parents took my sisters and I hiking and fishing at a big lake surrounded by a beautiful forest. We'd explore around the lake, learn about the trees and plants that grew there, watch for wildlife, and go trolling in our little motor boat. Mostly we'd cruise near the shoreline in the hopes of catching some fish. We'd always take a break at midday, pull up our boat on an island on the lake, sit on a rock, and eat some sandwiches. Then we'd hike in the woods some more, or just sit on the shoreline and admire the scenery.

As an adult, I never thought I'd find any place in urban California to match that lake of my memories. I thought that in order to take a hike near a peaceful, pretty lake, I'd have to travel far from the hustle and bustle of northern California's cities. But then I went to Loch Lomond Reservoir, just 10 miles north of Santa Cruz, and found out what I'd been missing.

The Loch Trail at Loch Lomond Recreation Area follows the shoreline of a large, deep blue reservoir through a Douglas fir and redwood forest. After a pleasant mile along the water's edge, the trail connects with a fire road (Highland Trail) that climbs up and around the hillside above the lake. More ambitious hikers will want to follow the latter and make a loop out of the hike. Less ambitious hikers will think the first mile is just fine. It's a level, easy, out-and-back hike from the boat launch ramp and park store.

The distance you hike is up to you; just follow the trail as far as you wish along the lake. You might stop to drop a line in the water or picnic at one of the many shaded tables near the shoreline, or you might just meander along, admiring the pretty lake as you walk. If you turn around before the trail starts to head seriously uphill, you'll have a two-mile round-trip. Go as far as Fir Cove, a little sandy inlet where a stream pours down from the hills into the lake. If you're in the mood for a longer trip, you can follow the trail until it connects with Highland Trail, then take Highland Trail uphill to a great view of the lake. You can make a five-mile loop by hiking back downhill on either the trail or the paved park road.

If the good hiking isn't enough to motivate you, here's the final selling point for Loch Lomond Reservoir: When you visit, not only do you get to take a peaceful lakeside stroll, but you can even rent a little motor boat, do some fishing for trout, bass, or bluegill, and then pull up your boat on the lake's island and have a picnic.

Pack up the peanut butter and jelly and the Audubon field guides—suddenly I feel like I'm 12 years old again.

Make it more challenging: Follow Loch Trail for 1.5 miles to its junction with Highland Trail. Take Highland Trail uphill, then loop back downhill on the park road for a five-mile round-trip.

Trip notes: A $3 entrance fee is charged at Loch Lomond. Check your calendar before you go: Loch Lomond Recreation Area is open only from

March 1 through September 15. Park hours are 6 a.m. to sunset. A free trail map/park brochure is available at the park entrance. For more information, contact Loch Lomond Recreation Area, 100 Loch Lomond Way, Felton, CA 95018; (831) 335-7424.

Directions: From Santa Cruz, take Highway 9 north and drive approximately seven miles to Felton. At Felton, turn right on Graham Hill Road and drive a half mile, then turn left on Zayante Road and drive 2.5 miles to Lompico Road. Turn left again and drive 1.5 miles to West Drive. Turn left one more time and drive to Sequoia Road, then enter the park. (The route is well signed for Loch Lomond Recreation Area.) Follow the park road all the way to the lake and park as close as possible to the boat ramp and park store. The trailhead for the Loch Trail begins by the boat ramp, right at the water's edge.

---

95. WATERFALL LOOP TRAIL
Uvas Canyon County Park
Off U.S. 101 near Morgan Hill
3.5 miles round-trip — 2 hours — mostly level terrain

Uvas Canyon County Park is a little slice of waterfall heaven on the east side of the Santa Cruz Mountains. Although the drive to reach it is a long journey from the freeway through grasslands and oaks, it leads you to a surprising redwood forest at the park entrance. Suddenly, you've entered another world.

Uvas Canyon is a small park, offering camping and picnicking facilities and a short stretch of hiking trails in its 1,200 acres, but it's living proof that good things come in small packages. You can walk the one-mile Waterfall Loop Trail and see Black Rock Falls and several smaller cascades on Swanson Creek, or you can add on an eighth-mile side trip to see Basin Falls and Upper Falls. If you're in the mood to stretch your legs, you can make a larger loop out to Alec Canyon, then take the uphill trail a half-mile to Triple Falls on Alec Creek.

The park has enough waterfalls to make any waterfall-lover happy. Just make sure you show up in the rainy season, because that's when Uvas Canyon is at its best. Water seems to pour from every crack in the hillsides. The canyon is filled with oaks, laurels, and Douglas firs, all thriving in the wet environment around Swanson Creek.

Start your trip at the Black Oak Group Picnic Area by the gated dirt road. Head straight (not uphill on the road) to connect to the short loop trail in the canyon. Cross Swanson Creek on a footbridge, then

---

bear right at the fork and head directly for Black Rock Falls, a quarter-mile away. You'll find the waterfall on your right, pouring 30 feet down a side canyon over—you guessed it—black rock. Take a few pictures, then continue on the trail, heading for Basin Falls. This waterfall is 20 feet high and surrounded by moss-covered rocks. It makes a lovely S-curve at it carves its way downcanyon. Next you'll reach Upper Falls, a little smaller in height but just as beautiful as the other falls.

At Upper Falls, it's decision time: Either head back and take the other side of the Waterfall Loop Trail for a short and level trip, or continue up Swanson Creek and follow the winding Contour Trail to Alec Canyon and Triple Falls. The latter adds 2.5 miles and a good hill climb to your mileage. If you're heading for Triple Falls, follow the Contour Trail until it meets up with Alec Canyon Fire Road. Turn right and hike a half-mile to Manzanita Point, where you get far-reaching views on clear days. Then turn right again on the spur trail to Triple Falls. True to its name, Triple Falls is a series of three cascades, totalling 40 feet in height. You can climb off-trail and sit right alongside the cascading fall, and maybe munch on a sandwich and think about how great it is to be alive. Then make a short return trip by following the fire road back to Black Oak Picnic Area, a steep three-quarter mile descent.

So which waterfall at Uvas Park is the best? Uvas Canyon's rangers say that if you're only going to see one cataract in the park, see Upper Falls, which is the widest of the bunch. My favorite was Basin Falls. My hiking partner's favorite was Triple Falls. Your favorite? Better go see them all and decide.

Make it easier: Skip the side trip along the Contour Trail to see Alec Canyon and Triple Falls; just stick to the short and easy Waterfall Loop for a one-mile round-trip.

Trip notes: There is no fee. Free maps are available at the park visitor center. For more information, contact Uvas Canyon County Park, 8515 Croy Road, Morgan Hill, CA 95037; (408) 779-9232.

Directions: From San Jose, take U.S. 101 south and exit at Bernal. At the stoplight, turn right, then right again, to access Monterey Highway. Turn left (south) on Monterey Highway. Turn right on Bailey Avenue and drive 2.8 miles to McKean Road. Turn left on McKean Road and drive six miles (McKean Road becomes Uvas Road). Turn right on Croy Road and drive 4.5 miles to the park (continue past Sveadal, a private camp/resort). Park near park headquarters or in one of the picnic area parking lots. The trailhead is the gated dirt road at Black Oak Picnic Area.

Yosemite &
Mammoth Lakes

(For locations of trails, see map on page 8.)

96. MERCED GROVE
Yosemite National Park
Off Highway 120 in Yosemite
3 miles round-trip — 1.5 hours — rolling terrain

🚶🚶

There are three giant Sequoia groves in Yosemite National Park—Merced, Tuolumne, and Mariposa. Because the Merced Grove is tucked into a western corner of the park and is the smallest of the groves, it is the least visited and most peaceful. Generally the Merced Grove only gets traffic from people who enter Yosemite at the Big Oak Flat entrance station, then drive by it on their way to Yosemite Valley. It's a fine place to go for an easy walk through a lovely mixed forest, and of course, to be awed by the big Sequoias. Think of this as a simple, beautiful nature walk, perfect on any day, in any season.

The hiking trail is a closed-off dirt road that was Yosemite's first carriage road. It makes for good cross-country skiing in winter. The trail is level for the first half-mile until it reaches a junction. Take the left fork and head downhill through a mixed forest of white firs, incense cedars, ponderosa pines, and sugar pines. Azaleas bloom in early summer beneath the conifers' branches.

You reach the beginning of the small Sequoia grove at 1.5 miles. First you see a group of six Sequoias along the trail to your right. They're not record-breaking trees, but they're certainly impressive in size. Walk a few more feet down the trail and you spot two more big trees on the left and one on the right—they're getting bigger as you go. A total of only 20 Sequoias are found in this grove, but because they grow extremely close together, they make a stately impression.

The Sequoias in the Merced Grove were "discovered" in 1833 by the Walker party, a group of explorers headed by Joseph Walker who were looking for the best route through the Sierra Nevada. Most likely, local Indian tribes had long known about the location of the big trees.

The largest, granddaddy Sequoias of the grove are found directly across the road from a handsome old log cabin. The cabin was originally built as a retreat for the park superintendent, but it is no longer used. Have a seat near the largest trees, pull a sandwich from your pack, and stay a while. For your return, simply retrace your steps from the cabin, hiking back uphill.

Make it more challenging: You can hike further, beyond the cabin, but the trail becomes more overgrown and obstacle-ridden with fallen trees.

Another option would be to combine this hike with a trip to the Tuolumne Grove of giant Sequoias, located a few miles away at Crane Flat.

Trip notes: There is a $20 day-use fee for entrance into Yosemite National Park. Keep your receipt because the fee is good for seven days. Park maps are available for free at the entrance kiosk. For more information, contact Yosemite National Park Public Information Office, P.O. Box 577, Yosemite National Park, CA 95389; (209) 372-0200.

Directions: From the Arch Rock entrance station at Yosemite National Park, drive east into the park for 4.5 miles to the turnoff for Tioga Road/Highway 120, which is Big Oak Flat Road. Turn left and drive 13.5 miles (past the Tioga Road/Highway 120 turnoff) to the Merced Grove parking area on the left.

Alternatively, from the Big Oak Flat entrance station on Highway 120, drive south into the park on Big Oak Flat Road for 4.3 miles to reach the Merced Grove on your right.

97. LUKENS LAKE TRAIL
Yosemite National Park
Off Highway 120 in Yosemite
1.5 miles round-trip — 1 hour — rolling terrain

The Lukens Lake Trail is the perfect introductory lake hike for families in Yosemite National Park. It has all the best features of a long backpacking trip to a remote alpine area, without the long miles, steep hills, and heavy weight to carry. Anyone can do it, and everyone will have a good time.

As you head out of the Yosemite Valley floor and up Tioga Road, the trailhead parking area for Lukens Lake is one of the first you'll reach. If you've been cruising around the valley, your body has become accustomed to a 4,000-foot elevation, but Lukens Lake is set at more than 8,000 feet. This can take some getting used to—don't be surprised if you're huffing and puffing a little more than you'd expect as you hike uphill. Fortunately, the trail to the lake is only three-quarters of a mile long and gains only 200 feet in elevation, so your body gets a chance to adapt to its new heights without much of a strain on your cardiovascular system.

After parking at the Lukens Lake pullout, cross the road to reach the trailhead. The wide trail climbs gently through a red fir forest for a half mile until it reaches a saddle, where it descends to the lake in another quarter mile. If this is your first hike on Tioga Road, you'll notice many differences in this forest environment from others at lower elevations. The red firs, with their red-brown, deeply ingrained bark, look a little like ponderosa pines but are more red in color and have distinctive needles and cones. While ponderosa pines grow at about 4,000 feet in elevation, red firs prefer areas of heavy winter snowfall, between 7,000 and 8,000 feet in elevation, where the soil is well-drained. They grow to be very large (more than 150 feet tall) and cluster in thick stands, making it nearly impossible for other plants to grow near or around them.

At this high elevation, you may find patches of snow along the trail and in the shady forest until late in July. This part of Yosemite can get 40 feet of snow per year, which doesn't melt quickly. The trail to Lukens Lake is one of those great Sierra trails where you may find yourself making snowballs while wearing shorts and a T-shirt. One early summer, I "skied" parts of this trail in my hiking boots—just perched myself on top of a downhill patch of snow and let 'er rip. Kids love doing this—big kids, too.

Lukens Lake is surrounded by a large and beautiful meadow, filled with mountain wildflowers such as shooting stars and bluebells. Soon after snowmelt, I found huge emerald-green corn lilies growing in five inches of water. The meadow can be totally flooded until midsummer, its shallow waters shimmering in the afternoon sun. If it's dry enough, you can cross the meadow and continue on the trail to the far side of the lake, where there are good picnic spots.

The trail continues from the back side of Lukens Lake to White Wolf Campground and then all the way to Ten Lakes and the Grand Canyon of the Tuolumne River, but your best bet is to stay right where you are. Sit by Lukens Lake for a while, enjoy the blue water and the deep green meadow, and then head back the way you came.

Make it easier: Take it slow if you're just getting used to the elevation.

Trip notes: There is a $20 day-use fee for entrance into Yosemite National Park. Keep your receipt because the fee is good for seven days. Park maps are available for free at the entrance kiosk. For more information, contact Yosemite National Park Public Information Office, P.O. Box 577, Yosemite National Park, CA 95389; (209) 372-0200.

Directions: From Merced, drive 70 miles northeast on Highway 140 to Yosemite National Park. Enter Yosemite at the Arch Rock entrance station, then drive 4.5 miles and turn west (left) on Big Oak Flat Road (signed for Highway 120). Drive 9.3 miles, then turn right on Tioga Road/Highway 120. Drive 16.3 miles on Tioga Road, past the entrance to White Wolf Campground, to the trailhead for Lukens Lake. Park in the turnout on the right side of the road, then cross the road to reach the trailhead.

98. TENAYA LAKE TRAIL
Yosemite National Park
Off Highway 120 in Yosemite
2 miles round-trip — 1 hour — mostly level terrain

Tenaya Lake is the big, beautiful lake you see right alongside the highway as you drive up Tioga Pass Road on your way to or from Tuolumne Meadows in Yosemite. It's set in a giant rock basin, rimmed by high, polished granite, and covers more than 150 surface acres. You can't help but notice it as you drive by. Almost no one can resist a stop to gaze at it, snap a few pictures, or picnic along its shores.

For all its spectacular beauty, the lake has a grim history. In the 1850s, members of the Ahwahneeche tribe, natives to the Yosemite Valley, fled here to avoid persecution by the federal government, who was sending soldiers to round up the Yosemite Indians and "resettle" them on reservations. The Ahwahneeches and their chief, Teneiya, were captured at Lake Tenaya and resettled on the Fresno River. Even there, angry whites continued to persecute them, seeking vigilante justice for alleged Indian crimes. Chief Teneiya died in 1853, and this lake was named for him. The Ahwahneeches had their own name for it: Pyweack, or Lake of Shining Rocks—a name well-earned by all the polished granite framing the water.

View from the picnic area at Tenaya Lake

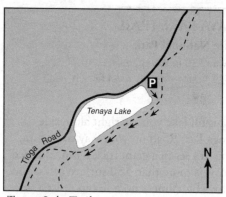

Tenaya Lake Trail

The level walk around the back side of the lake is a breeze, though you may have to wait for the snow to melt and the excess snowmelt to drain off. After a hard winter, the lake's picnic area and beach can be submerged under water until July.

The official trailhead is located at what used to be Tenaya Lake Campground, on the far east side of the lake. The camp was closed in 1992 because of environmental damage to the nearby meadow, but you can still park at its entrance (now a picnic area). Follow the trail from the parking lot to the picnic area to reach the lake's beach and the start of the trail.

When you get to the beach, you won't readily see the trail, which leads along the back side of the lake (away from the road). Take this as good news; the picnic area and beach are usually crowded with people, but few of them know about this trail. To access it, walk along the sand (to your left) to the end of the beach, where the south side of the lake is completely forested. You'll have to rock-hop across a small, shallow stream, or wade in to Tenaya Lake, to get there. At the intersection of beach and forest, you'll see the trail coming in from the east (it leads all the way from Tuolumne Meadows), and heading slightly uphill behind the lake. Take it—this is your ticket to your own private spot on popular Tenaya Lake.

The path meanders along, paralleling the lakeshore for its entire distance, then continues past the lake to Olmsted Point and beyond. You can hike as far as you wish and then turn around, although the best parts of the trail are in the first half-mile or so from the beach, before you reach the west end of the lake. The forest is very dense and lush, with plentiful wildflowers growing in the understory of Douglas firs, spruce, hemlocks, and pines. Several big rocks along the trail make perfect spots to sit and look out over the lake. While I took advantage of one of these rocky seats, five grebes floated by me, bobbing in the lake's light afternoon breeze.

On your return to the sandy beach, you may want to stay and hang out for a while. Tenaya Lake's strip of gorgeous white sand is ideal for picnickers or sun-lovers. Kids like to wade in to the cold lake water.

Adults focus their binoculars on 9,810-foot Polly Dome, that huge chunk of granite across the road from the lake, a favorite rock-climbing site. The daredevils on the dome can really grab your attention.

Don't bother bringing your fishing rod to Tenaya Lake. Although the lake was once stocked, park officials long ago stopped all fish plants in Yosemite's lakes, in an effort to keep the park in its natural state. Clearly not everyone is aware of this; on several trips, I've seen people sitting in lawn chairs with fishing lines in the water, hoping for something to happen. If only they knew, they would reel in their lures and go for this pretty lakeside walk instead.

Make it more challenging: Continue hiking beyond the lake's western edge, following the trail as far as you wish.

Trip notes: There is a $20 day-use fee for entrance into Yosemite National Park. Keep your receipt because the fee is good for seven days. Park maps are available for free at the entrance kiosk. For more information, contact Yosemite National Park Public Information Office, P.O. Box 577, Yosemite National Park, CA 95389; (209) 372-0200.

Directions: From Merced, drive 70 miles northeast on Highway 140 to Yosemite National Park. Enter Yosemite at the Arch Rock entrance station, then drive 4.5 miles and turn west (left) on Big Oak Flat Road (signed for Highway 120). Drive 9.3 miles, then turn right on Tioga Road/Highway 120. Drive 16.3 miles on Tioga Road, to the farthest (eastern) edge of Tenaya Lake. Park in the picnic area; the trailhead is located by the parking lot. (There is another Tenaya Lake picnic area a half-mile west of this one; make sure you drive all the way to the picnic area on the far east side of the lake.)

99. DOG LAKE TRAIL
Yosemite National Park
Off Highway 120 near Tuolumne Meadows
3.4 miles round-trip — 2 hours — some steep terrain

Here's one for the sad-but-true file: Yosemite Valley, with all its spectacular natural and geological wonders, is terrible for day-hiking. Yes, the crowds are a huge problem, but even worse is the incredible amount of asphalt leading to everywhere. It's as if the park forefathers decreed, "Gosh, this incredible land is holy country; let's pave over as much of it as possible."

Still, the valley is completely worth seeing, so travel through it via car, bike, or tram, then head out to Tuolumne Meadows on Tioga Pass

Road when you're ready to do some real hiking.

A perfect place to start is Dog Lake, one of the easy-to-reach trail destinations from Tuolumne Meadows that makes a great half-day hike. You've never heard of Dog Lake? Okay, so it's not one of the star attractions at Yosemite. That makes it even better; you'll leave the multitudes behind as you set off uphill from the trailhead, enjoying all the best features of this landscape at 9,000 feet in elevation.

Let's not understate the "uphill" part, though. This trail will definitely get your heart and lungs going, and keep them working aerobically for a good half-hour. And don't forget to factor in the high elevation as well. You'll be breathing hard for sure.

The trail begins with a walk through a pretty meadow, with views of snowy Cathedral Peak and Unicorn Peak in the distance. (Guess which is which—their names tell you all you need to know.) Notice how the trail is dug a few inches into the ground to keep hikers on a definitive route and protect the fragile meadow. In spring, colorful wildflowers add contrast to the emerald green grasses.

Immediately after crossing the meadow, you'll come to a huge horizontal slab of granite, marked by rock trail cairns that show the path across it. Beyond the granite comes a trail split—Dog Lake to the left and Lembert Dome to the right; you head left.

Now your climb begins in earnest, heading up the sandy and rocky trail to the top of a ridge directly behind Lembert Dome. The air is thin here, as your lungs will certainly note, and the trail is fairly steep. Lembert Dome is behind your right shoulder as you mount the ridge; you'll have plenty of opportunity to turn around and look at it when you stop to catch your breath. The surrounding forest is primarily lodgepole pines. Lodgepoles are one of the few trees that can grow at this high elevation, in a place of thin soil, thin air, and harsh exposure.

If you hike the Dog Lake Trail in early summer, a stream accompanies you on your left for much of the climb, but by September it goes dry. After a half mile of huffing and

Dog Lake Trail

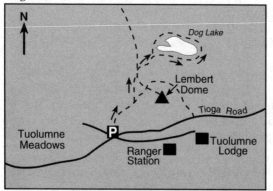

puffing, you'll cross the streambed and top the ridge. The trail levels out for a brief spell, but you're not done yet—to get to Dog Lake you must climb a little more, although not as steeply now, until you pass a junction with Young Lakes Trail to your left. Stay right at this junction and you'll reach Dog Lake in less than a quarter mile.

After the climb, Dog Lake is a joy to see. It's bigger than you might expect, deep blue in the center, and shallow around its edges. In late summer, some people picnic or swim at the lake, while others just sit and enjoy the view, or walk the trail that circles the lake's perimeter. I'd recommend heading around the lake to your right to reach the pretty meadow and sandy swimming area on the far side. The lake trail is peppered with wildflowers, including tiny lavender daisies with yellow centers, sierra lupine, and purple hiker's gentian. Multicolored dragonflies flit among the reeds by Dog Lake and its meadow.

If you have the energy, you can make a sidetrip to Lembert Dome on your return from Dog Lake. As you descend on the Dog Lake Trail, you'll pass the intersection with the Young Lakes Trail. About one-third mile further, you'll see a trail sign for Lembert Dome and Tuolumne Lodge pointing to the left. Following this trail leads you to the back side of Lembert Dome. Pass a small pond, then find an unmarked spur trail on your right that leads up the back side of the dome. This side trip takes some extra effort, and to return you must retrace your steps to the Dog Lake Trail, which will add another 1.5 miles to your trip. If you are feeling less ambitious, you can walk to Lembert Dome on another day, following the trail outlined in the story that follows.

Make it more challenging: Add on the side-trip to Lembert Dome.

Trip notes: There is a $20 day-use fee for entrance into Yosemite National Park. Keep your receipt because the fee is good for seven days. Park maps are available for free at the entrance kiosk. For more information, contact Yosemite National Park Public Information Office, P.O. Box 577, Yosemite National Park, CA 95389; (209) 372-0200.

Directions: From Merced, drive 70 miles northeast on Highway 140 to Yosemite National Park. Enter Yosemite at the Arch Rock entrance station, then drive 4.5 miles and turn west (left) on Big Oak Flat Road (signed for Highway 120). Drive 9.3 miles, then turn right on Tioga Road/Highway 120. Drive 39 miles on Tioga Road, past Tenaya Lake, to the east side of Tuolumne Meadows and the parking lot for Lembert Dome picnic area on the left (north) side of the road (the road sign also notes the trailheads for Soda Springs, Dog Lake and Glen Aulin). Park in the parking lot and locate the trailhead next to the rest rooms, on the west (left) side of Lembert Dome.

100. LEMBERT DOME TRAIL
Yosemite National Park
Off Highway 120 near Tuolumne Meadows
2.5 miles round-trip — 1.25 hours — some steep terrain

When you look up at 800-foot-high Lembert Dome from the trailhead parking area, you might not think you can make it to the top. It just looks too big and imposing to be scaled without ropes and carabiners.

For years I'd heard about Lembert Dome from an acquaintance who brags of having his picture taken on top of it. Quite the mountain man, he is. Well, guess what? I discovered that most people in half-decent shape can make it to the top of Lembert Dome. The west side of the dome may be an intimidating sheer face, but the northeast side is nicely sloped. Even if you don't choose to make the climb, you can always walk the trail that leads around the back of the dome for a great hike with an up-close look at this geological wonder.

Granite domes are a common geological feature in Yosemite. There's Half Dome, of course, and its neighbors Quarter Dome, North Dome, and Basket Dome. Then there's Sentinel Dome, which is another perfect easy hike (see page 230). But Lembert Dome is a standout—as grand in appearance as some of the larger domes, but more accessible.

Domes are essentially large rounded rocks, formed by the creation of slowly expanding granite. As the granite expands, cracks form, which create individual layers of rock near the surface. Over time a process called exfoliation takes place, in which these outer layers of rock break apart and fall off, removing all sharp corners and angles from the rock and leaving a smooth round dome.

To hike to Lembert Dome, take the trail by the rest rooms that is signed for both Dog Lake and Lembert Dome, then follow the trail signs to your right toward the dome. You'll climb in earnest on this route, and the sandy trail may be a little tricky to negotiate, but take it slow and give your lungs a rest every now and then. The trail around the west side of the dome offers amazing views of expert rock climbers plying their trade on the dome's most sheer face. On the south side of the dome, which is less somewhat less vertical, intermediate climbers practice their routes and hand-holds.

The trail becomes somewhat faint along the back of the dome, then disappears completely once you're on hard granite. If you have

On top of Lembert Dome

small children in tow, I wouldn't recommend taking them up on the dome, because a fall could be extremely dangerous. Sure-footed adults should pick a path and make their way to the top. If you're unsure of which way to go, watch for a while and see what routes other hikers take. Not being much for steep grades, I picked the flattest possible route to the top, which meant walking all the way around to the front of the dome, lateraling around the rock in a big circle.

Any way you get there, your efforts will be rewarded. The views from the top of Lembert Dome are outstanding, taking in all of Tuolumne Meadows and its surrounding peaks. The view can be downright dizzying, so if you're afraid of heights, keep a hand-hold on someone you love. The wind often howls on top of the dome, so come prepared with an extra layer of clothes. You're probably going to want to stay up top for a while.

Make it easier: Take it slow if you're getting used to the high elevation. Just walk around the base of the dome, or climb only part way.

Trip notes: There is a $20 day-use fee for entrance into Yosemite National Park. Keep your receipt because the fee is good for seven days. Park maps are available for free at the entrance kiosk. For more information, contact Yosemite National Park Public Information Office, P.O. Box 577, Yosemite National Park, CA 95389; (209) 372-0200.

Directions: From Merced, drive 70 miles northeast on Highway 140 to Yosemite National Park. Enter Yosemite at the Arch Rock entrance station, then drive 4.5 miles and turn west (left) on Big Oak Flat Road (signed for Highway 120). Drive 9.3 miles, then turn right on Tioga Road/Highway 120. Drive 39 miles on Tioga Road, past Tenaya Lake, to the east side of Tuolumne Meadows and the parking lot for Lembert Dome picnic area on the left (north) side of the road (the road sign also notes the trailheads for Soda Springs, Dog Lake and Glen Aulin). Park in the parking lot and locate the trailhead next to the rest rooms, on the west (left) side of Lembert Dome.

101. McGURK MEADOW TRAIL
Yosemite National Park
Off Glacier Point Road in Yosemite
2 miles round-trip — 1 hour — rolling terrain

👫

The McGurk Meadow Trail is an often-overlooked path that leads through a lovely fir and pine forest to a pristine, mile-long meadow with a stream meandering through its center. It's easily as beautiful (although not as large) as Tuolumne Meadows, but without all the people. If that's not enough to entice you to hike upon it, the trail also leads past an old pioneer cabin, a remnant of bygone days when sheep ranchers grazed their stock in Yosemite.

After parking at the pullout just beyond the trailhead, walk west along the road for about 70 yards to access the trail by the McGurk Meadow sign. Fifteen minutes of downhill hiking on a pleasant forested trail will bring you to the shepherd's cabin on the meadow's edge, only eight-tenths of a mile from the trailhead. Built with logs and nails, the cabin was probably used only in the summer. Its front door is so low that its opening would be covered by snow in winter months.

After passing the old cabin, you'll come to the edge of McGurk Meadow, where a trail sign points you to Dewey Point in three miles and Glacier Point in seven. No need to hike that far, though, because

Shooting stars in McGurk Meadow

this meadow is a perfect destination by itself. A footbridge carries you over a small stream, which cuts long, narrow "S" marks end over end through the tall grass.

Mountain meadows are remarkably fragile and important ecosystems. They function much as wetlands do in the low country: They provide food and spawning grounds for wildlife and they drain and cleanse the soil after snowmelt. When the thaw arrives, meadows turn green and lush with new life, a testament to the earth's power of renewal. For a short period, usually in July and August, subalpine meadows abound with wildflowers. One early July in McGurk Meadow, I saw a stunning display of purple alpine shooting stars with tiny rings of white and yellow, their stigma tips pointing to the ground like bowed heads. Hundreds of corn lilies had also already flowered, along with patches of purple penstemon.

My July walk revealed other signs of spring in the meadow, including several flitting butterflies and a centipede who was slowly making her way across the footbridge. Because the growing season is so short at this 7,000-foot elevation, plants and animals don't waste any time on warm days. They focus their efforts on growing, reproducing, and storing food for the long winter to come.

Like the centipede, you, too, should cross the footbridge and walk to the meadow's far side, where the trail turns right and skirts the meadow's edge. Add another quarter-mile or so to your trip by walking the trail along the length of this pristine meadow. When the trail leads away from the meadow and heads deeper into the forest, turn around and retrace your steps.

Make it more challenging: Continue following the trail as far as you please. Dewey Point, which is three miles further, is one of the best viewpoints in all of Yosemite.

Trip notes: There is a $20 day-use fee for entrance into Yosemite National Park. Keep your receipt because the fee is good for seven days. Park maps are available for free at the entrance kiosk. For more information, contact Yosemite National Park Public Information Office, P.O. Box 577, Yosemite National Park, CA 95389; (209) 372-0200.

Directions: From Merced, drive 70 miles northeast on Highway 140 to Yosemite National Park. Enter Yosemite at Arch Rock, then drive 6.3 miles into the valley and turn right at the fork for Highway 41/Wawona/Fresno. Drive 9.2 miles on the Wawona Road/Highway 41 and turn left on Glacier Point Road. Drive 7.5 miles to the trailhead for McGurk Meadow. The trailhead is on the left side of the road. A parking pullout is found about 70 yards further, also on the left.

---

102. SENTINEL DOME TRAIL
Yosemite National Park
Near Glacier Point in Yosemite
2.2 miles round-trip — 1 hour — rolling terrain

It's a weekend in early summer and you want to see Yosemite Falls. But you can't bear to face the crowds in Yosemite Valley, where you know you'll have to fight for a parking space and get your lungs filled with bus exhaust. Here's the good news: All of the valley's best attractions can be seen while hiking outside and above the valley, from spectacular lookouts that are far from the tour buses and parking lots.

In fact, if it's Yosemite Falls you seek, the best place to see it in all its grandeur is from the top of Sentinel Dome, an easy one-mile hike from Glacier Point Road. Along with a view of the falls, you'll also receive an unimpeded view of Half Dome and all its granite neighbors. Plus, you'll have the thrill of climbing to the top of mighty Sentinel Dome, elevation 8,122 feet.

The Sentinel Dome Trail gives you a complete understanding of the word "panorama." From the summit, you can view the whole spectacle of Yosemite's high country. You'd expect a view like this to come with a price, but since the trailhead is conveniently located at

7,700 feet in elevation, reaching the top of Sentinel Dome requires only a 400-foot climb. I've seen children as young as six on top of the dome.

Taft Point and Sentinel Dome share the same trailhead; take the Sentinel Dome Trail to the right. You'll hike gently uphill on an easy-to-follow trail, which is mostly exposed and sunny except for scattered Jeffrey pines and white firs. In summer, tiny purple and white mountain wildflowers, about two inches high, bring a splash of color to this hard granite environment.

As you near the dome, the valley views grow more spectacular. You'll enter a grove of old-growth fir trees and then approach Sentinel Dome from the southwest, meeting up with an old, once-paved road. The road leads you around to the dome's northeast side. Here you'll find a trail fork that leads to Glacier Point in a little over a mile, and the valley floor in five miles.

Forget about proceeding any further on the trail, because Sentinel Dome stands right at your feet. An imposing chunk of smooth granite—just an immense round boulder, really—the dome is quite steep on one side, but nicely sloped on the other. Although you won't find a

Young hiker on top of Sentinel Dome

formal trail up the side of the dome, the route is obvious (and you'll probably see other hikers ahead of you). Go for it.

From the very top of the dome you can see both lower and upper Yosemite Falls across the valley. After the heavy snowfall of the winter of 1998, I stood on Sentinel Dome and watched the waterfall *hurtle* over its cliff edge, not merely cascade or drop. Although Yosemite Falls is an easy mile away, the sound I heard was not a splash but an incredibly fierce pounding.

In addition to Yosemite Falls, many other sights are visible in all directions from Sentinel Dome's rounded top. Half Dome is easy to spot, and just to the left of it are two twin domes, Basket Dome and North Dome. Behind Half Dome is Quarter Dome, which is situated at the head of deep, forested Tenaya Canyon; behind Quarter Dome you can see Pywiack Cascade streaming down the mountainside. In front of Half Dome is Liberty Cap and Nevada Falls, and further to the right is Bunnell Cascade, which slides straight down to Bunnell Point. In case you weren't counting, that's five waterfalls in one peek (and on one peak).

Expect the wind to be fierce on top of Sentinel Dome. Although there's almost no soil structure at all, a few plants manage to dig their roots into the hard granite and survive. Among them are tiny wildflowers tucked into creases in the rock. Sentinel Dome used to have a very large and frequently photographed Jeffrey pine at its summit, but it finally gave way to the forces of nature.

Be sure to bring your camera for this trip. Few places in Yosemite offer such spectacular views.

Make it easier: Walk the trail to the back of the dome but don't climb on the dome itself. The views from the base of the dome are almost as good as from the top.

Trip notes: There is a $20 day-use fee for entrance into Yosemite National Park. Keep your receipt because the fee is good for seven days. Park maps are available for free at the entrance kiosk. For more information, contact Yosemite National Park Public Information Office, P.O. Box 577, Yosemite National Park, CA 95389; (209) 372-0200.

Directions: From Merced, drive 70 miles northeast on Highway 140 to Yosemite National Park. Enter Yosemite at Arch Rock, then drive 6.3 miles into the valley and turn right at the fork for Highway 41/Wawona/Fresno. Drive 9.2 miles on the Wawona Road/Highway 41 and turn left on Glacier Point Road. Drive 13.2 miles to the trailhead for Sentinel Dome and Taft Point (two miles before the end of the road at Glacier Point). The trailhead is on the left side of the road.

103. TAFT POINT TRAIL
Yosemite National Park
Near Glacier Point in Yosemite
2.2 miles round-trip — 1 hour — rolling terrain

👣👣

The sign at the Taft Point trailhead doesn't tell the whole story. It says something understated like: "Taft Point fissures, originally knifeblade thin, have eroded into dramatic chasms." Sounds like this might be some boring geology lesson. Until you take the hike and wind up shaking with fear in your hiking boots and giggling with exhilaration at the same time.

The Taft Point Trail starts off innocently enough from the same trailhead as the Sentinel Dome Trail (see page 230). It heads off to the left through a forest of Jeffrey pine, lodgepole pine, and white fir. If you've hiked the Sentinel Dome Trail previously, you'll notice the forest is much more dense here. In the first quarter-mile, you'll pass by a large pile of white quartz, its orange and grey veins visible upon closer inspection.

About a half mile in, pause to turn around and gain an impressive view of Sentinel Dome. When you see the dome from here, it looks so imposing that it's hard to believe you can walk right up to the top.

Continuing through the forest, you'll cross a couple of creeks, including one that is surrounded by dense corn lilies and grasses. At nearly one mile out, the trees disappear and you begin to descend along a rocky slope. The trail more or less vanishes on the granite; just head toward Yosemite Valley. In a few hundred feet, you come to the edge of the cliff you're standing on. You expect to be able to see some distance down, but nothing can prepare you for how far down it is.

If you can stop your knees from knocking, walk a few hundred feet farther, contouring along the edge of the cliff. Head for the metal railing you see at the high point (it's called Profile Cliff). On the way, you'll pass a few of The Fissures, which are remarkably skinny clefts in the cliff that drop straight down to the valley below. One of The Fissures has a couple of large granite boulders captured in its jaws; they're stuck there waiting for the next big earthquake or Ice Age to set them free. Then they'll make a half-mile, one-way journey to the valley floor.

The high overlook on Profile Cliff caps off the trip. Its railing, a meager piece of metal, performs an important psychological job. Although it's only a hand rail, it takes away some of the fear of peering 3,000 feet straight down, because you can clutch it tightly while you

One of the fissures on Taft Point

gawk at the view. If you have kids with you, be sure to keep a firm hand-hold on them.

At 7,503 feet in elevation, Profile Cliff is approximately the same height as 7,569-foot El Capitan, which means you get the same kind of unnerving view as those daring rock climbers on El Cap. Squint carefully, or pull out your binoculars, and you can see the El Capitan climbers almost directly across from you.

Also in view are Upper Yosemite Fall across the valley, the Merced River cutting down in front of El Capitan, and tiny cars parked near the meadow by its side. From this height you can't see Lower Yosemite Fall, which is obscured in the canyon, but you get a rare look at the stream that feeds the upper falls.

Make it easier: If heights frighten you, make the trip less scary by doing it with a friend. Children should definitely not go unsupervised at the fissures for even one second.

Trip notes: There is a $20 day-use fee for entrance into Yosemite National Park. Keep your receipt because the fee is good for seven days. Park maps are available for free at the entrance kiosk. For more information, contact Yosemite National Park Public Information Office, P.O. Box 577, Yosemite National Park, CA 95389; (209) 372-0200.

Directions: From Merced, drive 70 miles northeast on Highway 140 to Yosemite National Park. Enter Yosemite at Arch Rock, then drive 6.3 miles into the valley and turn right at the fork for Highway 41/Wawona/Fresno. Drive 9.2 miles on the Wawona Road/Highway 41 and turn left on Glacier Point Road. Drive 13.2 miles to the trailhead for Sentinel Dome and Taft Point (two miles before the end of the road at Glacier Point). The trailhead is on the left side of the road.

104. PANORAMA TRAIL
Yosemite National Park
Near Glacier Point in Yosemite
4 miles round-trip — 2 hours — some steep terrain

A trip to Yosemite always takes your breath away. It's one world-class natural wonder after another—Bridalveil Falls, Cathedral Rock, Half Dome, Yosemite Falls, El Capitan, Vernal and Nevada falls.... Every one of them is worthy of their very own park.

Tons of people drive their cars through the valley floor to visit these famous landmarks. Many of them also make the trip to Glacier Point to line up at the railing and see the splendor from up high. Then they have a corn dog at the refreshment stand, maybe buy a T-shirt, and drive away.

But these folks don't know what they're missing. Of all the ways to see Yosemite's sights, a short walk on Glacier Point's Panorama Trail is one of the best. And conveniently, the trailhead is located just steps away from the corn-dog-eating masses.

The Panorama Trail starts at 7,230 feet in elevation at Glacier Point, to the right of the viewing area and picnic tables. Several trails start from this trailhead, but you'll take the Panorama Trail, heading toward Illilouette Falls, a rushing cascade on Illilouette Creek. That's *ill-ill-ew-et,* accent on the second *"ill."* You don't have to go all the way to the waterfall to have a good trip, although it makes an excellent destination at two miles from the start. There are many rewards along the trail long before the falls, so you can customize this hike to your ambitions.

Head off downhill on the trail, switchbacking through a fire-scarred pine forest. You'll notice how the fire meandered on its route, burning some areas and sparing others. The sparse remaining forest provides an open view, which includes spectacular Vernal and Nevada falls. These two famous waterfalls, written about by John Muir and photographed by Ansel Adams, can't be seen simultaneously from the canyon bottom because one is lower and set back further than the other. But here on the Panorama Trail, you can see them both. Vernal Falls (the lower one), is a wide, block-shaped waterfall that drops more than 300 feet into a gorge. Nevada Falls, narrower and taller at 594 feet, is shaped like an inverted V.

No steps are taken on the Panorama Trail without a glimpse of something dramatic. You'll have continual chances to admire the gleaming granite of Half Dome, Quarter Dome, and Liberty Cap, plus

the glistening cascades of Vernal, Nevada, and Illilouette falls. You'll have a bird's eye view—3,000 feet down—of the entire east side of Yosemite Valley.

Keep an eye on your watch for this hike; because the trail leads downhill you should pay attention to how long you've walked, so you'll know how long your return climb will be. (Figure it will take you 1.3 times as long to climb out as it did to descend, as the grade is fairly steep.) If you choose to go all the way to Illilouette Falls, you'll have a long uphill on your return, with an

Vernal and Nevada Falls from the Panorama Trail

elevation gain of nearly 1,000 feet. Don't descend that far if you don't want to climb back up.

At 1.5 miles, you'll reach a trail junction; right leads to Mono Meadows and left leads to Illilouette Falls, Nevada Falls, and the valley floor. Head left and walk the last half-mile to an overlook of Illilouette Falls, where Illilouette Creek drops 370 feet over a granite lip. The trail deposits you at an overlook right across from the falls. You might want to pull out your sandwich and call this a picnic spot.

Make it easier: An easier turnaround spot is about 25 minutes down the trail, where you are directly across from Nevada and Vernal Falls— probably the best view you can get of them in the entire park. A turn-around here will make for a two-mile round-trip.

Trip notes: There is a $20 day-use fee for entrance into Yosemite National Park. Keep your receipt because the fee is good for seven days. Park maps are available for free at the entrance kiosk. For more information, contact Yosemite National Park Public Information Office, P.O. Box 577, Yosemite National Park, CA 95389; (209) 372-0200.

Directions: From Merced, drive 70 miles northeast on Highway 140 to Yosemite National Park. Enter Yosemite at Arch Rock, then drive 6.3 miles into the valley and turn right at the fork for Highway 41/Wawona/Fresno. Drive 9.2 miles on the Wawona Road/Highway 41 and turn left on Glacier Point Road. Drive 15.7 miles to Glacier Point (at the end of the road). Park in any of the parking lots, then walk to the viewing area. The trailhead is to the right of the viewing area, past the park store and picnic tables.

105. MARIPOSA GROVE of BIG TREES
Yosemite National Park
Off Highway 41 in southern Yosemite
2 miles round-trip — 1 hour — rolling terrain

If you think a redwood is a redwood is a redwood, it's time to think again. Think about taking a walk in the Mariposa Grove in southern Yosemite, for starters. Even if you've just returned from a week in Redwood National Park and feel you know all about big trees, the redwoods in Yosemite still give you a run for your money.

First, you need to understand the difference between redwoods. The coast redwood, or *Sequoia sempervirens,* is the most numerous of the redwoods, growing all over the foggy coast in northern California and Oregon. Coast redwoods are the tallest of trees—up to 375 feet tall. But they're not as large, or as old, as the redwoods you find in the Mariposa Grove, which are Sierra redwoods, or giant Sequoias.

And that's why you should come here. Giant Sequoias are the largest living things on earth in terms of volume. Whereas coast redwoods can grow 375 feet tall and up to 18 feet across, giant Sequoias can grow more than 300 feet tall and 30 feet across. That's big. The oldest Sequoias are around 3,000 years old. In contrast, coast redwoods are mere adolescents at 2,100 years old.

But as you walk on the Mariposa Grove Loop Trail, the main difference you're likely to notice between Sierra redwoods and coast redwoods is the forest they live in. While coast redwood forests are lush and green with an undergrowth of ferns and sorrel, the forest in the Mariposa Grove is drier and more sparse. The Sequoias are mixed in with other trees; they're like treasures to hunt for. The grove is full of ceanothus, dogwood, ponderosa pines, and firs, all competing with the Sequoias for sunlight and nutrients.

It's a harder life for Sequoias than coast redwoods. Their growing conditions are highly specialized, and they're now confined to only 75 small isolated groves on the western edge of the Sierra. Forest fires are essential for their reproduction; the extreme heat opens their cones and releases their seeds. You'll see evidence of past fires in the grove as you hike. Park rangers manage "control burns" in the Mariposa Grove to try to help the trees reproduce.

The entire loop around the Mariposa Grove is five-plus miles long with a fair elevation gain. That's why the park service runs motorized trams around the grove; this allows visitors to alternate riding and walking without getting too tired to see the forest for the trees, or the trees for the forest. But the loop trip suggested here is shorter and keeps you on your feet the whole time, so you can ignore the trams and see the highlights of the grove under your own power.

Begin hiking at the trailhead by the parking lot, heading immediately for the Fallen Monarch, a big Sequoia that fell more than 300 years ago. It was made famous by an 1899 photograph of the U.S. Cavalry and their horses standing on top of it. Even though the tree has been laying on the ground for centuries, its root ball and trunk are still intact—a testament to how long it takes for these trees to decay. It's because of a surfeit of tannic acid in the Sequoia's wood.

Next stop on the trail is the Grizzly Giant, after a right turn at the Bachelor and Three Graces (one big tree with three smaller trees at its side). The Grizzly Giant is the largest tree in this grove, with one particularly impressive branch measuring almost seven feet in diameter. The walk to the Grizzly Giant requires a 300-foot elevation gain, which should get your heart going.

Finally, head for the California Tunnel Tree, which was tunneled in 1895 so stagecoaches could drive through. Now you can walk through. This tree isn't quite as famous as the Wawona Tunnel Tree, which was tunneled in 1881 and is found in the upper grove at Mariposa. The Wawona Tree is no longer standing; it was crushed by the weight of a record snowpack in 1969. It may have died 1,000 years prematurely, enfeebled by the tunnel cut into its base.

Beyond the California Tree, you'll see a trail sign for the Upper Grove and Museum. Don't take that trail; instead turn left here to make a loop back to the parking area, passing the Bachelor and Three Graces and the Fallen Monarch again.

One important tip for getting the most out of your trip is to visit the Mariposa Grove either very early in the morning or late in the day, when the crowds are lessened and the forest is quiet. The Mariposa Grove is so popular that rangers sometimes close off the parking lot during midday, when visitation is highest. But in the early morning and late afternoon, you'll have a good chance of seeing more playful ground

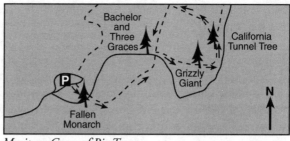

Mariposa Grove of Big Trees

squirrels than tourists with video cameras, and you'll get to experience the big trees in the best possible atmosphere.

Make it easier: Make your trip shorter by retracing your steps from the California Tunnel Tree. It's a 1.5-mile out-and-back trip.

Trip notes: There is a $20 day-use fee for entrance into Yosemite National Park. Keep your receipt because the fee is good for seven days. Park maps are available for free at the entrance kiosk. A guide and map to the Mariposa Grove of Giant Sequoias is available for 50 cents at the trailhead. For more information, contact Yosemite National Park Public Information Office, P.O. Box 577, Yosemite National Park, CA 95389; (209) 372-0200.

Directions: From Merced, drive 70 miles northeast on Highway 140 to Yosemite National Park. Enter Yosemite at Arch Rock, then drive 6.3 miles and turn right at the fork for Highway 41/Wawona. Drive 32 miles to the Mariposa Grove access road, then turn east and drive two miles to the grove parking lot. (If you enter Yosemite on Highway 41 at its southern entrance, the grove access road is on the right, just after you pass the southern entrance kiosk.)

---

106. MARK TWAIN SCENIC TUFA TRAIL
Mono Lake Tufa State Reserve
Off U.S. 395 near Lee Vining
1 mile round-trip — 30 minutes — level terrain

You'll never fully understand all the fuss about Mono Lake until you finally make the trip and see how strange and miraculous the place really is.

When you arrive, the first thing you notice is that the lake is immense in size and very beautiful. Gazing at it from the highway, you might feel as if you've gotten turned around and have driven west

---

instead of east, because here is this glorious, wide-open body of water that looks remarkably like the ocean.

But Mono Lake is three times as salty as the ocean and 80 times as alkaline. It's set in the middle of the high desert, just east of the crest of the Sierra and west of the Nevada state border. That means Mono Lake is framed by snow-capped mountains on one side and sagebrush plains on the other—a strange melding of extreme landscapes. Luckily for easy hikers, Mono Lake can be see via a terrific walk on the Mark Twain Scenic Tufa Trail in Mono Lake Tufa State Reserve.

Mark Twain visited Mono Lake in 1863 and wrote about it extensively in his book *Roughing It*. He was fascinated by the tufa structures found near the edges of the lake—off-white, coral-like formations that are formed when underwater springs containing calcium are released from the lake bottom and combine with the lake's water. This forms calcium carbonate, the chemical expression for tufa. The tufa formations grow upright, swelling into odd vertical shapes as much as six feet high as spring water pushes upward inside them. The tufas only stop growing when exposed to air, which in effect ruins the chemistry experiment.

The Mark Twain Scenic Tufa Trail takes you on a perfectly level one mile walk around the tufa formations and the southern edge of Mono Lake. You'll pass some high-and-dry inland tufas on your way to the lakeshore, where you'll see miniature tufa islands in the water. You can touch the tufa, which feels surprisingly hard, almost like concrete, although it appears brittle to the eye. Some hikers wade in to the lake or take a swim; others birdwatch along the shore. Most people just walk around feeling a bit dazed, amazed at this strange planet they've just discovered.

To the first-time visitor, Mono Lake, with 60,000 surface acres of water and 16,000 acres of exposed shoreline, really does seem like the ocean. In addition to its remarkable size, it's also one of the oldest lakes in North America, estimated at 700,000 years old. Swimming in Mono Lake is a unique experience because of the salinity of the water. You'll find it very easy to float; in fact, it's hard not to.

In addition to the tufa chemistry lesson, there's also a wildlife lesson to be learned on this trail. Mono Lake's islands are important nesting grounds for California gulls; in fact, 85 percent of the gulls that live on the California coast were born here. The lake's population of tiny brine shrimp feeds the gulls and the loons, grebes, pintails, and huge number of migratory birds that visit. From April to November, you can see brine shrimp clustered in thick masses near the lake surface.

Mono Lake from the Mark Twain Scenic Tufa Trail

The main controversy surrounding Mono Lake is regarding its water level. In 1941, four streams that fed Mono Lake were diverted into the California Aqueduct to provide water for Los Angeles. The lake started to shrink rapidly, losing an average of 18 inches per year. As the water level dropped, a land bridge to the islands was formed. Coyotes and other predators could now access the gulls' nesting area, which was bad news for the birds.

As you walk the Mark Twain Scenic Tufa Trail, you'll see elevation markers that mark the lake level in different years. In 1941, the lake's elevation was 6,417 feet. In 1993, it was down to 6,376 feet. Today, it's the job of the Water Resources Board to regulate the level of Mono Lake so that its resources remain protected. The lake level has been kept stable for the past decade, although it is not as high as it once was.

Mono Lake is unlike anything else you'll find in California. A hike along the shoreline of the huge turquoise lake with its bald islands and strange tufa structures leaves you with a great appreciation for what Mark Twain called "one of the strangest freaks of nature to be found in any land."

Make it more challenging: You can add on a three-mile round-trip hike to Panum Crater, a volcanic crater in the state reserve, by driving your car back (west) along Highway 120 for two miles to the turnoff for the Panum Crater trailhead.

Trip notes: There is no fee. For more information, contact Mono Lake Tufa

State Reserve, P.O. Box 99, Lee Vining, CA 93541; (760) 647-6331.

Directions: From the town of Mammoth Lakes, drive three miles east on Highway 203 to its junction with U.S. 395. Take U.S. 395 north for 20 miles to the Mono Lake South Tufa exit, which is also Highway 120 east. (If you're traveling south on U.S. 395, the Mono Lake South Tufa exit is five miles south of Lee Vining.) Turn east and drive 4.6 miles until you reach a dirt road on your left that is signed for South Tufa Area parking. Turn left and drive one mile to the parking area and trailhead.

107. PARKER LAKE TRAIL
Inyo National Forest/Ansel Adams Wilderness
Off U.S. 395 near Grant Lake
3.6 miles round-trip — 2 hours — rolling terrain

The Parker Lake Trail in the Ansel Adams Wilderness is a quintessential study in contrasts. The first part of the trip takes place in sunny high desert, the second part in a shady aspen forest along a stream, and the third part at a glacial lake where the mountain wind ricochets off the lake surface. You get a little bit of everything on this trail.

Parker Lake is located in a designated wilderness area, so no mechanized vehicles of any kind are permitted, including mountain bikes. Even airplanes have to keep their distance.

The trail has a 400-foot elevation gain, but unfortunately most of it occurs right at the beginning, giving you no opportunity for a warm-up. At the start, you'll climb hard for 15 to 20 minutes, but the rest of the hike is on a gently rolling trail. If you can manage the first half mile of trail, you can do the whole trip. As you ascend, you can stop, turn around, and catch your breath while you gaze at the far-off views of Mono Lake. If you just trudge up the hill without pausing, you'll miss out on the vistas.

In the first stretch of trail, the air is pungent with the smell of sage, which seems to grow everywhere. In spring and summer, the sage is joined by profusely flowering yellow mule's ears. As you walk, you may get buzzed by a cicada, a large insect that makes its home in the sagebrush. Cicadas create the constant buzzing and chirping sound you'll hear, welcoming you to the high desert.

As you ascend, you'll be joined by Parker Creek on your right, which can run quite forcefully after snowmelt. But soon the trail levels out and things begin to change. You come closer to the stream, then enter a grove of quaking aspens, bearing white bark and small, round leaves that quake in the wind. The aspens are a refreshing sight on the trail, signifying shade and nearby water.

Wildflowers are more varied and profuse in this wetter area—blue and purple forget-me-nots, yellow alpine butterweed, light lavender hooker's onion, dark blue irises, pale orange paintbrush, and dark blue brewer's lupine with its silver-tipped leaves. Even mariposa lilies, with their tulip shape and yellow and red spots, make an appearance.

As you keep walking, the surrounding forest changes again. You'll enter a grove of immense Jeffrey pines, mixed in with tall and narrow lodgepole pines. You may hear the sound of busy woodpeckers at work in the pines.

Pass by a trail spur on your left that leads to Silver Lake, then head into a peaceful, shady dell close to Parker Creek. The raging stream you saw at the beginning of your hike is now tamed and quieted; you're closer to its headwaters. Aspens, pines, and wildflowers abound. Now the trail levels out completely for the last quarter-mile to Parker Lake.

Prepare for another abrupt scenery change as you arrive. The lake is a picturesque glacial water set in a basin below Mount Lewis at 12,300 feet, Parker Peak at 12,600 feet, and Mount Wood at 12,900 feet. When I visited, two loons were floating peacefully across the water, despite the nearly gale-force winds that whipped down the snow-capped mountains and across the lake's surface. With a grove of aspen at the far end of the lake completing the picture, the scene was like a postcard, too beautiful to be believed.

If the wind is too strong for a picnic at Parker Lake, head back down the trail for a quarter-mile to the protected and peaceful aspen grove.

Make it easier: You can cut this hike short if you like, but remember that the toughest part is in the first half-mile. If you make it that far, you can do the whole trip.

Trip notes: There is no fee. For more information, contact Inyo National Forest, Mono Lake Ranger District, P.O. Box 429, Lee Vining, CA 93541; (760) 647-3044.

Directions: From Lee Vining, drive five miles south on U.S. 395 to the Highway 158 turnoff for the June Lake Loop. Travel 1.3 miles southwest on Highway 158, then turn right and take Forest Service Road 25 for one-half mile, then Forest Service Road 26 for 1.9 miles to the parking area for Parker Lake. Both of the Forest Service roads are dirt roads and are signed for Parker Lake. The trail to Parker Lake begins from the trail sign at the parking area.

108. DEVILS POSTPILE & RAINBOW FALLS TRAIL
Devils Postpile National Monument
Off U.S. 395 near Mammoth Lakes
5 miles round-trip — 2.5 hours — rolling terrain

What the heck is the Devils Postpile? People ask themselves this question time and time again as they read the road signs while driving up U.S. 395 on their way to Mammoth Lakes for skiing or fishing vacations. Getting the answer requires only a short walk in Devils Postpile National Monument—three-quarters of a mile round-trip—but if you add in a few more miles, you'll see spectacular Rainbow Falls as well.

There's one catch, though. The road into the park is narrow, steep, and winding, and because of that, the park closes the road from 7:30 A.M. until 5:30 P.M. each day. During these hours, visitors must pony up eight bucks to ride a shuttle bus in and out. You have a choice: you can get up early or stay out late and drive your own car into the park, or you can take the shuttle bus.

Lava columns make up Devils Postpile

Note that solitude lovers should seriously consider the pre-7:30 A.M. option, and visit on a weekday besides. The trail to Devils Postpile and Rainbow Falls is incredibly popular; summer weekends bring a continual parade of hikers.

Once you're in the park, go straight to the Devils Postpile parking area and set out on the trail by the ranger station. The footpath begins in a pretty meadow alongside the headwaters of the San Joaquin River. If you time your trip right, you will be wowed by the meadow wildflowers, especially the masses of shooting stars and Indian paintbrush. In a mere four-tenths of a mile on a level, easy trail, your curiosity will be sated as you reach the base of the Devils Postpile. What is it? It's a pile of volcanic rock posts or columns made from lava that was forced up from the earth's core. At the base of the standing columns is a huge pile of rubble—the crumbled

Rainbow Falls at Devils Postpile

remains of columns that collapsed. Notice the shapes of the various lava columns; some are almost perfectly straight, while others curve like tall candles that have been left out in the sun.

The Mammoth Lakes area is volcano country. Less than 100,000 years ago, lava filled this river valley more than 400 feet deep. As the lava began to cool from the air flow on top, it simultaneously cooled from the hard granite bedrock below. This caused the lava to harden and crack into tall, narrow pieces, forming nearly perfect columns or posts. The Devils Postpile is considered to be the finest example of lava columns in the world.

After examining the base of the Postpile, take the trail on either side of it up to its top. You can stand on the columns and marvel at the fact that they are all nearly the same height. Under your feet, the tops of the columns look like honeycomb, or tiles that have been laid side by side. A bonus is that the view of the San Joaquin River from the top of the Postpile is quite lovely.

When you're ready, return to the base of the Postpile and continue past it on the well-marked trail to Rainbow Falls. You'll skirt in and out of the monument boundary and Inyo National Forest as the trail descends gently through lodgepole pines. The forest fire damage you'll notice was caused by a wildfire in 1992. The sound of the San Joaquin River is always apparent, although you won't see the stream again until you get close to the waterfall.

At a trail junction directing you straight to Rainbow Falls or left to Reds Meadows, continue straight. After a stream crossing on a two-log bridge, the path begins its final descent to Rainbow Falls.

The anticipation mounts as you walk closer to a big channel in the river gorge. The gorge is cut very steeply, with almost no foliage on its walls—just stark, vertical rock. The roar of Rainbow Falls can be heard before you see it; the trail brings you in above the falls. If you're hiking in the late morning, you'll see Rainbow Falls' namesake—two big, beautiful rainbows arcing over the falls' mist. The angle of the midday sun on the water droplets creates the perfect recipe for a rainbow.

Keep walking past the lip of the falls. You'll see that Rainbow Falls' drop makes a grand statement, plunging 101 feet over hard rock. The trail has two viewing areas for the falls, about 30 yards apart. A path from the second viewpoint descends steep granite steps to the base of the falls. Ferns and moss grow on the rock at the cliff bottom; they benefit from the waterfall's constant mist.

Make it easier: Just hike to Devils Postpile and back for a less than one mile round-trip. Or start your trip further down the road at Reds Meadows; hiking to Rainbow Falls from there is a two-mile round-trip. The trailhead isn't at the resort proper, but just before it on the road to the resort. There is a signed parking area for the trailhead.

Trip notes: There is no fee, unless you arrive between 7:30 A.M. and 5:30 P.M. and have to take the shuttle bus (see below). For more information, contact Devils Postpile National Monument, P.O. Box 501, Mammoth Lakes, CA 93546; (760) 934-2289, or Inyo National Forest, Mammoth Ranger District, P.O. Box 148, Mammoth Lakes, CA 93546; (760) 924-5500.

Directions: From U.S. 395 in Lee Vining, drive 25 miles south to the Mammoth Lakes/Highway 203 cutoff. Take Highway 203 west for four miles, through the town of Mammoth Lakes, then turn right at Minaret Road (which is still Highway 203) and drive for 4.5 miles to the Devils Postpile entrance kiosk. At the kiosk, either park and take the bus or continue driving for 7.8 miles to an intersection where you turn right to head to Devils Postpile. From there, it's another quarter mile to the parking lot. The trail begins from the left (south) side of the parking area, just past the ranger station.

If you arrive between the hours of 7:30 A.M. and 5:30 P.M., you'll be stopped by rangers at the entrance kiosk. Between these hours, you must ride a shuttle bus into the park. The cost of the shuttle is $8 for adults, $5 for children ages 5 to 12, and free for children under five. Get off the bus at the Devils Postpile parking area.

109. EMERALD LAKE TRAIL
Inyo National Forest
Off U.S. 395 near Mammoth Lakes
2 miles round-trip — 1 hour — rolling terrain

Normally I'm not a lawbreaker; in fact I'm generally a pretty upstanding citizen. But I almost broke the rules when it came to hiking at Emerald Lake. I'd driven all the way to Mammoth Lakes in July, eager to find a few good easy hikes, and several people had recommended taking the walk to Emerald Lake. It's beautiful, they said. It's pristine. It's easy to hike to. It's a perfect little lake.

But everywhere I went around Mammoth it was the same story: The trails were still snowed in. The campgrounds were still closed. It was warm and sunny, but there was 10 feet of snow everywhere. I was getting frustrated.

So I made the drive out to Cold Water Campground, where the Emerald Lake trailhead is located. When I got there, I found a big sign across the access road: CLOSED. But the sign was the kind of wooden placard you could just pick up and move, and I knew my car could make it down the access road, snow or no snow. I considered my options. "It's for the good of the book," I rationalized.

Just as I was making myself feel justified, a woman and two little kids came trudging along. They, too, wanted to hike to Emerald Lake.

"We parked our car along the road," the woman told me. "We're going to walk in to the trailhead. It adds an extra mile to the hike, but it's worth it."

Feeling rather ashamed of myself, and relieved they didn't catch me in the act of moving the sign, I parked my car and followed them. Hey, if two five-year-olds can walk an extra mile, so can I.

And Emerald Lake is worth it. It's a simple out-and-back hike to reach it, walking alongside Cold Water Creek most of the way. The elevation gain is 400 feet spread out over one mile, which means your heart and lungs get a decent workout. And the trail is nicely shaded the whole way. You'll notice many pines and firs in the forest—mostly

Climbing on boulders at Emerald Lake

Jeffrey pines at the lake and lodgepole pines along the trail. You climb from 8,900 feet at the trailhead to 9,300 feet at the lake.

As you hike through the forest, you have a good chance of seeing belding ground squirrels—light brown squirrels that are often mistaken for chipmunks. They have a shrill whistle and are usually spotted running along the ground or sitting upright on their back haunches.

Water ouzels or dippers can be seen around Cold Water Creek. You'll recognize them easily by the way they fearlessly fly right into the streaming water. The birds can dive underwater, then walk along the streambed in search of a few insects for lunch.

Emerald Lake lives up to its name; it is a pretty emerald color. But its best feature is a gorgeous backdrop of craggy granite peaks rising straight up to the sky, framing the blue water. The lake is small and C-shaped, and surrounded by big boulders—perfect spots for sunbathing or reading a book.

After you've visited the lake, head downhill the way you came. On your way back, look closely at the mountains on either side of you. On the east side, the peaks are volcanic in origin. Their soil appears reddish in color and there is sparse vegetation and few trees. On the west side, the peaks are hard granite, carved by glaciers. They are snow-covered most of the year. You're witnessing an unusual geological occurrence— a place where glacial and volcanic rocks are visible in the same canyon.

Make it easier: If you don't want to climb all the way to the lake, take the trail anyway and just walk as far as you like. There are many nice picnic spots along Cold Water Creek.

Trip notes: There is no fee. For more information, contact Inyo National Forest, Mammoth Ranger District, P.O. Box 148, Mammoth Lakes, CA 93546; (760) 924-5500.

Directions: From U.S. 395 in Lee Vining, drive 25 miles south to the Mammoth Lakes/Highway 203 cutoff. Take Highway 203 west for four miles, through the town of Mammoth Lakes, to the intersection of Highway 203/Minaret Road and Lake Mary Road. Drive straight at this intersection (do not continue on Highway 203 which heads to the right), following Lake Mary Road for 3.8 miles until you come to a fork that is signed for Cold Water Campground. Turn left and drive six-tenths of a mile on Forest Service Road 4S09, around the southeast side of Lake Mary, then turn left into Cold Water Campground and drive through the camp to the day-use parking area and trailhead.

---

110. HOT CREEK GEOTHERMAL AREA TRAIL
Inyo National Forest
Off U.S. 395 near Mammoth Lakes
2 miles round-trip — 1 hour — rolling terrain

The only problem with relaxing in a hot tub is that after a while, you always get too hot. But that rule doesn't apply at Hot Creek, where you can soak in a natural hot spring while cold river water flows past you and regulates your temperature. Sounds good? It is good. But before you jump in to the soothing waters, take a walk on one of the prettiest and most unusual streamside trails in Northern California.

Your adventure starts with a three-mile drive on a dirt and gravel road to the Hot Creek Geothermal Area parking lot. There you'll find changing rooms and rest rooms for bathers, and interpretive signs explaining what makes this area bubble and boil. Looking down at Hot Creek from the parking area above, you get a glimpse of what you'll see on your hike: Clear and narrow Hot Creek curves gracefully through a canyon of sagebrush and volcanic rocks, intersected by a footbridge where hot springs aficionados clamber in to the warm water.

To the right of the footbridge, two bright aqua pools are isolated from the stream's flow. Their full-boil status can be seen even from 100 feet above. The pools' steam rises ominously upward, giving full warning to visitors of their ferocious heat. Without Hot Creek flowing through these hot springs to cool their boil, the pools are liquid fire, unfit for humans or animals.

Posted signs and fences indicate where you can and can't roam, because of the unstable nature and unpredictable temperatures of this geologic area. Your dog may accompany you on your walk, but you must keep him leashed and under control to keep him safe. Children, too, should be watched very carefully, as their natural curiosity could lead them into dangerously hot water.

Hot Creek Geothermal Area is a great place to go for a geology lesson. The area is what's left of a 700,000-year-old volcanic eruption. The creek canyon is part of a 10 by 18 mile depression called a caldera, which was formed when eruptions blasted molted rock from beneath the earth's surface and caused the ground to sink hundreds of feet. The hot springs are the result of mountain runoff filtering down through the earth's crust and being heated by molten rock or magma, then being pushed back up to the surface in the caldera.

Hot Creek

The hiking trail along Hot Creek is completely level, but to access it you'll need to walk downhill about 100 yards on the short paved trail from the parking lot. When you reach the bottom of the canyon, the first thing you'll notice is the pervasive smell of sulphur. Take a look at the hot pools and vents, then cross the footbridge to the north side of the stream and walk to your left (west) on the dirt trail. A parallel trail is located on the south side of the stream, but it's usually occupied by fly fishermen. (If you walk the north side of the creek, you'll have less chance of disturbing anybody's casting. Fishing Hot Creek is hard enough as is.)

Although there are almost always people at the hot springs area, the crowds fade away as you walk westward along Hot Creek. Suddenly you're in your own world, wandering along a clear and shallow stream neatly bordered by fascinating rock formations, sagebrush, and thick reeds at the stream's edge. Ground squirrels and lizards scurry among the rocks, startled by your footsteps. Hot Creek's canyon is very narrow, and at every curve you gain spectacular views of the snowy Sierra Nevada straight ahead. If ever a place reflected the juxtaposition of desert and alpine environments, this is it.

Walk as far as you like and then retrace your steps back to the hot springs area. If you've brought your bathing suit, you can finish up your walk with a dip in the warm waters in the middle of the river.

Make it more challenging: You can extend your walk much further along Hot Creek, as this trail leads almost three miles one-way towards the Hot Creek Fish Hatchery.

Trip notes: There is no fee. For more information, contact Inyo National Forest, Mammoth Ranger District, P.O. Box 148, Mammoth Lakes, CA 93546; (760) 924-5500.

Directions: From U.S. 395 in Lee Vining, drive 28 miles south, 2.8 miles past the Mammoth Lakes/Highway 203 cutoff, to the Hot Creek Fish Hatchery exit, where you turn left (northeast). Drive three miles on Hot Creek Hatchery Road, past the Fish Hatchery, to the Hot Creek Geothermal Area. Turn left into the parking lot. The trailhead is located by the rest rooms.

INDEX

About the Author

Ann Marie Brown is an outdoors writer who lives in Marin County, California. She is the author of eight books with Foghorn Press:

California Waterfalls
California Hiking (with Tom Stienstra)
Day-Hiking California's National Parks
101 Great Hikes of the San Francisco Bay Area
Easy Hiking in Northern California
Easy Hiking in Southern California
Easy Biking in Northern California
Easy Camping in Southern California

FOGHORN ✹ OUTDOORS

Founded in 1985, Foghorn Press has become one of the country's premier publishers of outdoor recreation guidebooks. Foghorn Press books are available throughout the United states in bookstores and some outdoor retailers. If you cannot find the title you are looking for, visit Foghorn's website at www.foghorn.com or call 1-800-FOGHORN.

The Complete Guide Series

- *Easy Hiking in Southern California*—(256 pp) $ 12.95—1st Edition
- *Easy Camping in Northern California*—(256 pp) $ 12.95—2nd Edition
- *Easy Camping in Southern California*—(256 pp) $ 12.95—1st Edition
- *Easy Biking in Northern California*—(224 pp) $ 12.95—2nd Edition
- *California Hiking* (720 pp) $20.95—4th edition
- *Tom Stienstra's Outdoor Getaway Guide for Northern California* (448 pp) $ 18.95—5th Edition
- *The Outdoor Getaway Guide for Southern California* (344 pp) $14.95—1st ed.
- *California Waterfalls* (408 pp) $17.95—1st edition
- *California Camping* (776 pp) $20.95—11th edition
- *California Fishing* (768 pp) $20.95—5th edition
- *California Recreational Lakes and Rivers* (600 pp) $19.95—3rd edition
- *California Beaches* (640 pp) $19.95—2nd edition
- *Pacific Northwest Camping* (656 pp) $20.95—6th edition
- *Pacific Northwest Hiking* (648 pp) $20.95—3rd edition
- *Tahoe* (678 pp) $20.95—2nd edition
- *Utah and Nevada Camping* (384 pp) $18.95—1st edition
- *Utah Hiking* (320 pp) $15.95—1st edition
- *Arizona/New Mexico Camping* (500 pp) $18.95—3rd edition
- *Colorado Camping* (480 pp) $16.95—1st edition
- *Baja Camping* (288 pp) $14.95—2nd edition
- *Florida Camping* (672 pp) $20.95—1st edition
- *Florida Beaches* (792pp) $19.95—1st edition
- *New England Hiking* (448 pp) $18.95—2nd edition
- *New England Camping* (520 pp) $19.95—2nd edition

The National Outdoors Series

- *The Camper's Companion—The Pack-Along Guide for Better Outdoor Trips* (458 pp) $15.95
- *Wild Places: 20 Journeys Into the North American Outdoors* (320 pp) $15.95

A book's page count and availability are subject to change.
For more information, call 1-800-FOGHORN,
email: foghorn@well.com, or write to:
Foghorn Press
PO Box 2036
Santa Rosa, CA 95405-0036